Embedded Systems
Firmware Demystified

Ed Sutter

CMP Books
Lawrence, Kansas 66046

CMP Books
CMP Media LLC
1601 West 23rd Street, Suite 200
Lawrence, Kansas 66046
USA
www.cmpbooks.com

Acquisition Editor:	Robert Ward
Editors:	Joe Casad and Catherine Janzen
Layout production:	James Hoyt, Justin Fulmer, and Madeleine Reardon Dimond
Managing Editor:	Michelle O'Neal
Cover art:	Rupert Adley (www.solidimages.com)
Cover design:	Damien Castaneda

Distributed in the U.S. by:
Publishers Group West
1700 Fourth Street
Berkeley, California 94710
1-800-788-3123
www.pgw.com

Distributed in Canada by:
Jaguar Book Group
100 Armstrong Avenue
Georgetown, Ontario M6K 3E7 Canada
905-877-4483

ISBN: 1-57820-099-7

CMPBooks

VH #2 7/02

Table of Contents

Preface

An embedded system is just a computer buried inside some other product. Surprisingly, you can know a great deal about programming and computing and still get lost in the arcane world of embedded systems. In the world of embedded systems programming, countless details — both hardware- and software-related — make the development process seem like a path that few have traveled and even fewer have survived. How do software, hardware, and firmware differ? How in the world does a 100,000-line program end up inside a device smaller than my fingernail? What is flash memory and why do I need a cache? What is the difference between a task and a process? Do I need to worry about reentrancy? As we progress through *Embedded Systems Firmware Demystified*, you will come to see that these questions are not as complex as they first appear.

Embedded systems programming spans a wide range of activities from building programmable logic at the most concrete end to writing a UNIX™ process at the most abstract end. Bracketed by these poles, the industry has exploded in the last 20 years. In the late seventies, assemblers were considered luxuries. A typical embedded system used less than 64Kb of system memory (bits, not bytes!). There was no hardware hand-off to the firmware developer. The same person that drew the schematics and soldered the prototype also wrote the firmware that pulled the whole thing together. By the time Intel introduced the 8085 chip, it was clear that those pesky microprocessors were here to stay. In the eighties, the Motorola versus Intel CPU wars started, and C became a popular choice for the elite few who dared to mess with a high-level language and an EPROM programmer. Today, microprocessors are everywhere and range from the 4- and 8-bit workhorses still dominating the industry to 1GHz 64-bit processors that almost need a freezer (microprocessor-controlled, no doubt) to keep them cool.

Over the years, the complexity of these systems has snowballed. The industry has transitioned from programming a DEC PDP machine with binary codes on the front panel to applying object-oriented design to a microcontroller in a toaster. If you let the trend get to you, the changes can seem frazzling. There are microprocessors and microcontrollers; RAM, DRAM, and SDRAM; pipelining and superscalar; EPROM and flash memory; RISC and CISC; and RAS and CAS and cache — and that's just the beginning.

Now, everything from toothbrushes (no kidding) to fighter jets are likely to have a version controlled by a microprocessor of some kind. With this trend come tools and technologies. One can easily be overwhelmed by the available choices in hardware (integrated circuits that the firmware must make work) and software (tools that are used to build the firmware application).

The goal of this book is to prepare you for a real embedded systems project by walking you through an entire embedded systems design. Not coincidentally, the project source code included is a piece of firmware — an embedded boot platform — that can simplify all your future projects. I assume a small hardware design with CPU, memory, and some peripherals. I present a basic schematic and walk you through the method in which instructions are fetched from memory. I discuss devices, as well as concepts. I examine flash memory versus EPROM, SRAM versus DRAM, microcontroller versus microprocessor, and data bus versus address bus. I also explain how you convert your C and assembly language source code to a binary image that ends up in the memory device from which the CPU boots (the boot flash memory).

Several chapters cover the basic steps of starting up an embedded system and getting a working application (including the basic boot in assembler), exception handling, flash memory drivers, a flash file system, and serial and Ethernet connections. The result is an understanding of how an embedded systems project gets started and how to build a platform on which an embedded systems application can reside.

Sound exciting? Great! Sound scary? It's not! The intent of this book is not to discuss the latest superscalar architecture or the antenna effects of copper routes on a printed circuit board, nor does it present a high-level abstract design process. (Advanced architectures and transmission-line effects are certainly important, but they are not the topic of this book.) This book is for those who want to get their hands dirty without being overwhelmed by industry jargon or design-specific technical details. By the end of this book, you will know how to read a basic schematic, know what goes into the boot flash device, and understand the major components of a complete embedded systems development platform.

Who Is the Reader?

At the minimum, I assume the reader has some experience with C and basic assembly language concepts. I do not assume any electronics or hardware background. Thus, readers with a wide range of programming backgrounds will find this book useful.

Computer science or electrical engineering students without a significant background in firmware development, but at least an interest, can obviously benefit from this book.

Low-level firmware developers will find the working example helpful, as it includes documentation and code explanations for an extensible firmware development platform. I explain the details associated with booting new hardware and the way in which the CPU interacts with peripherals. Topics range from the lowest-level boot to a Trivial File Transfer Protocol (TFTP) implementation over Ethernet. You can port the code in this book to your own target system or integrate snippets of this code with your existing firmware platform.

Hardware developers will find the completed platform useful for helping analyze and debug hardware beyond the CPU complex. For those inquisitive enough to step away from hardware to learn more about the firmware process, this book provides a way to get started without getting too far from the hardware. (Hardware designers regularly make the transition to programming in the firmware/software world.)

Project leaders will also find this book useful, as the firmware package presented is a mature platform. The platform is applicable to a wide range of real-time operating systems (RTOS) and target architectures, and it is extremely easy to port to new systems. The fact that the platform is fairly target- and RTOS-independent makes the transition to a different target or RTOS much less painful.

What's Covered in this Book?

Chapter 1: A Hard Start describes a basic CPU structure, with support peripherals, on which the firmware discussed in this book can execute. The design includes, among other things, a core microprocessor, RAM, flash memory, serial I/O, and CPU supervision. Each element of the design is discussed (for example, CPU supervision and types of volatile and non-volatile memory devices). This chapter also examines the basics of how microprocessors fetch instructions from the memory device and how cache makes these fetches more efficient. The chapter covers the typical peripherals found in many microprocessors today, without being specific to a particular device.

Chapter 2: Getting Started introduces the writing and building of programs for embedded devices. This chapter explains the differences between a native-compilation and a cross-compilation environment. I discuss file formats and break down the task of burning the boot flash memory into simple steps. I also explain the importance of the link editor file and show how it is used to allocate sections of the application code to portions of the target memory. The chapter also discusses some preliminary tests and preparations you must undertake before you start programming the firmware.

Chapter 3: Introducing MicroMonitor introduces the boot platform, or boot monitor, used in embedded systems. This monitor, called MicroMonitor, has a full list of features and serves as a learning tool to teach you about the firmware development process.

Chapter 4: Assembly Required describes MicroMonitor's reset vector, or startup code. I then build some serial drivers and discuss an implementation for establishing exception handlers.

Chapter 5: Command Line Interface describes how to build a shell around the core functionality introduced in Chapter 4. I start with the command line interface (CLI). Next, I explain the processing that parses the input command line and that eventually (through the table of structures) calls a function corresponding to the command line. The command line interface includes shell variables and symbols, command line editing and history, user levels, and password protection.

Chapter 6: Interfacing to Flash Memory is the first of three chapters dealing primarily with flash memory. I describe a sample platform with (potentially several) banks of flash memory. This chapter discusses the lowest-level details involved in programming flash memory and presents a useful approach for target hardware with different flash memory configurations.

Chapter 7: A Flash File System discusses the creation of a tiny file system (TFS) which resides in flash memory. This simple file system is offered as an alternative to some of the more complicated approaches taken by many flash file system designers. I also describe some of the advantages and disadvantages of the trade-offs made in the design of TFS.

Chapter 8: Executing Scripts describes a feature that, with a CLI for command execution and a TFS for file storage, lets a file execute as a script or small program. This chapter examines the surprisingly simple details that combine the CLI and TFS to create a simple interpreter. The CLI commands are chosen to provide the CLI/TFS user with a simple but useful programming environment. Conditional branching and subroutines are just a few of the capabilities of this system.

Chapter 9: Network Connectivity examines the elements needed to connect as a node on a network. Just as flash memory is becoming a standard boot memory device, so too is Ethernet becoming a standard interface on many embedded systems. This chapter discusses several protocols used with embedded systems, including Ethernet, ARP, ICMP, IP, UDP, and BOOTP/DHCP. Finally, the chapter examines encapsulation of network layers — one on top of another — by small blocks of code that know only about their own piece of the packet payload.

Chapter 10: File/Data Transfer discusses two common file-transfer protocols: Xmodem for serial interfaces and TFTP for networks. Here I explain each of these protocols as implemented in the boot monitor package. The Xmodem and TFTP implementations presented in this book can transfer files and raw memory both to and from the target.

Chapter 11: Adding the Application shows you how the platform provides the base on which applications reside. The example in this chapter is a simple application with no RTOS, but it is clear that this platform supports just about any environment. You, as the developer, decide how much of the platform remains accessible by the application after the application takes over the system. This chapter discusses how the application is built to reside within the TFS and how the platform's loader automatically transfers the file from flash memory space to RAM space for execution.

Chapter 12: Monitor-Based Debugging discusses some of the monitor's on-board debugging capabilities and shows the implementation of these capabilities because, whether you want to admit it or not, you're going to have to debug your code. Here you'll learn how to create a basic symbolic debugger that can display memory as a structure (instead of as raw data), set breakpoints, single-step through a program, profile a program's execution, and dump a stack trace. The debugging techniques described in this chapter do not require in-chip support or an external debugger.

Chapter 13: Porting MicroMonitor to the ColdFire™ MCF5272 explains the process of porting the MicroMonitor firmware package to a Motorola MCF5272 (ColdFire) evaluation board. The text introduces the directory structure of the source code on the CD and walks through the monitor-specific details of the porting process. This chapter completes the process begun in earlier chapters.

Appendix A: Building a Host-Based Toolbox provides snippets of code that might prove useful for interfacing to files, serial ports, and sockets. Despite the fact that this book is about firmware, you are likely to have to do some native programming eventually. Even if you've already done a lot of native programming, the code presented here should speed your work.

Appendix B: RTOS Overview introduces some of the basic concepts of a real-time operating system (RTOS), which lets you expand your environment from supporting single-threaded programs to multi-threaded ones. Several books are available on this subject, so this appendix is not intended as an exhaustive study. I, however, present a fundamental explanation of what multi-tasking can do for you and why preemption is a beautiful yet dangerous feature.

Conventions

Throughout the book, I use different typefaces to differentiate between a) the book's regular text and b) special software tools, code, and so forth. General text is in roman font. Terms used for the first time are in *italic*. A `monospaced font` indicates code, software tools, hexadecimal numbers, filenames, data types, variables, and other identifiers, as well as other special items.

Source Code

This book covers a lot of source code. When the text describes various portions of the code in detail, snippets or entire functions are included. All code in this text has been transferred from the original working C source code and is included on the CD. Some implementation details that were not applicable to the discussion were removed from the text listings to make the presentation clearer. I have made every effort to maintain accuracy between the original code and the code presented in the text; however, the code on the CD is the complete working version. If you have questions, please refer to the code on the CD.

Acknowledgments

I want to thank my good friends and managers at Lucent — Roger Levy and Paul Wilford — for their support and encouragement. Also, much thanks to my good friends Patricia Dunkin and Agesino Primatic, Jr. for reviewing the text and providing a lot of good comments and suggestions.

My appreciation goes to the team at CMP Books. Thanks to Joe Casad, Catherine Janzen, and Robert Ward for editorial and technical contributions (special thanks to Robert for dealing with my many questions and paranoias throughout this whole process). Thanks to Michelle O'Neal, Justin Fulmer, James Hoyt, and Madeleine Reardon Dimond for typesetting, illustrating, and indexing the book.

Finally, I want to thank my wife, Lucy, for her endless encouragement through this project. I also want to thank my son, Tommy, for helping me keep my priorities in line. Most of all, I want to thank my Lord and Savior, Jesus Christ, for the sacrifice that He made to provide me with eternal salvation. It just doesn't get any better than that!

Chapter 1

A Hard Start

Although the primary focus of this book is firmware development, a good firmware developer must have a reasonable understanding of the hardware on which the firmware resides. You could compare a firmware programmer to someone who changes oil at a gas station: if all that person knows is how to perform an oil change, he won't have the skills to notice warning signs that a fully trained mechanic would pick up right away. A narrowly trained technician may change the oil competently but not notice other problems like a leaky head gasket. Sooner or later something else will go wrong, remain unnoticed, and cause additional trouble due to the technician's limited knowledge.

This chapter explains what a firmware engineer needs to know about the hardware in a typical system. The goal is not to turn you into a hardware designer but simply to explain enough so that you can do more than "change the oil." To achieve this goal, this chapter discusses some of the common CPU support peripherals and examines how the hardware processor does its job. I will start by focusing in on the type of system that this book addresses. You will learn about some of the most common features of today's microprocessor-based systems, some of which reside within the CPU silicon itself and others which are usually external to the CPU. I will also discuss the sequence of steps that the CPU takes to retrieve an instruction and the advantages and snags that are introduced by the use of cache.

At the end of this chapter (although you will still not be a qualified hardware designer) you will hopefully have a better understanding of the hardware platform onto which you will be installing your firmware.

System Requirements

The hardware required for an embedded system varies greatly depending on its intended use. Some tiny systems have barely 1K data space and 16K of instruction space, while high-performance systems might run a 1GHz 64-bit processing engine with 32MB CompactFlash and 128MB DRAM. In this book, I focus mostly on systems with capabilities that fall somewhere in the middle. The firmware I'll discuss does require some memory space (ranging from 32K to 256K of flash memory and 8K to 128K of RAM) depending on what capabilities are built in, so it is not appropriate for small microcontroller (8051, 68HC05/11/12, etc.) projects. On the other hand, this code doesn't need (or want!) a large machine to work successfully.

Figure 1.1 represents a complete system. Using this system model, you can program your own devices, talk to the PC, and even serve HTML pages to a network browser. If you need to skimp, you can eliminate the reset/watchdog and battery-backed-RAM/time-of-day (BBRAM/TOD) clock controller and still have the capabilities I listed! I include these capabilities in our model because they are extremely useful. They're also quickly becoming standard equipment on most microprocessor designs.

Figure 1.1 Block Diagram of a Typical Embedded System.

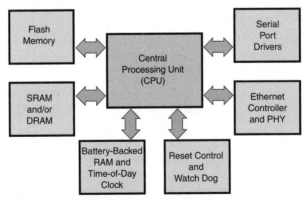

These are the components most common in embedded systems. All embedded systems use some kind of nonvolatile storage (flash memory, EPROM, ROM) and some form of RAM. Most have some channel they can use to communicate with a development host (a serial port, Ethernet port, or JTAG port.).

Central Processing Unit

Embedded systems are designed around either a microcontroller or a microprocessor. For our purposes, this distinction isn't really significant, partly because the line drawn between the two is getting a bit blurred with current development. A few years ago, microprocessors were defined as execution units and everything else was an external peripheral device. A microcontroller, on the other hand, was distinguished by the fact that it had everything it needed on one chip. This distinction isn't as clear today. Chips we once called microprocessors are becoming more and more integrated with added peripherals. These chips include things like serial ports, programmable chip selects, interrupt controllers, DRAM controllers, internal timers, and programmable I/O pins. Some chips go even further with a built-in Ethernet device and PCI controller in the same chip. Some chip vendors refer to these chips as microcontrollers, and others refer to them as microprocessors. (Some say pot*ae*to and some say pot*ah*to... Either way, it still makes french fries!) Don't let the names confuse you. In this text, I stick to the following usage:

- *Microcontroller* — those devices that can be configured to run 100 percent on their own. With a microcontroller, there is no need for any other peripheral devices (except maybe a power supply and crystal). Microcontrollers contain some small amount of nonvolatile memory for program storage and volatile memory for program use and typically come with an 8- or 16- bit internal CPU. Devices that fall into this category include the 8051 and 68HCXX families.

- *Desktop Microprocessor* — those devices that contain almost nothing except the processing engine. They immediately require complex support chips as their peripherals. The low end of these devices are 32-bit chips, but 64- and 128- bit processors are getting more and more common. This category includes devices like the K6, Pentium, and G4 processors.

- *Embedded Microprocessor* — those devices that contain a processing unit and some set of peripherals typically seen in an embedded system. These devices generally fall in the 16- and 32- bit category and include processors like the 68332, PPC860, and SH2.

- *CPU (Central Processing Unit)* — this term can refer to any of the above, or it can refer to just the processing section of a microcontroller or embedded microprocessor.

Keep in mind that these definitions are not the rule in the industry. You should also note that there is some overlap between the different terms. Both microcontrollers and desktop microprocessors are used in embedded systems. In fact, back in the 1980s, microcontrollers were even used in some of the first desktop machines.

Microcontrollers, as defined above, dominate the embedded systems market by several orders of magnitude. However, silicon (both processor and memory) prices are dropping, and the larger 16- and 32-bit processors are gaining ground in embedded applications. This book generally focuses on systems based on embedded microprocessors.

Embedded microprocessors come in a variety of shapes and sizes. They are even becoming available as logic cores designed for integration into very large programmable devices called field programmable gate arrays (FPGA). Companies that were producing programmable logic at one time are now producing programmable logic with a built-in processor.

Following is a brief description of some of the typical peripherals that are included with today's embedded microprocessors. I discuss each item using the analogy of a similar process in an office environment.

Programmable Chip Selects

Like a committee chairperson, programmable chip selects reduce confusion by coordinating communication. Imagine you are in a meeting and you are trying to speak to one person in the group. In this situation, you need some way to let that person know that you want to talk to them. Ideally, this mechanism should also let all the other people know that you are not addressing them. Chip selects perform this task for the microprocessor. Devices that are peripheral to the processor occupy some amount of space within the processor's address range. When a peripheral device's chip enable input line is not active, its data bus is in a high-impedance state, or disconnected, condition. This idea is very important because electrically there can only be one device actually writing data onto the data bus at any one time. (The term *bus contention* refers to the illegal condition that occurs if more than one device is attempting to write on the data bus at a given time.)

The firmware must know the address range for each peripheral device, which is typically decided at the hardware design stage. Each peripheral has some set of characteristics with which the processor must deal so that the two can interact with each other. Some peripherals use a very small amount of address space while others can use several kilobytes. Some peripherals are fast enough to keep up with the processor, and others force the processor to wait. In some cases, the peripheral tells the processor asynchronously when the peripheral has done its task, and, in other cases, a defined number of clock cycles must elapse between accesses to the peripheral device. All of these pesky little details can add up to a significant amount of extra glue logic between the processor silicon and the peripheral silicon. To reduce the need for glue logic, most processors intended for the embedded market offer pins called *programmable chip selects*. The chip select is a pin that the CPU uses to access a unique address range on the processor bus. There are typically three to six of these lines on an embedded processor, and the hardware attached to these lines can provide a simple one-device-per-chip select. Alternatively, there may be additional logic between the CPU and peripheral that performs additional address decoding to allow multiple devices to connect to a single chip select.

Glue logic refers to the extra circuitry (logic) that would be necessary to connect (or glue) two devices together.

Interrupt Controller

An interrupt controller helps prioritize incoming messages, which is a task that any office worker can appreciate. Consider the following small office scenario. Person_A is in an office behind a desk, talking on the phone. Person_B walks down the hall directly into Person_A's office and asks a question. Person_A can do one of several things:

• Totally ignore Person_B and continue the phone conversation.

• Quickly acknowledge Person_B's request but respond with something like "OK, I'll get to that in a little while," placing the request into a pile with a bunch of others.

• Tell the person on the phone that the conversation will have to continue later and then respond to Person_B. This outcome is likely if Person_A considers Person_B to be more important than whomever is on the phone.

• End the conversation. This outcome occurs automatically, regardless of whom is on the phone, if Person_B is the boss.

You can say that Person_A processes the interrupt from Person_B. Several factors determine whether or not Person_B is acknowledged, including the importance of the person on the phone, the fact that Person_A's door might have been closed, and so on. Somehow Person_A must prioritize the interrupt based on what is currently going on.

Now, consider Person_A having the phone conversation to be the CPU currently executing instructions and Person_B to be a peripheral device that needs the CPU's attention. An integrated interrupt controller provides the CPU with this ability to enable, disable, and prioritize incoming interrupts from both internal and external peripherals. Usually all incoming interrupts are maskable (can be disabled) except the NMI (non-maskable interrupt) and reset lines (the bosses).

Timer-Counter Unit

Consider a scenario with several typists working in an office. For a little fun, they decide to see who can type the most words in one minute. They gather around a computer terminal, and each one gets a shot at the one-minute trial. However, they find that they need some way to keep track of the 60-second interval of time from the beginning to the end of the test. Alternatively, they might just count the number of seconds taken to type a specific block of text. In this case, they are not measuring a fixed amount of time but the elapsed time it takes each individual to complete the challenge.

The timer-counter unit within an embedded system can help with this process. The unit provides the CPU with capability related to elapsed time. The timer-counter unit provides the firmware with the ability to generate periodic events, including events based on incoming pulse counts.

NOTE

It is important to note that the microprocessor's timer-counter unit usually does not deal with time of day on its own, so don't assume that "timer" means "wall clock." In most cases, "timer" means "stop watch." A stop watch can be converted to a wall clock if at some starting point the stop watch is synchronized with a wall clock. This process is what is done with the microprocessor's timer if time-of-day is needed.

DMA Controller

Consider an office that contains a file cabinet. In that file cabinet is paperwork that several office workers need to access. Some only need to access it once in a while, while others require the paperwork much more often. The manager of the office sets up a policy so that some of the individuals have a personal key to get into the file cabinet, while others must get a shared key from the manager. In other words, some office workers have direct access to the file cabinet, and others have indirect access.

In many embedded system designs, the CPU is the only device that is connected to the memory. This means that all transactions that deal with memory must use the CPU to get the data portion of that transaction stored in memory, just as some office workers had to obtain the manager's key. Direct memory access (DMA) is a feature that allows peripherals to access memory directly without CPU intervention. These peripherals correspond to the office workers with their own keys.

For example, without DMA, an incoming character on a serial port would generate an interrupt to the CPU, and the firmware would branch to the interrupt handler, retrieve the character from the peripheral device, and then place the character in a memory location. With DMA, the serial port places the incoming character in memory directly. When a certain programmed threshold is reached, the DMA controller (not the serial port) interrupts the CPU and forces it to act on the data in memory. DMA is a much more efficient process. Many integrated microprocessors have multiple DMA channels that they can use to perform I/O-to-memory, memory-to-I/O, or memory-to-memory transfers.

Serial Port

Consider the front door of an office building. The front door is where people can come in and out and easily interact with the facilities provided by the business. This fact doesn't mean that there aren't other ways to contact the business, but the front door is a very convenient and standard way of doing it.

This task of providing access is the serial port's job. The serial port provides basic communication to a console or some other device that understands the same protocol. The serial port or universal asynchronous receiver transmitter (UART) provides the CPU with an RS-232 bit stream, which is the same technology used for the PC's COM port. Different processors have different variations on this standard, but, in almost all cases, the minimum is a basic asynchronous serial bit stream (using RS-232 levels) consisting of one start bit, some number of data bits (usually between five and nine), and one or two stop bits.

DRAM Control Unit

Imagine that you are a manager with some employees who have many useful talents but also need the time to take care of their children. You could just tell them you can't deal with the kids in the office (and lose their talents), or you could be a bit more flexible and offer to have some other employees in the office take care of their kids.

This is the dynamic RAM (DRAM) story. RAM is very useful in all microprocessor-based projects. DRAM is a much cheaper alternative to SRAM, but, unlike SRAM and flash memory, DRAM requires baby-sitting or extra logic in the hardware to keep the bits in the DRAM stable. The type and size of the DRAM determine how complex the baby-sitting needs to be. The DRAM control unit does the the babysitting so that the CPU can interact directly with the dynamic RAM.

Memory Management Unit

A memory mangement unit's (MMU) main responsibility is to define and enforce the boundaries that separate different tasks or processes. To understand the effect of separating tasks, consider two different office environments. In the first one (the *formal* environment), there is an individual office for each employee. Each employee has a key to the door of his or her office and is considered the owner of that space. The second environment (the *informal* environment) uses a bullpen setup. There are no walls between employees, and everyone is on the same floor in the same air space. Each one of these configurations has its particular advantages and disadvantages. In the formal environment, you don't have to worry about one employee bothering another employee because there are walls between them. No matter how noisy one employee gets, the neighboring worker does not hear the disturbance. This is not the case for an informal setup. If an employee is talking loudly on the phone in the open environment, this inconsiderate individual distracts the other workers. If, on the other hand, the employees are considerate, two employees can quickly communicate with each other without needing to leave their seats. Similarly, if one employee needs to borrow another employee's stapler, it's just a toss away. In the formal environment, each time communication needs to take place, the communicating employee needs to go through some series of steps, like making a phone call or walking to the other office.

Each employee can be compared to a block of code (or task) that is designed to perform some specified job in an embedded systems program. The air space equates to the memory space of the target system, and the noise generated by a misbehaving employee can be equated to a bug that corrupts the memory space used by some other task. The MMU in hardware, if configured properly, can be compared to the walls of the formal office environment. Each task is bounded by the limitations placed on it by the MMU, which means that a task that somehow has a bad pointer cannot corrupt the memory space of any other task. However, it also means that when one process wants to talk to another process, more overhead is required.

Later, in this book, you will see that code bounded by the MMU protection is called a process and code not bounded by an MMU is called a task. A few years ago, the full use of an MMU in an embedded system was rare. Even today, most embedded systems don't fully use the capabilities of the MMU; however, as embedded systems become more and more complex and CPU speeds continue to rise, the use of an MMU to provide walls between processes is becoming more common.

Cache

Let's say you work at a desk and you regularly access folders from a file cabinet near your desk. Some folders you access regularly, others you access less frequently. You could return each folder to the file cabinet after each access. On the other hand, you might decide to use some smaller shelf right on your desk for those folders that you access frequently so that you don't have to get up to get them as often. On any given day, the set of folders that are in the shelf on your desk may change based on how much you plan to access them on that day. When properly organized, the local shelf can save you several trips to your file cabinet.

The microprocessor and memory story is similar. Microprocessors have been speeding up at a much faster pace than have the large memory subsystems with which they interact. To compensate for this difference, smaller blocks of really fast (and more expensive) memory are put between the microprocessor and system memory so that fetches to memory that happen frequently can be done through this faster cache memory instead of through the slower standard memory.

Programmable I/O Pins

As the manager of an office, you know that the ideal hiring scenario is to hire individuals that have multiple skill sets. Though each employee can only do one thing at any one time, hiring multi-talented individuals gives you the option of using the same group of people in several different ways.

The pin set of most modern processors also gives you this option. All of the previously mentioned peripherals require the use of a certain set of pins on the processor. In many cases, the majority of those pins can be used for their specific function (serial port receiver, timer output, DMA control signal, etc.), or they can be programmed to just act as a simple input or output pin (PIO). This flexibility allows the silicon to be configured based on the needs of the design. For example, if you don't need two serial ports (and the processor comes with two), then the pins that are allocated to the second port (RX2, TX2, and maybe DTR2, CTS2, etc…) can be programmed to function as simple PIO pins and used to drive an LED or read a switch.

NOTE

Programmable pins are sometimes referred to as dual function. Note that this dual functionality should not be assumed. How each pin is configured and the ability to configure it to run in different modes is dependent on the processor implementation. Often a pin name is chosen to reflect the pin's dual personality. For example if RX2 can be configured as a serial port 2 receiver or as a PIO pin, then it will probably be labeled as RX2/PION (or something similar), where N is some number between one and M, and M is the number of PIO pins on the processor. You should be aware that some microprocessors may be advertised as having a set of features but actually provide these features on dual-function pins. Hence, the full set of advertised features (two serial ports and 32 PIO lines) may not be simultaneously available (because the pins used for the second serial port are dual-functioned as PIO lines). Make sure you read the datasheet carefully!

Putting It All Together

The essential point of all these office analogies is that different offices can be configured in quite a variety of different ways depending on the needs of the business that the office supports. The same thing applies to embedded microprocessors.

The discussion so far has assumed that these components exist on the chip with the CPU, but they can also appear as physically separate components. The next sections discuss components that are usually found outside the microprocessor.

System Memory

Aside from the CPU itself, memory is the most fundamental building block in any microprocessor-based system. The CPU fetches instructions from the memory, and these instructions tell the CPU what to do. If the memory is programmed incorrectly or connected to the CPU incorrectly, then even the most sophisticated processor will be confused!

There are several different types of memory available. This range of selection exists for the same reason that there are several varieties of almost anything in the electronics industry: price/performance/density trade-offs. Different designs have different requirements that make different memory architectures attractive. For example, some systems need a lot of memory, but not really fast memory; others require small amounts of really fast memory; some need memory that does not lose its data when the power is removed; and so on. Following is a discussion of the most common types of memory used today, along with some of their characteristics.

ROM, PROM, EPROM and EEPROM

The term ROM is an acronym for Read-Only-Memory. This type of device is programmed as part of the manufacturing process and cannot be changed by the CPU or by any in-house device programmer. A programmable read only memory (PROM) can be programmed by an in-house device programmer, but cannot be erased. A PROM gives the user of the device one shot at programming the device. If there is an error in the program or if the program needs to be updated, the old PROM must be discarded and replaced with a new, properly programmed device. An erasable programmable read only memory (EPROM) can be programmed and erased in-house, with the limitation that the programming is done with an external device programmer and erasure must be done with some ultra-violet light source. Finally, an electrically erasable PROM (EEPROM) is in-system byte-writable and byte-erasable. At first glance, the EEPROM would appear to be the ideal storage device; however, EEPROMs are relatively slow and fairly expensive, even at lower package densities.

Generally, ROM, PROM and even EPROM are slowly fading into the sunset as new emerging technologies (i.e., flash) gain in popularity and drop in price.

RAM

This name is also an acronym: random access memory (RAM). Unlike the ROM acronyms of the previous section, the term *RAM* doesn't give a very good indication of its characteristics, at least not from our point of view. The name reflects the fact that any byte can be accessed at any time, which was a step ahead of its predecessor, sequential access memory, when it first appeared on the electronics scene. For the sake of our discussion, we assume that all memory is random access, but not all memory is writable by the CPU. Therefore for us, the differentiating characteristic (compared to EPROM) is the fact that the processor can write to RAM. RAM is read/writable but is also *volatile*, which means that when power is removed, the data is not retained.

There are two fundamental types of RAM: static (SRAM) and dynamic (DRAM). SRAM is the easier of the two to interface with because it is "static," meaning that it does not require any baby-sitting from the processor to do its job. Simply wire it up to the processor and use it. DRAM, on the other hand, requires external hardware to refresh it periodically so that the internal capacitors hold their charge. DRAM technology is much cheaper, but it is also slower and requires additional hardware to keep it running (the DRAM controller mentioned earlier). Because of these issues, DRAM is typically used in systems that require large amounts (> 1MB) of memory so that the added expense of the controller is justified. SRAM is simple but has a higher cost per byte of storage. It is typically used in systems that require small amounts of memory or in systems that need a small amount of fast writable memory (like a cache). For example, on your typical PC, some DRAM is available for general use, and a much smaller amount of SRAM is available for the CPU cache.

Flash Memory

Like EPROM, flash memory is also nonvolatile memory. The big advantage of flash memory over EPROM is that it is in-system programmable, which means that no separate device is needed to modify its contents. Early devices required a higher voltage (usually 12V), but today's parts require the same voltage as the rest of the board. Since the flash memory is in-system writable, no UV eraser is needed.

The architecture of flash memory comes in a few varieties, and although modern flash memory is in-system programmable, it is still not as convenient as using RAM. Typically, an erase procedure deals with a single "sector" of the memory. Sector sizes are usually relatively large, and an erasure sets all the bits within that sector to one (all bytes = $0xff$). Writing to the individual bytes changes only some of the bits within each byte to a zero state. Each operation (erase, write, and so on) except read is performed with a special programming algorithm. This algorithm is unique enough that it does not interfere with the typical interaction between the CPU and the memory.

Flash memory is quickly becoming the standard nonvolatile memory choice for new designs. Aside from the algorithm needed to write/erase the memory, the only other drawback of flash memory is that it has an upper limit to the number of times a sector can be erased. Usually the limit is high (100,000 or 1,000,000 cycles), but, nevertheless, it must be considered in the design.

Still Others

There are several other types of memory, most of which are some derivative of one or more of the above types. These other standards are not as popular, but they typically satisfy some niche in the market. For example, PSRAM (pseudo-static RAM) is a DRAM with some kind of refresh controller built into it. It satisfies a system that needs more SRAM than a single SRAM device supports but doesn't need the densities offered by DRAM. Nonvolatile SRAM (NVRAM) is static RAM with a battery backup. Some devices actually have the battery built into the plastic; others are non-volatile simply because the hardware design has battery backup protecting the device; still others provide some type of automatic backup of RAM to on-chip flash when power is removed. Serial EEPROM is a type of EEPROM that communicates with the CPU usually using two to four I/O pins. Access is slow, but physical size is extremely small because there is no address or data bus.

CPU Supervision

This section discusses functions that help the CPU maintain itself through some otherwise catastrophic situations. The functions covered here are (in order of importance) a power monitor for reset pulse generation, a watchdog timer, a power monitor for SRAM nonvolatility, and a time-of-day clock. The latter two are not actually considered part of CPU supervision, but it is very common to see various combinations of these functions in the class of integrated circuits which are referred to as "CPU supervisors."

Reset

Before the CPU can do anything at all, it needs to be powered up, which simply requires a connection to the power and ground pins on the device. Once powered up, it's essential that the internals of the device are allowed to synchronize and start up in a sane state. A RESET signal forces key CPU components to a known initial state. Typical requirements on a reset input line of a processor are that it be held in a constant active (usually low) state for some duration (say 100ms). In some designs, a simple resistor/capacitor (RC) combination is used to keep the RESET line in a low state for the 100ms time period when power is applied to the system (this is referred to as power-on reset).

Without getting into a lot of detail, assume that the resistor/capacitor (RC) circuit of Figure 1.2 provides a time-delay power-up. While the other pins have the supply voltage applied immediately (Signal A), the RC connection to the RESET pin holds it low for some delay longer (Signal B), thereby providing the minimum 100ms of low state to RESET after power-up. Unfortunately, the RC pair is not very good at detecting when it should apply the low level to the RESET pin. That means that it doesn't work well for systems that are in remote locations and must be automatically reset after power outages and dips. In these situations, the power could dip and cause the power supply level to fall, which would in turn cause the CPU to go insane, but would not cause the RC circuit to pull the RESET line low enough to bring the CPU out of its insane state. In some respects, the RC combination is an analog solution for a digital problem. The real solution for a safe power-up reset is to monitor the supply line and pulse the RESET line for the designated amount of time whenever it transitions from "out of" to "within" CPU tolerance. Fortunately, there are components out there that do just that! There are several different components available that monitor the supply voltage and automatically generate a clean reset pulse into the CPU when the supply drops below a certain level.

Figure 1.2   Conditioned Reset Input.

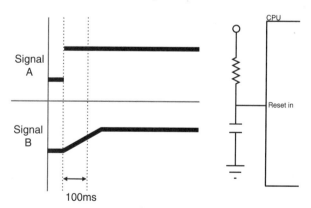

When power is applied to the system (Signal A), the charge time of the RC circuit attached to the reset input (Signal B) delays the reset activation. While this reset mechanism works when the power is cycled cleanly, it can cause problems when power is momentarily interrupted.

Watchdog Timer

The watchdog timer (WDT) acts as a safety net for the system. If the software stops responding or attending to the task at hand, the watchdog timer detects that something is amiss and resets the software automatically. The system might stop responding as a result of any number of difficult-to-detect hardware or firmware defects. For example, if an unusual condition causes a buffer overrun that corrupts the stack frame, some function's return address could be overwritten. When that function completes, it then returns to the wrong spot leaving the system utterly confused. Runaway pointers (firmware) or a glitch on the data bus (hardware) can cause similar crashes. Different external factors can cause "glitches." For example, even a small electrostatic discharge near the device might cause enough interference to momentarily change the state of one bit on the address or data bus. Unfortunately, these kinds of defects can be very intermittent, making them easy to miss during the project's system test stage.

The watchdog timer is a great protector. Its sole purpose is to monitor the CPU with a "you scratch my back and I'll scratch yours" kind of relationship. The typical watchdog (see Figure 1.3) has an input pin that must be toggled periodically (for example, once every second). If the watchdog is not toggled within that period, it pulses one of its output pins. Typically, this output pin is tied either to the CPU's reset line or to some nonmaskable interrupt (NMI), and the input pin is tied to an I/O line of the CPU. Consequently, if the firmware does not keep the watchdog input line toggling at the specified rate, the watchdog assumes that the firmware has stopped working, complains, and causes the CPU to be restarted.

Figure 1.3   External Watchdog Timer.

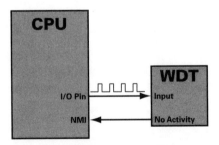

The watchdog timer is a simple re-triggerable timer. When the application is operating normally, it periodically resets the WDT by toggling the WDT's input. If something causes the application to hang or crash, the WDT times out and forces the CPU to restart by toggling the CPU's reset line.

Battery-Backed SRAM

Not all systems need to maintain the integrity of their SRAM when power is turned off, but this requirement is becoming more and more common because the components that provide that capability are getting cheaper and easier to use. Not too long ago, embedded systems used an arrangement of discrete components to determine what voltage was higher (power supply or battery) and properly steer the higher supply to the power pin of the SRAM (or the whole system). Now a handful of companies provide nonvolatile SRAM modules that have the battery and the power supply monitoring circuitry built right into the part. These parts are guaranteed to retain data for up to 10 years (with certain restrictions regarding the actual amount of time the internal battery is powering the SRAM, of course). Modules with built-in batteries are often available in versions that are pin-compatible with standard SRAM chips. These pin-compatible packages can be a life-saver if you need to add nonvolatile read/write storage to an existing design.

Time-of-Day Clock

For most embedded systems, the CPU provides all that is needed for maintaining time. Typically, there is no need to keep track of the time of day; nevertheless, when you need the time of day, you can't get it without some type of battery-backed time-of-day clock function. Even though the CPU has its own crystal and can keep relatively good time, the CPU's notion of time only persists as long as the CPU is powered up and running. When the board is reset, the CPU's clock is reset as well, making it impossible for the CPU to maintain the time on its own. If you need time of day in your system, then you need a battery and a time-of-day chip. An exception to this case is if the embedded system knows that it has an external device from which it can get the current time after being reset.

Serial Port Drivers

Many embedded systems use serial ports as an interface to the outside world. Despite the serial port's age (it has been around longer than dirt), serial ports are still found on most modern single-board computers. The serial device on an embedded system has two portions: the protocol and the physical interface. The protocol portion takes care of start and stop bits, bits per character, the width of each bit based on a configured baud rate, and the conversion of the serial bit stream into a parallel byte stream easily digested by the CPU. The physical interface takes care of converting voltage levels on the CPU to the voltage levels needed by the interface. In many cases, the physical interface also provides some electrical isolation between the physical connector and the CPU. Embedded systems use two fundamentally different transmission mechanisms for their serial ports: single wire and differential drive transmission.

Single Wire Data Transfer

Single wire systems dedicate one wire to each direction of data transfer and use a common ground reference. While simpler than differential drive transmission, single wire transfer has limitations with regard to transmission speed and the length of the wire from sender to receiver. The most common single wire standard is RS-232. RS-232 is the serial interface used by the COM port on a PC and the TTY ports on UNIX systems. RS-232 is by far the most common serial communications standard in the industry.

The Many Flavors of RS-232

RS-232 is brought to the external world as a data terminal equipment (DTE) or data communications equipment (DCE) connection. If you want to connect two RS-232 ports together pin-to-pin and you want these two ports to be able to exchange data, one side must be configured as DTE, and one side must be configured as DCE. This terminology originates from one of the earliest uses of the interface: connecting a dumb terminal port to a modem to provide remote access to a computer. In this scenario, the terminal is the DTE, and the modem is the DCE.

If there weren't a DTE and DCE side to the interface and you tried to connect the two devices pin-to-pin (through a cable), the transmitter line on one would be tied to the transmitter line on the other, and the receiver line on one would also be tied to the receiver on the other. This wouldn't be pretty! Configuring one side as DTE and the other side as DCE allows a straight-through cable to connect the two devices. The physical difference between DTE and DCE is the pinout of the connector. For example, on DTE, pin 2 might be transmit, and on DCE, pin 2 would be receive. Similarly, pin 3 on DTE might be receive, and pin 3 on DCE would be transmit.

So what do you do if you have two devices that both have an RS-232 connection, but both are of the same type? That's what a null-modem is for. The null-modem does all the required pin swapping through a special cable or a small adapter that is inserted between the cable and one of the device connectors.

Differential Drive Interface

Differential drive is not as widely used. It requires a few more wires, increases the drive length substantially, and also supports transmission speeds in excess of 1MB.

Differential drive interface can drive faster signals through greater distances because of its inherent noise immunity. The idea behind differential drive is that opposite polarity signals (a signal and its inverse) are applied to two wires that travel the same path as a twisted pair. These wires are wrapped around each other, which minimizes interference. The receiver determines the state of the signal based on the voltage difference between the two wires. If noise hits the cable, it is likely to inject the same corrupting signal on each wire, so it doesn't contribute to the detected difference (see Figure 1.4).

The most common embedded interfaces that use this technique are RS-422 and RS-485. RS-422 is a differential drive replacement for RS-232. With no other changes in firmware, an RS-232 interface could be replaced with RS-422, and its maximum line drive and line speed would be increased. RS-485 adds the ability to have more than a single transmitter and receiver on the connection. RS-485 can support single-master/multiple-slave or multi-master modes of communication between serveral devices. RS-485 is commonly used on factory floor networks because of the noise immunity and ability to connect multiple devices.

Figure 1.4   Differential Drive and Noise Immunity.

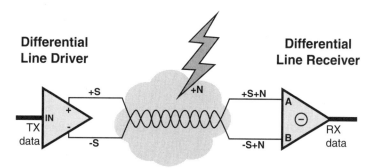

The line receiver uses analog techniques to compute A-B, giving (+S+N)-(-S+N)=2S. Thus all induced transmission line noise is cancelled at the receiver.

Ethernet Interface

While there are a few processor chips that include a portion of the Ethernet interface on the chip, it's still more common to find the Ethernet interface on a separate device. Like the serial port, the Ethernet interface is partitioned into two layers (protocol and physical). The protocol layer is implemented as a single block called the Media Access Layer (MAC). The physical layer consists of two blocks: a PHY and a transformer. It is becoming more common to see the PHY and Ethernet controller integrated into one device, but the transformer is still separate; hence, the Ethernet interface can consist of two or three distinct devices.

The Ethernet controller is the portion of the interface that does the packet-level work. For incoming packets, it verifies that the incoming frame has a valid cyclic redundancy check (CRC), ignores packets that do not match a specified MAC address, organizes the incoming frames as packets that can be retrieved by the CPU (usually through either a FIFO or DMA transfer), and generates interrupts based on various configuration parameters established by the driver. For outgoing packets, the Ethernet controller calculates the CRC, transfers data from memory to the PHY, adds padding to small packets, and interrupts the CPU to indicate that the packet has been sent.

The PHY takes care of the lowest level of the interface protocol. It is responsible for various parameters (like bit rate) specific to the environment.

The transformer provides isolation and electrical conversion of the signals passed over the cable.

Flash Device Options

All flash devices are structured as a number of sectors. On some devices, the sectors are all the same size; on others the sector sizes vary. Some have features that allow the firmware to lock a sector so that it cannot be erased unless a physical connection is inserted onto the hardware. Some devices have reset input lines, and others do not. Densities vary from 64KB to 8MB in a single flash device.

Flash Locking Facilities

Erasing or writing flash memory involves a special, nontrivial algorithm. Thus, it is relatively safe to assume that this algorithm will not be executed accidentally. However, it is still nice to have the option to protect certain sectors from misbehaving code. Many of the available flash devices have the ability to protect one or more sectors from write operations. Some of these devices allow you to protect a specified sector or group of sectors by placing the device in an external programming device and applying a high voltage to one of the pins. Others have a more flexible configuration that uses an external write protect pin and a lock sequence. In this latter type of device, a sector is write-protected or locked by executing a specific command sequence. Once locked, a sector can only be modified after first being unlocked. This process makes it even more difficult to corrupt a sector accidentally. Locking can be used to assure that some very basic boot code is always available for the CPU regardless of what happens to the programming of the other sectors.

If this safeguard is still not enough, an alternate technique can prevent a sector from being modified until a power cycle occurs. This method is typically accomplished by enabling the write-protect pin and then initiating the lock sequence to a particular device sector. Because there is no unlock sequence that works when the write-protect pin is enabled and the write protect pin can not change state until the next hard reset, the sector is protected from all erroneous writes except those that happen immediately upon boot. If you need more protection than this method provides, use EPROM!

Bottom-Boot and Top-Boot Flash Devices

Some devices are organized as a few small sectors at the bottom address space, followed by large sectors that fill the remaining space. Some devices have a few small sectors at the top of the device's address space and use large sectors in the lower address space. Since boot code is typically placed in small sectors, flash memory is some times described as bottom-boot or top-boot, depending on where the smaller sectors are located.

Ultimately, one sector contains the memory space that the CPU accesses as a result of a power cycle or reset (boot). This sector is usually referred to as the *boot sector*. Because some CPUs have a reset vector that is at the top of memory space and others have a reset vector at the bottom of memory space, the flash devices come in bottom-boot and top-boot flavors. A processor that boots to the top of memory space would probably use a top-boot device, and a processor that boots to the bottom of its memory space would be more suited to a bottom-boot device.

When the boot sector of the flash device exists in the boot-time address space of the CPU, it can be protected by making the boot sectors unmodifiable. Since only a small amount of code is typically needed to provide a basic boot, there is little wasted space if you dedicate a small sector to an unmodifiable boot routine. This supports the ability to make as much of the flash space in-system reprogrammable without losing the security of knowing that if all of the reprogrammable flash was accidentally corrupted, the system would still be able to boot through the small amount of code in the unmodifiable boot sector.

The CPU/Memory Interface

The most critical interface in any computing system is the connection between memory and the CPU. If this interface doesn't function properly, the CPU cannot function because it cannot retrieve instructions. If the processor can't reliably retrieve instructions, it really doesn't matter if anything else on the board works — you won't be using it anyway.

Understanding the CPU/memory interface is important to more than just the data and instruction stream. In most systems, peripherals share the data and address buses with memory. Thus, understanding the protocol for these buses is an important first step toward understanding much of the hardware.

This section explains, in general terms, how the CPU uses the address and data buses to communicate with other parts of the system. To make the discussion more concrete, I describe the operation in terms of the hypothetical machine detailed in the simplified schematics in Figure 1.5 and Figure 1.6. Don't worry, you won't need an electrical engineering degree to interpret these drawings. I've omitted everything except the relevant connections. The result is only slightly more detailed than the typical functional block diagram, but it is also representative of the portion of a real schematic that you would need to understand to work with most embedded processors. If you can identify the control, data, and address lines in your system, you probably know all you need to know about how to read a schematic.

Figure 1.5   Schematic CPU.

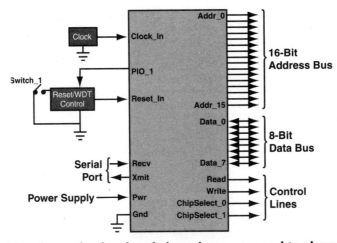

In this schematic, the signals have been grouped to show how they relate to the various system buses. Notice that nearly all of the CPU pins are dedicated to creating these buses.

The CPU

In the CPU diagram (Figure 1.5), there is only one "big" part: the CPU. There are also two other blocks of components on this page: the clock and the reset circuit. The clock provides the CPU with the ability to step through processing states, which can vary from one cycle per instruction (RISC) to sometimes over a dozen cycles per instruction (CISC). The clock can be a crystal, or it can be a complete clock circuit, depending on the needs of the CPU. The reset/WDT circuit provides the processor with a logic level on the reset pin that forces the CPU back to its starting point. This particular circuit uses separate logic to assure that the processor's reset pin is held low for the required amount of time after a power-up or when the Switch_1 switch is pressed. Notice that a PIO line out of the CPU feeds into this circuit to provide the WDT with a periodic sanity pulse.

Figure 1.6   Schematic Flash and RAM.

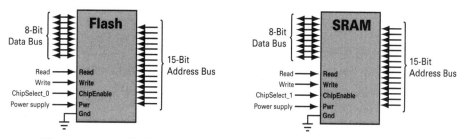

The memory devices connect directly to the system buses. Because each device is only 32K, each uses only 15 address lines. Notice how each device is activated by a separate chip select.

The CPU in this design uses 16-bit addresses but transfers data eight bits at a time. Thus, it has a 16-bit address bus and an 8-bit data bus. Using these 16 bits, the processor can address a 64K memory space. In this design, half of that space is occupied by 32K of flash memory and the other half by 32K of SRAM (Figure 1.6).

Each CPU pin belongs to one of four groups: address, data, control, or I/O.

In this simple design, the majority of the CPU pins are committed to creating address and data buses. Since each memory component houses only 32K of address space the memory chips have only 15 address lines. In this design, the low-order 15 address bits are directly connected to these 15 lines on the memory components. Two additional CPU control signals — ChipSelect_0 and ChipSelect_1 — are used to activate the appropriate memory device. The most significant bit Addr_15 is unused. (If the CPU did not provide conveniently decoded chip select lines, we could have used the high-order bit of the address bus and some additional logic (called *address decode logic*) to activate the appropriate memory device.

Whenever the CPU wants to read or write a particular byte of memory, it places the address of that byte on the address lines. If the address is 0x0000, the CPU would drive all address lines to a low voltage, logic 0 state. If the address were 0xFFFE, the CPU would drive all except the least significant address line to a high voltage, logic 1 state.

When a device is not selected, it is in a high-impedance state (electrically discon-nected) mode. Two more control lines (read and write) on the CPU control how a selected device connects to the data bus. If the read line is active, then the selected memory chip's output circuits are enabled, allowing it to drive a data value onto the data bus. If the write line is active, the CPU's output circuits are enabled, and the selected memory chip connects only its input circuits to the data bus.

Collectively the read, write, and chip select pins are called the control/status lines.

Hexadecimal and Bus Signals

It's common to refer to address and data bus values in ASCII-coded hex, for example "Put 0xBE at 0x26A4". In this usage "put 0xBE" means place 0xBE on the data bus, while at "0x26A4" means place the address 0x26A4 on the address bus. To find out what happens to individual address or data lines, you need to expand the hex to its binary equivalent. Each hex digit represents four bits as in the following chart:

Hexadecimal	Binary	Hexadecimal	Binary
0x0	0000	0x1	0001
0x2	0010	0x3	0011
0x4	0100	0x5	0101
0x6	0110	0x7	0111
0x8	1000	0x9	1001
0xA	1010	0xB	1011
0xC	1100	0xD	1101
0xE	1110	0xF	1111

Thus, 0xBE represents the eight bits 1011 1110.

Note that the number of hexadecimal digits implies the size of the bus. 0xBE con-tains only two hexadecimal digits, implying that the data bus is only eight bits wide. The four hexadecimal digits in 0x26A4, on the other hand, suggest that the address bus is 16 bits wide. Because of this implicit relationship between the hex representation and the bus size, it is accepted convention to pad addresses and data values with zeros so that all bits in the bus are specified. For example, when referencing address 1 in a machine with 32-bit addresses, one would write 0x00000001, not 0x1.

Figure 1.7 summarizes the connections between the CPU and the flash device. If you compare this diagram to the schematic, you can see that the only additional con-nections on the flash device are for power and ground.

Figure 1.7   Connection Between CPU and Boot Flash Device.

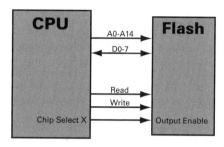

The CPU uses the read and write signals to control the output drivers on the various memory and peripheral devices, and thus, controls the direction of the data bus.

The CPU-to-flash device interaction can be summarized with the following steps:

1. CPU places the desired address on the address pins.
2. CPU brings the read line active.
3. CPU brings the appropriate chip select line active.
4. The flash device places the data located at the specified address onto the data bus.
5. CPU reads in the data that has been placed on the bus by the flash device.
6. CPU releases the chip select line and processes the data.

This sequence of steps allows the CPU to retrieve the bytes from memory that ultimately become instructions. It's commonly referred to as *instruction fetching*. If you understand this interface, it's easy to connect to other devices, because they are all fundamentally the same. The SRAM interface is identical except that a different chip select line is activated. The different chip select lines are configured so that each line is active for a 32K address space. (ChipSelect_0 is used for the 0–32K range, and ChipSelect_1 is used for the 32K–64K range.) A write access is essentially the same thing except that now the Write line is used and the data flow is from CPU to memory, not memory to CPU.

So that's essentially it for the address, data, and control. You have a certain number of address bits (dependent on the actual size of the device), 8 data bits (16 or 32 if you were using a different device), and a few control lines (read, write, and chip select). All that remains in the schematic is the serial port. Since most modern processors have a UART built in, there's only a driver to attach, and that does not involve any CPU interaction. In other words, you now understand the fundamentals of a simple microprocessor-based hardware design!

The Power (and Pitfalls) of Cache

For standard programming environments, cache is a blessing. It provides a real speed increase for code that is written to use it properly (refer to Figure 1.8). Caching takes advantage of a phenomenon known as *locality of reference*.[1] Locality of reference states that at any given point in a program's execution, the CPU is accessing some small block of memory repeatedly. The ability to pull that small block of memory into a faster memory area is a very effective way to speed up what would otherwise be a relatively slow rate of memory access.

Figure 1.8   Cache Between CPU and External Devices.

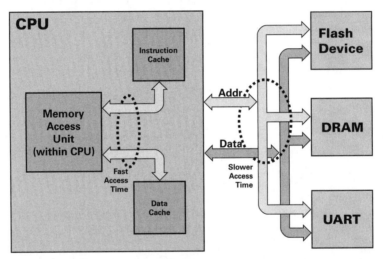

There are different levels of cache, the fastest (usually called level 1) cache used by the CPU is located on the CPU chip.

Cache is a fast chunk of memory placed between the memory access portion of the CPU and the real memory system in order to provide an enhancement to the access time between the CPU and external memory. There are several different types of cache implementations. Discussion of these various implementations is beyond the scope of this text. Instead, this section focuses on the two major types of caches used in today's embedded systems: instruction cache (I-cache) and data cache (D-cache).

As the names imply, the two different caches are used for the two different types of CPU memory access: accesses to instruction space and accesses to data space, respectively. Caches are divided into these two major types because of the difference in the way the CPU accesses these two areas of memory. The CPU reads and writes

1. M. Morris Mano, *Computer System Architecture*, Second Ed. (Englewood Cliffs, NJ: Prentice Hall, 1982), pg 501.

to data space but tends to read from instruction space much more often than it writes to it.

The only limitation that cache puts on typical high-level system programmers is that it can be dangerous to modify instruction space, sometimes called *self-modifying code*. This is because any modification to memory space is done through a data access.

The D-cache is involved in the transaction; hence, the instruction destined for physical memory can reside in the D-cache for some undetermined amount of time after the code that actually made the access has completed. This behavior presents a double chance of error: the data written to the instruction space might not be in physical memory (because it is still in the D-cache), or the contents of the instruction's address might already be in the I-cache, which means the fetch for the instruction does not actually access the physical memory that contains the new instruction.

Figure 1.9   Data-Cache Instruction-Cache Inconsistency.

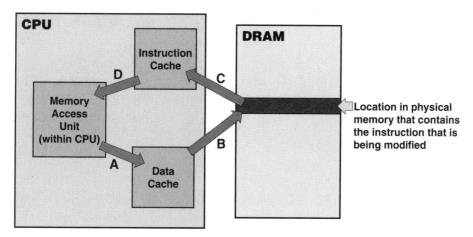

Cache increases performance by allowing the CPU to fetch frequently used values from fast, internal cache instead of from slower external memory. However, because the cache control mechanism makes different assumptions about how data and instruction spaces are manipulated, self-modifying code can create problems. Cache can also create problems if it masks changes in peripheral registers.

Figure 1.9 shows how the cache gets between the data write and the instruction read. Step A shows the CPU writing to memory through the D-cache. Step B shows the transfer of the contents of that D-cache location to physical memory. Step C represents the transfer of the physical memory to the I-cache, and step D shows the CPU's memory access unit retrieving the instruction from the I-cache. If the sequence of events was guaranteed to be A-B-C-D, then everything would work fine. However, this sequence cannot be guaranteed, because that would eliminate the efficiency gained by using the cache. The whole point behind cache is to attempt to eliminate the B and C steps whenever possible. The ultimate result is that the instruction fetch may be corrupted as a result of skipping step B , step C, or both.

For embedded systems, the problem just gets worse. Understanding the above problem makes the secondary problems fairly clear. Notice in Figure 1.8 that there is a flash device, DRAM, and a UART. Two additional complexities become apparent:

1. The UART is on the same address/data bus as the memory, which means that accesses to a UART or any other physical device outside the CPU must deal with the fact that cache can "get in the way." Hardware must be designed with this consideration in mind (or the firmware must configure the hardware) so that certain devices external to the CPU can easily be accessed without the data cache being involved.

2. The UART may be configured to use DMA to place incoming characters into memory space. In many systems, DMA and cache are independent of each other. The data cache is likely to be unaware of memory changes due to DMA transfers, which means that if the data cache sits between the CPU and this memory space, more inconsistencies must be dealt with.

The complexity of the hardware and the "need for speed" make these issues tricky but not insurmountable. Most of the prior problems are solved through good hardware and firmware design. The initial issue of I-cache and D-cache inconsistency can be resolved by invoking a *flush* of the data cache and an *invalidation* of the instruction cache. A flush forces the content of the data cache out to the real memory. An invalidation empties the instruction cache so that future CPU requests retrieve a fresh copy of corresponding memory.

Also, there are some characteristics of cache that can help resolve these problems. For example, a *write through* data cache ensures that data written to memory is placed in cache but also written out to physical memory. This guarantees that data writes will be loaded to cache and will pass through the cache to real memory; hence it really only provides a speed improvement for data reads. Also, a facility in some CPUs called *bus snooping* helps with the memory inconsistency issues related to DMA and cache. Bus snooping hardware detects when DMA is used to access memory space that is cached and automatically invalidates the corresponding cache locations. Bus snooping hardware isn't available on all systems however. Additionally, to avoid the problem with cache being between the CPU and the UART, devices can usually be mapped to a memory location that doesn't involve the cache at all. It is very common for a CPU to restrict caching to certain specific cachable regions of memory, rather than designating its entire memory space cacheable. The bottom line is that the firmware developer must be aware of these hardware and firmware capabilities and limitations in order to deal with these complexities efficiently.

Summary

While embedded systems come in a fascinating array of variations, at the lowest hardware levels they usually have many general similarities. Memory systems interface with CPU via address and data buses. Systems interface with development hosts via serial ports. Watchdog timers supply robust operation even in the presence of intermittent software and hardware bugs. Knowing the general structure of these common facilities gives you a useful framework for learning the specifics of new systems.

The hardware coverage in this chapter won't make you a hardware guru, but it should prepare you to better understand the documentation for your particular hardware. More importantly (for the purposes of the book), it should prepare you to understand the hardware issues discussed in later chapters.

Where this chapter described primarily hardware features, the next chapter focuses on software issues — specifically on how to compile and load programs for an embedded target. More than anything else, these two issues, the need for greater knowledge about the hardware and the need for tools that work in a cross-development environment, separate embedded systems from application development.

Chapter 2

Getting Started

The last chapter presented hardware design options for a typical embedded system. This chapter concentrates on how to write and build a program destined for an embedded device.

Because you will be working in a cross-development environment on potentially untested hardware, the first programs are very small, very limited test programs. Even though the first test may be trivial programs, getting them into the target is not trivial. Before you can hope to begin testing your firmware, you must:

- understand the hardware environment;

- make sure you have the necessary programming and debugging tools;

- make sure your programming and debugging tools are compatible with the hardware environment;

- perform some simple tests to verify that the hardware is working.

You'll learn more about these considerations later in this chapter. First, I'll begin with a look at the cross-platform compilation process and how the embedded systems environment differs from the conventional PC environment.

Before going any further, you should be aware that the build procedure discussed in this book does not involve any fancy graphical user interface (GUI) nor does it require any expensive tools. The development environment used throughout this text is the Microcross GNU X-Tools™, a fully functional set of cross-compilation tools is provided on the book CD. Supplying the completed tool set should eliminate the headaches typically associated with build environment incompatibilities. The examples in this chapter use tools like gcc, objcopy, objdump, and make. You can pick your own editor. I use elvis, a vi clone, that allows me to edit binary files in a convenient way. (You will see later that this is very handy.) If you are accustomed to working with a modern desktop application development environment, these tools may seem primitive, at first. Their sparseness, though, is their strength. Using a GUI development environment for this stage of firmware development is like working in the rain with an umbrella. You spend more time figuring out how to hold the umbrella than you do working on the project. It's much better to just get wet. The point is that you don't want anything sheltering you from the bare metal. Working with simple command-line tools may seem a little cold at first, but, in order to understand the firmware development process, you need to put down the umbrella.

How Is It Done on a PC?

To create a convenient execution context on the target machine, the developer needs to implement substitutes for many of the key operating system services that both users and programmers tend to take for granted in the desktop world. A PC uses DOS and BIOS to perform many tasks that the average user takes for granted. You begin to realize just how much the PC does once you try to duplicate some of its functionality in an embedded systems project so to start off the discussion, we will quickly overview the process of program development on a "native" PC environment.

Consider the sample program shown in Listing 2.1.

Listing 2.1   A Simple Sample.

```
int
PrintAMessage(void)
{
    return(printf("This is a message\n"));
}

int
main(int argc,char *argv[])
{
    int msize;
```

```
    sleep(1);
    msize = PrintAMessage();
    return(msize);
}
```

Typically, this program exists as an executable file with the extension .exe. When the user types in the file name, a search is made through the file system directories (specified by the PATH shell variable) looking for a match. The information in the file header is checked to verify that the file is a valid executable. Lastly, the executable file is loaded into DRAM of the PC and executed.

This process requires four significant steps:

- the shell takes the incoming program name from the keyboard and determines that it is not a command within the local shell;
- the shell searches the file system until the program name is found;
- the loader verifies the program and loads it into DRAM;
- the loader transfers control to the program in DRAM, and the program executes.

These four steps describe the process of running a program from the highest level. If you really want to get inquisitive, there are certainly more details to consider. For example, how does the shell start up in the first place? How does a character get from the keyboard to the CPU inside the PC? How does the CPU retrieve the file from the disk drive? Some of these questions are relevant because they must be translated into some process or sequence of steps in our embedded system, and other questions are not especially relevant to an embedded system. So, although a desktop PC is quite a bit different from a typical embedded system, there are many fundamental similarities. If you understand how the PC works, you will find it a lot easier to understand firmware.

Four concepts from the PC world are particularly helpful for an understanding of the embedded systems environment:

- *Command line interface* — In DOS, the file command.com is one of the first files retrieved from the disk when the PC is turned on. The command.com program is a shell that provides an interface between the user and the PC hardware. In an embedded system, there is no insulation (shell) between the program and the hardware. The program must interact with the hardware directly. In other words, you need to create the equivalent of a command.com interpreter for your embedded system. You can't just write a `printf("hello world\n")` statement and take the rest for granted.

- *File system* — The file system allows programs to be stored in some large capacity device and pulled into the processor's memory space only when needed. In an embedded system, the program is typically stored in flash memory all the time, as there is seldom any other storage device from which you can retrieve a program. As you will see later, this doesn't mean that the flash device can't look and act like a file system.

- *Loader* — Because the PC can have more than one application active at a time (through the use of interrupts and the vector table), there is no way to predict just where the program will reside in memory when it is executed. The loader takes care of the memory location details using the relocation information in the `.exe` file. In an embedded system, you *can* assume that an application runs at a specific point in memory, so you can build the program to reside at a specific location in target memory. A program that is built to run at some dynamically chosen point in system memory is called *relocatable*. A program built to run at a fixed location in memory is called *absolute*.

- *Services* — On a PC, the application can assume that certain services are provided by trap handlers already loaded into the vector table of the CPU. These handlers are an important part of the service layer created by the BIOS. Because an embedded target has no BIOS, the application obviously can't assume there is one! The implication is that some of the standard libraries provided with the compilers cannot be used, or, if they are, they must not assume any underlying facilities exist in the platform. For example, your embedded application can't call `fopen()` and expect a file to magically open somewhere. You can't even count on being able to use use `putchar()` because the fundamental system calls that interface to the serial port may depend on BIOS services (or some equivalent). If you wish to make these types of functions available on an embedded system, you must provide these services yourself.

To summarize, many of the features you take for granted on a PC are features you must build for yourself on an embedded system. You'll learn how to build these features later in this book.

The program in Listing 2.1 makes several other implicit assumptions about the execution context, for example:

- Upon entry into `main()`, the stack pointer must be pointing to memory space that can be used for temporary storage.

- Something from somewhere must be able to pass arguments to `main()` (the function that is supposedly the starting point of the program).

- Some notion of time must be established to allow functions like `sleep()` to work properly.

- When `main()` returns, some supervisor such as the operating sytem (OS) will resume control.

The Cross-Compilation Process

Within the context of this discussion, there are two different types of compilation: native and cross. Both kinds of compilation produce a file containing binary machine code (called an `executable`), but that's where the similarity ends.

You are probably most familiar with *native compilation*. With native compilation, the programmer writes a program on a PC, compiles it on a PC, and runs it on a PC. The environment in which the program was compiled is the same environment in which it is executed. Embedded systems developers, on the other hand, usually generate code using *cross -compilation*. You write a program on a PC, compile it on a PC, and run it on some other target. (The host platform for compilation doesn't have to be a PC, it can be a UNIX machine or other operating system.) Not only is the host a different machine, but the target and host CPUs are probably totally different beasts.

The end result of the native compilation process is a file (the executable) in a format that the operating system's loader understands. (The loader is the tool in the host system that takes the executable and does what is necessary to execute it on the host system.) Depending on the host OS, the executable may be *relocatable* or *absolute*. If an executable is relocatable, it is built so that the loader can place it anywhere in the memory space of the host system. If the executable is absolute, it is built to run starting at some fixed address in memory (usually zero). Obviously, there is only one real location zero in the memory space, but the loader knows that the host's MMU will take the necessary steps so that the program "thinks" it is running from location zero. Consequently, in a native environment, the programmer cannot know where the program will be loaded in memory.

The end result of the cross-compilation process is also an executable file, and prior to some final processing, this file may actually look a lot like a standard executable file for a UNIX or DOS machine. When building a program that is to boot a target system, the file is not relocatable.[1] This is because boot code is always destined to reside at some fixed memory location in the target's memory space (not necessarily zero), and, when boot code is executed, the MMU (if there is one) is disabled. At

---

1. In general, programs destined for embedded systems are not relocatable; however, if the program is destined for an embedded system that already has some underlying platform, relocation becomes an option if the platform supports it.

boot time, there is no underlying loader; the only layer "below" the bootcode is the solder and circuit board. Various toolsets might compile the executable to any of several different commonly used file formats. Rather than covering each of these formats, this book examines a generic file format that represents most of the common file formats used today. The executable file is divided into two main parts: a series of headers, followed by a series of sections. The first header in the series describes the file. The remaining headers describe the following sections. Each section header contains information about the physical location of the section, the section size, whether or not the section is instruction or data, and, if it is data, whether or not it is assumed to be writable. The section header that corresponds to the RAM space needed for uninitialized data, usually called BSS,[2] does not actually have a corresponding section, because it does not have any associated data. This space is simply cleared at startup. Some of the other sections contain binary data destined for the boot device. Other sections contain symbolic information used by a debugger to debug the program. Since the current focus is on providing information to the boot device, I do not detail the sections that contain debug information.

On its own, the file header information doesn't offer much help for the CPU. The CPU doesn't know what a file header is, it just wants to be able to fetch instructions from the reset location in target memory space and start executing them. The cross-compilation process requires an additional step to convert the executable file from the format illustrated in Figure 2.1 to one that presents the data in a way the CPU understands.

Since the executable file represents an absolute memory map, the code behind it has been compiled and linked to run at a specific location in memory. The linker extracts the necessary location information from the memory map input file. This file tells the linker where to put the different output sections (text, data and BSS).

The final step is to convert the executable file into a single binary image that will look to the processor like raw instructions and data. This is usually a fairly easy step, but its complexity depends on the complexity of the memory map. For the sake of our discussion, you can assume that the system's boot-flash-device starts at location 0x000000 and its RAM starts at location 0x800000 (assuming our CPU has a 24-bit address bus). In addition, you can assume that the .text section resides at 0 and all the other non-BSS sections are concatenated above this location. This layout makes the transition to a true binary image fairly simple. The raw data in the .text section becomes the beginning of the image file, the raw data of .data and .rodata sections are appended to the raw data of .text image.

---

2. *BSS* means block started by symbol. This term originates from the old IBM mainframe world and refers to a block of memory that is not initialized. Gintaras R. Gircys, Understanding and Using COFF, (Sebastopol, CA: O'Reilly & Associates, 1988), pg 9.

Figure 2.1   Example Executable File Format.

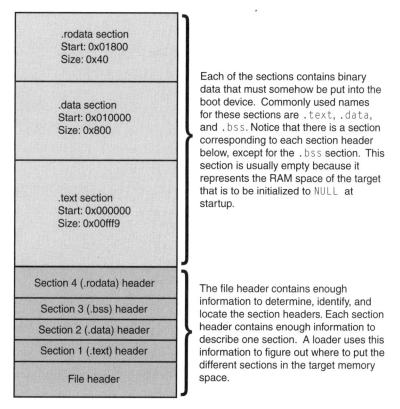

.rodata section
Start: 0x01800
Size: 0x40

.data section
Start: 0x010000
Size: 0x800

.text section
Start: 0x000000
Size: 0x00fff9

Each of the sections contains binary data that must somehow be put into the boot device. Commonly used names for these sections are `.text`, `.data`, and `.bss`. Notice that there is a section corresponding to each section header below, except for the `.bss` section. This section is usually empty because it represents the RAM space of the target that is to be initialized to `NULL` at startup.

Section 4 (.rodata) header

Section 3 (.bss) header

Section 2 (.data) header

Section 1 (.text) header

File header

The file header contains enough information to determine, identify, and locate the section headers. Each section header contains enough information to describe one section. A loader uses this information to figure out where to put the different sections in the target memory space.

Typically, executable files are partitioned into sections, where each section represents a contiguous block of memory. For purposes of discussion, I assume executable files follow the simple structure shown in this illustration.

Note that even though you instruct the linker to place each of the sections back-to-back in memory, there still may be a hole between any two sections. You can determine the size of this hole by observing the starting address and size of each of the sections. If the `.text` section is `0xfff9` bytes, starts at address `0x0000`, and has the `.data` section directly appended to it, the starting address for the `.data` section will be `0xfff9`. If the address is higher, then for one reason or another (usually alignment), the linker has shifted the start address of the section. This shift must be accounted for with padding in the image file. For example, if the `.data` section starts at `0x10000`, you must insert `0x10000-0xfff9` bytes of padding before appending the content of the `.data` section to the new image file. You also need to take the shifting into account for each of the remaining sections. The end result is a binary file that looks something like Figure 2.2.

Figure 2.2   File Containing Raw Binary Data Destined for Boot Flash Memory.

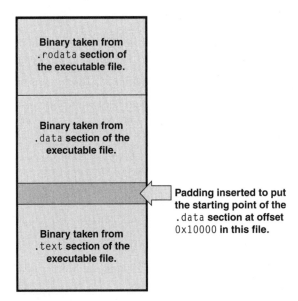

This figure shows how the sections of Figure 2.1 map into the eventual binary image that is to programmed to flash memory. Notice that the headers are gone!

The file of Figure 2.2 contains the actual instructions and data that the CPU will fetch out of memory and convert into some logical operation. Using a device programmer, a developer can transfer this binary image, unchanged, to the non-volatile storage space of the flash device. After the flash device is placed in the target system, on reset the CPU begins to fetch the binary data that represents the program.

You now know a little bit about what an embedded system "executable" looks like on the inside. Initially, the file looks similar to those on a UNIX or DOS machine, but the similarities fade abruptly on closer examination. There is no shell to invoke the loader and no file system from which to load the executable. Intead, the embedded system has an empty socket into which you insert a programmed memory device.

The "loader" (if you dare call it that) in a typical embedded system works something like this:

1. Transfer the raw binary file to a floppy disk.
2. Take the floppy disk to some flash device programmer.

3. Install the floppy disk and copy the file as binary data to a local buffer on the programmer.

4. Insert the flash device into the programmer socket.

5. Erase the flash memory and then transfer the content of the local buffer to the flash device.

6. Wait for completion, then remove the floppy disk and flash device and insert the flash device into the socket on the target board.

7. Turn on the power and pray.

It's quite a different loader from what was described for the PC earlier!

Today most, but not all, cross-development environments offer friendlier, faster alternatives to this device-substitution approach. Some device programmers have a network connection so that the file can be transferred over a network, thereby eliminating the floppy disk steps. If you are really lucky, the target system has a JTAG or BDM interface that you can use to connect directly to load the program image. These interfaces can eliminate the need for an external programming device.

Establishing the Memory Map

The memory map describes (in terms of address space ranges) where the designer has placed memory and peripheral devices. The memory map may be simple flash memory and RAM. On the other hand, the processor may boot out of the top of memory, and there may be multiple devices that are not necessarily in contiguous memory space.

Usually, the hardware is designed so that the firmware can use all the memory of any one type contiguously. All flash memory is located as a contiguous block, as is all RAM, EPROM, etc. The processor also requires a block of non-volatile memory in hardware at the location where it resets. This block of memory is typically called a *boot block*, and it is a requirement, not an option. The CPU must reset and access valid memory; hence, the boot block must be non-volatile.

The details of the memory map are determined by the hardware designers (hopefully with some input from the firmware developers!). The firmware developer communicates these design decisions to the linker and other tools through entries in a configuration file called the link editor file or memory map file. Depending on the target and some of the needs of the firmware, this file can get quite complicated.

The Link Editor File

The following example is basic, but complete. It shows how the link editor file tells the linker where the physical memory is (the MEMORY directive) and where within that memory each section is to be placed (the SECTION directive). Each line in the MEMORY description specifies a name, start address, and length for each block of memory within the system being mapped. In the case of Listing 2.2, there is 256K of flash memory (0x40000) starting at location zero and 512K of dynamic RAM (0x80000) starting at location 0x80000. Note that the names flash and dram have no meaning other than to tag the block of memory. The example code could just as easily call these memory blocks "bill" and "mary." Also, note that comments are usually allowed in these files, and you should use them to describe what you are trying to configure. As with any piece of code, other developers might need to modify it.

Listing 2.2   Link Editor File

```
/* Memory Map File for widget.  This hardware has .25Meg of FLASH
 * from 0-0x3ffff and .5Meg of DRAM from at 0x80000-0xfffff.
 * This program is built such that initialized data is left in
 * ROM space.  This keeps things simple, but does require
 * that no initialized data be written at runtime.
 */

MEMORY
{
    flash : org = 0,        len = 0x40000
    dram  : org = 0x80000,  len = 0x80000
}


/* Note the use of boot_base, bss_start and bss_end to tag beginning
 * of flash, and boundaries of .bss space respectively.  These tags
 * can be used by the program to reference the hard-coded memory locations
 * they represent.
 */
SECTIONS
{
    .text   :
    {
        boot_base = .;
        *(.text)
    } >flash
```

```
    .data   :
    {
        *(.data)
    } >flash

    .bss    :
    {
        bss_start = .;
        *(.bss)
        bss_end = .;
    } >dram

}
```

The blocks in the SECTIONS portion of the file establish where each of the fundamental sections are placed in real memory space (see Listing 2.2). The *(.text), *(.data) and *(.bss) lines tell the linker to put all of the text, data, and BSS portions (respectively) of the image into the referenced memory area. If needed, the user can also list the object file names in the order they should be placed in memory. The other alternative is to specify the order on the linker command line.

The boot_base = ., bss_start = ., and bss_end = . lines are used to create labels that can be referenced by C code. These labels look like variables located at the current location (.) in the memory map. In this example, boot_base corresponds to address 0x0000 (in the flash memory block). The bss_start tag maps to the begining of BSS space, while bss_end corresponds to the last DRAM address allocated to BSS.

NOTE

Some toolsets provide these tags; others don't. So the consistent thing to do is provide your own set of tags and use them regardless of what the toolset provides.

Text, Data, and BSS

So far this chapter has concentrated on the memory sections .text, .data, and .bss. There can actually be several more sections aside from these three; however, these are the basic sections (or section types). A text section usually contains code (instructions that are fetched from memory and executed by the CPU). A BSS section is a section of memory that does not contain any initialized data. Usually, this section is cleared to zero at run-time startup. A data section usually holds initialized data. The data section includes the space used by variables that are declared with an initial value. The data section can also house all the initialized strings used throughout the code.

What further complicates the data section is that some initialized data may also be writable. Nonwritable initialized data can be part of flash memory. The initial state of writable initialized data must also be part of flash memory, but for this data to be writable, its run-time value must be stored in RAM. To accomodate this dual personality, when the program starts all writable initial values are copied from flash to matching data blocks in RAM. The program manipulates only the values in RAM.

The code of Listing 2.3 illustrates the varieties of data. The actual instructions that make up the function called func are placed in the text section. The strings passed to printf() represent initialized, read-only data, so this information is placed in a data section that does not need to be copied to RAM. The variable justStarted is initialized, but the code wants to be able to modify it, so the variable must be assigned to a data section that starts off in flash memory and is copied to RAM. Finally, the variable sysClock is not initialized but is writable, so it is assigned to the BSS section, which represents RAM space that is cleared to zero at startup.

Listing 2.3   A Program That Uses Text, Data, and BSS Sections.

```
int justStarted = 1;
int sysClock;

int
func()
{
    if (justStarted == 1) {
        printf("Hey, we just started!\n");
        justStarted = 0;
    }
    else {
        printf("Hello sysclock = %d\n",sysClock);
    }
}
```

One last note regarding these sections: in assembly language, you can put code in data space and data in code space if you want to. The directives in the assembler allow this; however, standard C compilers place the different types of binary data in the sections as described above, so it only makes sense to follow that lead.

Different Reset Vectors Equate to Different Memory Maps

It is worth noting that different CPUs branch to different points in memory as a result of a reset or power-up. Some jump to the bottom of memory, some to the top, and some jump somewhere in between. Wherever the reset vector goes, so goes the boot flash memory. For this and other reasons, the reset vector position can complicate the memory map.

Clearly, the CPU's reset philosophy plays a major role in establishing the memory map of the system. For top-boot CPUs, boot flash memory occupies the top of physical memory space, and everything else is below it. For mid-boot CPUs, additional memory could be on either side, and, for bottom-boot CPUs, all additional memory is above. Figure 2.3 shows these three different scenarios.

Figure 2.3   Reset Vector <-> Boot Flash Configuration.

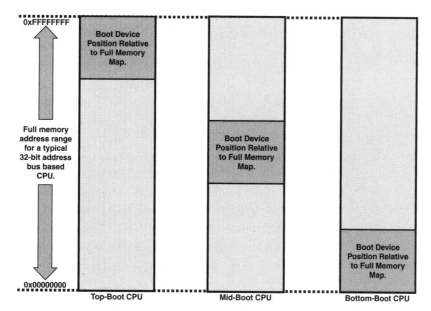

The reset behavior of the processor determines the location (in address space) of the boot device and therefore, of the flash memory.

The make File

As with many of the examples in this book, I will discuss a simplified make file. The goal of this section is to introduce the build procedure for a cross-compilation environment, not to provide a tutorial on make.

The sample makefile (Listings 2.4–2.7) assumes the programmer is using the GNU cross-compilation tools for a ColdFire 5272 microprocessor under the bash shell environment. This toolset generates an output file format known as Common Object File Format (COFF). COFF is one specific example of the many different output file formats that are available. Typically, the GNU tools produce COFF, ELF, or AOUT file formats. The bash shell provides an environment that looks very much like a typical UNIX shell; hence, you see commands like rm instead of delete and cp instead of copy.

I've divided the make file into four sections: initialization, linkage, modules, and miscellaneous.

The basic format of the makefile is the same for cross-compilation as it would be in a native environment. On closer examination, however, you can see that there are quite a few subtle differences that make the typical cross-compilation makefile more complicated.

Listing 2.4   Initialization Section for the ColdFire 5206 Makefile.

```
#HHHHHHHHHHHHHHHHHHHHHHHHHHHHHHHHHHHHHHHHHHHHHHHHHHHHHHHHHHHHHHHHHHHHHHHHHHH
#
# Makefile for building M5272C3 based system.
#

PROG        = myprog
OBJCOPY     = m68k-coff-objcopy
OBJDUMP     = m68k-coff-objdump
NM          = m68k-coff-nm
CC          = m68k-coff-gcc
ASM         = m68k-coff-as
ASMCPP      = cpp -D ASSEMBLY_ONLY
LD          = m68k-coff-ld
CCOPTS      = -Wall -g -c -m5200 -o $@
ASMOPTS     = -m5200 -o $@

OBJS=obj/reset.o obj/start.o obj/cpuio.o obj/main.o
```

The initialization section of the makefile (Listing 2.4) shows the GNU/Cold-Fire-specific commands that replace the standard cc and ld commands. The code also defines additional commands to create a variety of different output files. The first PROG definition serves as a standard output file prefix. You will see shortly that there are a variety of different output files that can be created based on the final executable produced by ld, so the PROG definition specifies a common base name for these different files. Most of the tools have simple one-to-one mappings. For example, for the ColdFire, the CC macro is simply m68k-coff-gcc, ld is simply m68k-coff-ld, and so on. Most of the options are also pretty standard: -g to include symbolic information in the final output file, -c to tell the compiler that this module is incomplete and will be linked later with additional modules, and -o to tell the tools where to put the output. Notice that CCOPTS includes -m5200 to let the compiler know what type of ColdFire microprocessor will use the code.

Listing 2.5   **Top Level** all **Target.**

```
#############################################################################
#
# Top level target to create executable image:
#
all: $(OBJS) makefile
     $(LD) -Map=$(PROG).map -TROM.lnk -nostartfiles -ecoldstart \
        -o $(PROG) $(OBJS)
     coff -B $(PROG).bin $(PROG)
     $(NM) --numeric-sort $(PROG) > $(PROG).sym
```

The top level, all target (see Listing 2.5), depends on all of the individual object modules (OBJS) that must be compiled or assembled prior to performing the linkage (LD). The LD line takes all of the modules (reset, start, cpuio, and main) and links them together in the order of their listing. It establishes an absolute memory map based on the memory map specified by -TROM.lnk (where ROM.lnk is the name of the memory map file). The -Map option tells the linker to generate a file (myprog.map) that describes, in detail, the memory map of the image being created. Typically, a loader automatically includes code that does some initialization prior to turning over control to the application's main() function. Because embedded systems run on the bare metal, you must write custom code to initialize your particular hardware (in reset.s and start.c). The -nostartfile option tells the linker to omit the default startup module (crt0.o). The -ecoldstart option tells the linker to use coldstart as the entry point (instead of the default entry point in crt0.o).

The coff command converts the output COFF file produced by ld into the binary image that the CPU requires. (The source and executable for the coff tool are supplied on the CD but are not part of the standard GNU toolset.) Finally, the NM command is a convenience that allows the developer to query the myprog.sym file immediately for symbolic information about individual variables in the final load image.

Listing 2.6   Rules Section.

```
#############################################################################
#
# Individual rules:
#

obj/cpuio.o: cpuio.c cpuio.h
    $(CC) $(CCOPTS) cpuio.c

obj/start.o: start.c config.h
    $(CC) $(CCOPTS) start.c

obj/main.o: main.c config.h
    $(CC) $(CCOPTS) main.c

obj/reset.o:    reset.s  config.h
    $(ASMCPP) reset.s >tmp.s
    $(ASM) $(ASMOPTS) tmp.s
```

The rules section (Listing 2.6) is pretty standard, except in the way that it uses both CPP and ASM for the reset.s file. Invoking both tools allows the developer to include header files in both C and assembly language. Though some assemblers support a CPP pass as an option, I have coded two separate steps to emphasize the two passes.

The final section of the makefile (see Listing 2.7) shows some of the options that are typically not needed for native compilation. This section also demonstrates how defining a PROG prefix can keep things more organized. The make targets in this correspond to different output files that can be generated by the ld step. The S-record file format could be used in place of the binary format generated by the coff tool. The showmap target simply dumps the content of the section headers. Because the section headers contain information about each of the sections, the showmap target can be useful when trying to diagnose incorrect memory map file settings. Finally, the dis and disx targets dump a listing that includes the source and disassembly intermingled. This listing is useful when using a primitive debugger to set breakpoints within functions.

Listing 2.7   **Miscellaneous Section.**

```
################################################################################
#
# Miscellaneous utilities:
#
clean:
    rm -f obj/*

clobber:    clean
    rm -f $(PROG) $(PROG).map
    rm -f $(PROG).bin $(PROG).srec $(PROG).dis $(PROG).sym

gnusrec:
    $(OBJCOPY) -F srec $(PROG) $(PROG).srec

showmap:
    $(OBJDUMP) --section-headers $(PROG)

dis:
    $(OBJDUMP) --source --disassemble $(PROG) >$(PROG).dis

disx:
    $(OBJDUMP) --source --disassemble --show-raw-insn $(PROG) >$(PROG).dis
```

Building Libraries

A library is a collection of frequently used functions (for example, functions like strcpy(), printf(), strcmp(), and atoi()), that can be incorporated into a program on an as-needed basis. For example, if a program used strcmp(), then the code for strcmp() would be pulled from the appropriate library and included in the application. Regardless of how many functions are in the library, only the code for functions actually referenced by the program is pulled into the program. So, at least two things are gained as a result of using a library:

- A library saves a project from having to add strcmp.o, printf.o, atoi.o, etc. to the link line. The programming team does not even need to be aware of what functions they are getting from the library. The programmers merely include something like -lc on the linker line, and the rest is magic.

- A library reduces the size of the final program module (as compared to including the library source) because unneeded functions are not pulled into the executable.

In some cases, you might want to build your own library. For example, if the code that interfaces to some peripheral widget is to be used by several projects and you want the benefits mentioned above, it might make sense to package the interface functions as a library.

If you know only a little about the process, you might attempt to create a library by putting all of the related functions (widget_funcA(), widget_funcB(), and widget_funcC()) into a single file, compiling it with -c to generate an object (.o) file, and then using some tool (lib or ar usually) to create a library (.a) file from the .o file.

Unfortunately, this approach doesn't have the desired effect because all of the functions were compiled to a single .o file. A library is basically a concatenation of object modules (or .o files). When the linker goes to the library looking for a currently unresolved reference, it looks through each of the object modules for a match. When it finds a match, it pulls that *entire* object module into the program code, regardless of the number of functions in that module. If several functions were originally compiled together into a common .o file, referencing one of those functions results in all of the functions being incorporated into the finished program. The users of such a library are unknowingly getting more for their money! Unfortunately, more is not good in a tight-memory space embedded system. Fortunately, this problem is easily resolved. When building a library, put each function in a separate file that gets built separately.

Wasted space isn't the only reason to avoid monolithic libraries. Suppose that I want to use the previously mentioned library to interface to my widget; however, I have a special case where I want to write my own widget_funcB() and use the library's widget_funcA(). With a monolithic build, I'll end up with two widget_funcB()s in my program because when the linker goes to the library to get widget_funcA(), the other function comes with it. Now there is a name clash between the widget_funcB() in the library and the widget_funcB() that I wrote.

In my experience, this problem is most common when trying to use my own printf(). (Yes, you will need to write your own printf() sooner or later in embedded systems programming!) I want my printf() to call vsprintf() (provided by the library), but, unfortunately, printf() and vsprintf() are in the same object module in the library. I can't call vsprintf() because the linker says that there are two printf() functions (mine and the one pulled in as a result of using vsprintf()).

The important thing to remember is that whenever you build your own library, you build it as a lot of individual one-function-per-file modules. You'll save headaches and memory space!

Up Front: Prior to Loading the Code

Before even considering burning a flash device, make sure you've made adequate preparations for the development process. The following sections discuss some preliminary measures. Many of these measures might seem obvious, but they are nevertheless important enough to mention. The tips discussed in the following sections include:

- Get involved with the hardware design
- Get to know the hardware and be nice to the designer
- Have local copies of all data sheets
- Make sure the hardware is working
- Start slowly
- Look at what you've created

It is also important to consider what tools you need for the development process and to ensure that the design is compatible with those tools. Several hardware-based development and debugging tools are available to assist with the embedded systems development process, including emulators, logic analyzers, JTAG and BDM interfaces, memulators, and logic probes. Many of these tools attach directly to the target device.

Emulators

The in-circuit emulator (ICE) is a device that usually plugs into the CPU's socket on the target hardware. An emulator is designed for a specific CPU. It emulates the CPU closer than any other tool available. The emulator provides a lot of really nice features, such as an instruction trace buffer (which collects previously executed instructions), complex breakpoints, and knowledge of the CPU's instruction cache. If you really need sophisticated debugging, you need an emulator.

If an emulator provides the most insight and flexibility for firmware debugging, why use anything else? This sophistication doesn't come for free. Emulators are usually quite expensive.

Because the emulator typically plugs into the same socket that normally contains the CPU, the target board must be prepared for the emulator. For example, the board designers might need to leave extra space around the CPU to accommodate the emulator's sometimes bulky connector.

If you plan to use an emulator, make sure your hardware can deal with the physical requirements of the pod that connects the emulator with the target board. These physical access issues sometimes extend to the enclosure as well. The pod usually hangs within 12 inches of the target by some shielded multi-pin ribbon cable. So, if your target sits in a card cage and there is another card right next to it, you may be in trouble.

Because it replaces the CPU on the target, the emulator, of necessity, is quite sophisticated. Emulators are very CPU-specific, and you cannot use an emulator with a different processor without incurring substantial additional cost. Because the memory steering logic of the emulator lengthens the memory access cycle, emulators are sometimes not able to run at the full rated speed of the CPU. Also, emulators tend to become available after the CPU is already out and available, so if you are working with a bleeding-edge processor, there is a good chance the emulator will not be available when you need it.

Another problem with plugging into the socket on the target board is that the load that the emulator presents to the target system might be quite different from the load that the CPU would have put on the target. This difference in load can both mask and induce problems. In some situations, the difference in load can reduce induced noise, allowing your system to run in noisy environments — until the emulator is removed. Sometimes the difference in load disturbs the target hardware, creating problems that would otherwise not be present.

Despite all of these warnings, emulators, are still very handy, and the degree to which each of these issues matters depends very much on the environment.

Get Involved with the Hardware Design

First of all, make sure the boot device is conveniently reprogrammable. This point might seem obvious, but it's not unusual to find systems that have the boot device soldered to the board with no reprogramming mechanism except to unsolder the device. Such a design can be painful, especially for the person writing the boot firmware. Understandably, some cost-sensitive projects must avoid sockets and other expensive components. Even so, at least one or two early versions of the board can be built with boot device sockets or a JTAG-like interface so that the boot device can be reprogrammed without the need for a soldering iron.

The design should also include some mechanism that allows the boot firmware to easily communicate with the boot firmware designer. Ideally, this communication would be via a serial port and a few LEDs. If the application is extremely cost sensitive and these extra parts are out of the question for the deliverable hardware, consider the possibility of including some expansion connector that is not populated on the final product. During development, the connector can provide additional interfaces for debugging. The only unit cost is a small increase in board size. Once again, this decision hinges on cost restrictions and other factors but providing some means of connectivity can save a lot of time in the development process.

I mentioned JTAG in the preceding section. If the CPU has some type of debug interface, then make sure that the associated pins are accessible. These interfaces become quite useful, especially if there is no other communication device tied to the processor. When the hardware is laid out, find out what JTAG-like tools are available for your CPU. Get the pinout for the tool you plan to use and make certain the hardware has a connector for it.

The Logic Analyzer

A logic analyzer is used for general purpose logic analysis of digital hardware designs. The logic analyzer views the CPU and its address and data bus as just a collection of digital logic signals. This perspective debugging makes a logic analyzer useful for debugging firmware. As demand for these firmware debug tools has grown, companies that build logic analyzers have added hooks and extensions to the tools to make them look like firmware development tools. For example, with the analyzer connected to the address and data bus of the processor while the CPU is executing, the logic analyzer is collecting (and storing) the accesses. When this trace buffer is later observed by the developer, it can be viewed as a disassembly instead of just a buffer of address bus and data bus values.

Many of the disadvantages of the emulator apply to the logic analyzer as well. Logic analyzers are usually quite expensive, they too require bulky connections (if you plan to use them for tracing instruction and data accesses), and they can introduce load into the system. An added point to keep in mind when you are using a logic analyzer for firmware debugging is that you are monitoring external, physical accesses to the address and data bus of the processor. These external transactions do not reflect data or instructions retrieved from cache. Thus, if cache is enabled, the trace buffer is really not telling the whole story. Even with the cache disabled, the user must be aware of the fact that many processors fetch blocks of instructions rather than one instruction at a time and that some of the instructions in a block might not be executed. This feature is sometimes called *instruction prefetch* in a processor. On the positive side, although a logic analyzer is rather expensive, it is an expense that can be distributed over hardware and firmware development and over several different hardware platforms, regardless of the CPU.

Get to Know the Hardware and Be Nice to the Designer

Hey, I'm not kidding! A good mutual friendship between the firmware and hardware folks can save a lot of frustration and time over the lifetime of a project. Let me say from experience that chances are, it's not a hardware problem! A lot of small, sneaky bugs might tempt you to be suspicious of the hardware but investigate before you accuse! This advice amounts to common sense etiquette that will improve relations in any development environment.

Getting to know the hardware doesn't mean that you should look over the shoulder of the hardware designers as they are writing VHSIC Hardware Description Language (VHDL), but it certainly does help if you are familiar with at least the CPU section of the schematics. Take some time with the hardware designer and ask questions. Establish a good working relationship with the designer and the schematics. Get your own copy of the schematics and mark them up. This is important for the target hardware as well as the target CPU itself. You must also spend some time reading about the processor you are trying to tame.

JTAG and BDM Interfaces

JTAG and BDM interfaces are becoming popular for firmware development. JTAG, or Joint Test Access Group, is a standard interface that was originally intended for hardware BIST (built-in self-test) but has been extended so that it can be used for debugging embedded systems. Background Debug Mode (BDM) is similar (implemented by Motorola) in that it is strictly dedicated to CPU-related debugging. JTAG and BDM interfaces only work with CPUs that support them, so you can't assume this option is available on every project — it depends on the processor choice. The beauty of JTAG and BDM interfaces is that they usually cost less than $1,000, they are usually applicable to a processor family (not just one processor), and they require only a small, low-pin-count ribbon cable to connect to the processor. One disadvantage of these tools is that they are very dependent on the CPU's implementation of the interface. Another issue is that JTAG and BDM interfaces typically do not provide any kind of trace buffering capability. JTAG and BDM interfaces can be used to help debug firmware, and they can also be used as a means of programming flash memory. You can usually justify a tool that costs less than $1,000 and could potentially save you a lot of development legwork.

Have Local Copies of all Data Sheets

You must know more than just the schematic. Each device on the schematic may come with a 200-page manual. As silicon gets denser, more and more complexity is built into the devices. It is vitally important for you, the firmware developer, to master the device behavior. In this age of electronic paper, I still find it handy to print the sections of the manual that I will be referring to the most. Printing the manual also allows you to document errors or strange behavior of a device.

This issue raises another point: make sure you check with the device vendor to see if there are any errata outstanding. It is not at all unusual to use a device that has bugs, especially if your design uses some new device from a silicon manufacturer. Worse than that, you may be the one that finds new errata. This doesn't happen often, so don't be too quick to blame the silicon, but it does happen.

Make Sure the Hardware is Working

If the hardware design is brand new and the board is fresh from the factory, make certain the designer has blessed it before you start assuming it's valid. Our first run–time step makes the assumption that the connection from the CPU to the flash device is correct. If you're using the board for the first time, make sure you know how to connect the power supply properly. This point may sound silly, but you sure won't get on the good side of the hardware designer if you toast the board on the first day by connecting the power incorrectly.

Start Slowly

I can't emphasize this point enough... TAKE BABY STEPS!!! Don't even consider testing a large program until you have tested several small versions of the boot code. Consider the things you haven't proven yet:

- Is your program mapped to the correct memory space?
- Do you really understand how this CPU deals with a reset/powerup?
- Is your conversion of the executable file to binary done correctly?
- Are you sure you configured the device programmer properly?
- If your boot memory is wider than eight bits and it involves more than one device, are you sure you inserted the bytes into the correct device? Is the odd byte the most significant byte (MSB) or least significant byte (LSB)?
- Does the hardware work?

A little humility here is likely to save you a lot of extra loader passes. Search the CPU manufacturer's website for example boot code. In almost all cases, you will find something. Check out user groups. Do some web hunting. If possible, get some hardware assistance. If you don't know how to use an oscilloscope or logic analyzer, then get cushy with someone who does. These are priceless tools at this stage of the game.

NOTE

While a logic probe is somewhat limited in capability, its convenience and price make it worth mentioning. A logic probe is an very inexpensive, hand-held instrument that allows you to read the logic level (high or low) at the probed connection. Most logic probes also support the ability to detect a clock. A logic probe is a simple pencil-like gizmo (usually with power and ground connections) that you clip onto appropriate sources. You read a pin's logic level by touching the pin with the tip of this "pencil." A readout (often just LEDs) on the probe will then indicate whether the pin is logical high or low, high impedance, or changing. A logic probe is very handy if you have already verified that the hardware is stable and you are just writing code to wiggle some PIO pins or a chip select.

Look at What You've Created

The build tools allow you to dump a memory map. See if the memory map makes sense for your target. Look at the actual S-record or binary file before you write it to the flash device. Does it make sense? Even the file size can give you a clue. If your program consists of only a very tight busy loop in assembly language, the final binary file should be very small.

Find some tool (I use elvis) that allows you to visually display a binary file in some ASCII format. You can use this tool to confirm certain aspects of the build process. For example, to prove that flash-resident code is being placed correctly, you can modify the source to insert some easily recognized pattern at what should be the base of the flash memory (see Listing 2.8). After converting the source to binary (using the normal build process), use your dump tool to examine the file. You should find the marker pattern at the offset corresponding to the beginning for your flash memory.

Listing 2.8   "Marking" Code to Confirm Position.

```
coldstart:
    .byte   0x31, 0x32, 0x33, 0x34
    assembler code here
```

Listing 2.9 is a sample dump from the elvis vi clone that displays the offset into the file, the data in ASCII-coded-hexadecimal, and the data in regular ASCII (if printable). Hence, the flash memory begins at offset 0x0000.

Listing 2.9   **Sample Dump**

```
OFFSET      ASCII_CODED_HEX_DATA                               ASCII_DATA
 000000:  31 32 33 34 ff fd 78 14   38 60 00 30 4b fc 00 0e   1234..x.8`.OK"..
 000010:  38 80 00 00 38 a0 00 00   38 c0 00 00 3c e0 00 04   8C..8a..*1..<x..
```

The only thing you need to see in Listing 2.9 is that the first four bytes of the file are as you expected (0x31, 0x32, 0x33, and 0x34).

TIP

This binary dump is also very useful if you have to split your data into separate files so you can program multiple devices that are in parallel in the hardware. Before the split, you have what is shown in Listing 2.9, and, after the split (assume a split into two files), one file is as shown in the display labeled "Split A" and the other file is as shown in "Split B", clearly indicating that the single file was properly split.

Split A

```
OFFSET    ASCII_CODED_HEX_DATA                             ASCII_DATA
 000000: 31 33 ff 78 38 00 4b 00   38 00 38 00 38 00 3c 00   13.x8.K.8.8.*.<.
```

Split B

```
OFFSET    ASCII_CODED_HEX_DATA                             ASCII_DATA
 000000: 32 34 fd 14 60 30 fc 0e   80 00 a0 00 c0 00 e0 04   24..`0".C.a.1.x.
```

Device-Relative vs. CPU-Relative Addressing

Some tools create binary files, and some tools create S-record files. As I have discussed, a raw binary file contains the exact data that is destined for the flash device, so that binary file can be transferred directly to the device programmer to be burned into the flash memory. S-records, on the other hand, are lines of text (in a file) that must be converted to the raw binary format before being written to the flash device. This conversion is usually done by the device programmer, so you would typically just transfer the S-record file to the programmer. Your toolset is likely to contain a complete description of the S-Record format, but, briefly, the format looks like this:

```
<S><T><LL><AAAA...><DDDDDDDDDDDD...><CC>
```

Where S denotes S-record, T is usually a value of 1, 2, or 3 indicating the size of the AAAA field. The LL field contains the length of the record; the AAAA field is a hexadecimal address that is usually 4, 6, or 8 bytes of address (16, 24, and 32 bits of address). DDDD... is data to be placed at the specified address, and the final CC is a checksum of the line. That's a nice quick summary of S-records, now the warning: If the toolset you are using builds an S-record file for your program, the result may not work without some adjustment. This is because the AAAA field that the toolset creates is relative to the CPU not the flash device. Depending on the CPU, it is very likely that the boot device does not reside at physical address 0x00000000 in CPU address space.

Figure 2.4   Flash Relative vs. CPU Relative Address Space.

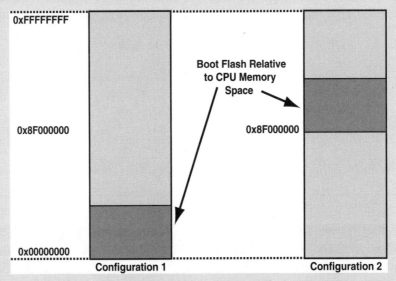

Since memory devices usually span only a portion of the processor address space, the absolute addresses in an object format (like S-records) might need to be adjusted to be interpreted correctly by the device programmer. This requirement is because the device programmer often knows only about the memory device's address space not the processor's.

Referring to Figure 2.4, in the case of Configuration 1, where the boot device resides at location zero of CPU-relative memory, the S-record CPU-relative addresses also correspond to flash device addresses, so all works well.

Configuration 2 however, does not work. Here the CPU boots from some location other than zero, so offset zero within the flash device no longer corresponds to physical address zero. Assume that this CPU boots at 0x8F000000, so the S-record file has AAAA... fields starting at 0x8F000000 because that's where the CPU sees the instructions. However, when I step away from the hardware design and go program the flash device, I must adjust the S-record address of 0x8F000000 to 0x0000000 because 0x8F000000 in CPU address space is the same as 0x00000000 in the flash device's address space. This adjustment to the S-record address can be performed in some post-processing step or in the programmer if it supports the ability to adjust the base. My personal preference is to avoid this complexity by using raw binary files instead of S-records.

Run Time

Now that you've covered some of the preliminary details, you can touch the hardware with a clear conscience knowing that you did your homework. The following sections discuss some of the first steps you take when you finally start working directly with your embedded device.

Hardware Sanity Tests for the Firmware Developer

So what do you do if you're all alone and you suspect the target hardware has a problem? Realistically, if the target is a complex hardware design, you probably won't be able to do much, but here are a few high-level tests that identify some common problems. This section assumes you can read a schematic and handle a multimeter, oscilloscope, and maybe a logic analyzer. Don't expect too much, though. Even if you do actually find something, chances are that you will need to wait for the hardware person to verify your findings. But, hey, it's still fun, and, in the meantime, you get to know the hardware a bit better, which always helps.

Verify Power Supply Voltage

The first step is to make sure that the power supply is plugged in. I'm not kidding! Use a meter to verify that power supply voltage is what it's supposed to be. Next, try an oscilloscope to make sure that the voltage is stable and not noisy or oscillating. A meter alone is not going to detect dirty power.

Verify a Valid Clock

Use an oscilloscope to verify that the clock input to the processor is toggling and that the frequency is about what you would expect. Normally, as long as the clock is toggling the system will run, but an incorrect clock frequency or duty cycle can sometimes cause trouble, so don't just assume that because it is toggling it is OK.

Check the Boot Chip Select and Read

With a scope probe on the boot device chip select, push the reset button and verify that, at least momentarily, the line toggles to the active state. Repeat this process for the read line of the same device.

Get Out the Magnifying Glass

If you've looked at hardware recently, you'll understand why you need a magnifying glass. Those pins are awfully close together! Look at the pins on the CPU and boot device. Check for raised pins, solder globs across pins, or cold solder joints (which look much duller than other good joints). If you do find what appears to be a bad connection, report it to the lab person that takes care of solder rework. Unless you have experience with the equipment used to rework these tiny solder joints, you are better off leaving the solder joints alone. If you misuse these tools, you could easily damage the device (or worse, damage the printed circuit board).

Be Aware of Electrostatic Discharge

If you are handling the target hardware in any way, take electrostatic discharge (ESD) precautions. Wear a wrist or ankle strap and check with the designer on other precautionary steps. ESD will not necessarily kill a device; it may just make it flaky. There's nothing worse than flaky in embedded systems.

Simple Loop at the Reset Vector

Start with a very basic loop at the reset vector and verify that the chip-select to the boot flash device is constantly toggling. This step can be as simple as one line of assembly language(see Listing 2.10).

Listing 2.10   Confirming the Boot Address

```
coldstart:
    jmp coldstart
```

Without external test equipment to observe the chip select toggle when running, the test in Listing 2.10 may not prove much. Depending on the CPU and how it deals with an unprogrammed boot device, the CPU might still be perfectly happy to execute NOPS or whatever garbage pattern is in the flash device. So seeing the flash chip select line toggling does not guarantee that the CPU is executing the test program. On the other hand, if the chip select line is not toggling, you can be sure that something has failed. If you can connect a logic analyzer to the device, the logic analyzer can shed a bit more light on the state of things.

A Simple LED Is Priceless at This Point!

Previously I mentioned the usefulness of an oscilloscope or logic analyzer. If neither an oscilloscope nor a logic analyzer is available, then hopefully you thought ahead and had the design include an accessible LED. This LED could be used to monitor state based on some type of blink rate or on/off state. An LED is not a perfect tool because until you get going, you don't really know if the LED is on or is blinking so fast that it appears to be on. On top of that, if the LED is on, is it on because you turned it on or would it be on even without the flash device plugged into the socket? Once you do get to a point where you know that access to the LED is working, you can use the LED as a convenient replacement for the oscilloscope by turning on the LED at the end of some test and then sitting in a busy loop (leaving the LED on). This way the LED can be used to indicate that whatever you tried to do worked.

Build on this. Create three small assemblly language routines: LED_on, LED_bslow, and LED_bfast. The blink rate between the slow and fast routines should be extreme so that it is easy to tell which routine you are accessing. These three routines can then be used to indicate in-progress, pass, and fail status of additional tests. Also, consider the possibilities if you had more than one LED. If you had four LEDs, you could track 16 unique states while trying to bootup.

RAM and a "No-Stack-Required" Serial Out

The next set of steps depends on what you have on your hardware. These tests are designed to demonstrate the minimum functionality necessary to support compiled C programs. The primary issue is to determine whether the run-time stack is reliable. If your processor has any internal RAM, you should use that internal RAM if possible, since internal RAM does not involve the external address or data bus. Test external SRAM with a loop that fills all the RAM space with 0x55, then reads it back, then writes it with 0xAA, and then reads it back in an endless loop. A scope can be used to trigger on the read line and write line as two different tests; make sure the data appears to be always 0x55 or 0xaa.

If your system does not have any SRAM, the next routine to work on would be interfacing to the serial port. Start by writing a simple loop that just pumps a character out the serial port, ignoring status for now. Even if you are overrunning the transmit buffer, you should still see an occasional character appear on the RS-232 interface. If not, connect the scope to the TX line of the serial connection and see if there is any activity at all. If you get no activity, troubleshooting can be tricky. You may have the write to the device working but have the UART blocked because some parameter is not configured properly (baud rate, for example). Also, if the device is connected to a terminal, be aware of the possible need for a null modem connector.

If your hardware only has DRAM, you are left with the difficult task of initializing DRAM on a target that is still unproven. This isn't easy and probably requires discussion with the hardware designer. The details of initializing DRAM are beyond the scope of this text because it is very dependent on the device. Having LED and/or serial port access at this point is very useful for determining the state of the DRAM initialization.

Get to C-Level

At this point you have verified execution out of the boot device, tested some memory, blinked an LED, and sent a few characters out the serial port. Believe it or not, this progress is good on new hardware. It's now time to transition to C-level. Because you have working RAM, it should be easy to transition to C. Create a simple C function that does not use any global data, only stack. The function uses a for loop to insert a delay between changing the state of the LED. If you assume the LED is accessible at address 0xff8000, bit 0, and setting bit 0 turns on the LED, the C function should look something like the function shown in Listing 2.11.

Now, in assembly language, initialize the stack pointer register to a location in memory that is divisible by 16. Allow for a few hundred bytes of space to grow into. Make sure you know which way your stack grows and branch to the address of the C function. Hopefully your LED is blinking.

Next, repeat the same test, but this time make the loopcnt variable static. If this works, then you know you have properly established the BSS space in the linker memory map. (By making the loopcnt variable a static variable, you are telling the compiler not to put the variable on the local stack; hence, the variable is mapped to the space that is allocated for use by the .bss section.)

Listing 2.11   Blinking a LED.

```
#define LED_ADDRESS 0xff8000
#define LED_ON      0x0001
#define LED_OFF     0x0000


void
```

```
First_C_Function(void)
{

    volatile int loopcnt;

    while(1)
    {
        *(unsigned short *)LED_ADDRESS = LED_ON;
        for(loopcnt=0;loopcnt < 500000; loopcnt++);
        *(unsigned short *)LED_ADDRESS = LED_OFF;
        for(loopcnt=0;loopcnt < 500000; loopcnt++);
    }

}
```

TIP

Avoid Modification of Initialized Data in C
By the time you get the serial port working, your test program might have about 100 lines of assembly code and a handful of C functions. Things start to move faster now, but, to keep things simple, you need to make one easy sacrifice. Don't write any code for a while that assumes that initialized data is writable. Initialized variables are one of those things that a programmer on a workstation can always take for granted. Initialized data in an embedded system implies that the data in its initialized state exists somewhere in memory when the target is powered up. This point implies that initialized data must be in non-volatile memory. Now, if the data is to be writable in C, then it can't be in non-volatile memory once you begin executing C-level code because non-volatile memory is not writable. The solution to this dilemma is that the initialized data section of memory is located in non-volatile storage and must be copied to volatile space at startup (prior to C-level) so that the data is initialized but writable. This step isn't very hard, but, from one toolset (compiler/linker) to another, the process is slightly different. The easier thing to do at this point is just avoid the problem, so don't assume that your initialized data is writable.

Summary

If you've gotten this far, many of the riskiest, most tedious steps are behind you. A few blinking LEDs and ASCII characters on a terminal might not impress your great aunt, but rest assured, they represent significant progress.

You've verified basic access to the essential devices (memory and serial port) and you've created a function in C. The next step is to build a simple putchar() and getchar() in C, based on what you've already done in assembly language. This allows you to throw printf on top. In short, you have a working computer!

Finally, I've said this before, but it continues to be very important. Take very small steps throughout this early boot stage. Do nothing fancy. Make sure cache is turned off and do not optimize any of the C functions. Slow and steady progress is good progress here.

Chapter 3

Introducing MicroMonitor

The goal of the next few chapters is to build a large program that provides an extensible firmware platform onto (or into) which you can add application programs. This chapter assumes you've successfully gone through the pain of the previous chapter. If you're booting a new target system, then don't start here, start with the much smaller, more precise steps of the preceding chapter. At this point, I assume you have a solid base of knowledge and working hardware onto which you can start to build the real boot code.

An Embedded System Boot Platform

The term *boot monitor* refers to the code that is run on a computer system as the lowest level of firmware resident to the hardware platform. You can find various types of boot monitors on a wide range of computer systems, certainly not limited to embedded systems. In general, a typical boot monitor provides the system with some very basic startup capabilities, and provides a bit of insurance to the user because if all else fails (meaning the upper layers of the installed OS), the boot monitor will still be there to fall back on. Typically, a boot monitor is built to provide a basic set of capabilities for diagnostic and system startup, and once the system has started up, the boot monitor is no longer in the picture. This is where I would like to introduce the term *embedded system boot platform* as a superset of a typical boot monitor.

An embedded system boot platform, like a boot monitor, is a target-resident environment that provides a suite of capabilities that enhances the development process. In its simplest form, the platform speeds up some of the early stages of embedded system development. In more elaborate configurations, the platform can provide a simple flash file system, Trivial File Transfer Protocol (TFTP)/Xmodem interfaces for application transfer, and a variety of additional commands and capabilities that provide enhancements to the development environment. As a part of a development strategy for an organization, an embedded system boot platform provides a common base on which to build a project. It is an integral part of the application itself, providing the system with a core set of features that are generic in nature and should be usable by application code regardless of the operating system. With that definition in mind, MicroMonitor is an embedded system boot platform.

MicroMonitor is the firmware that the CPU executes immediately after a reset or power-up. MicroMonitor resides in the non-volatile flash memory of the target system. It is responsible for booting the CPU and getting the system to a state where a user can access the target through some interface (typically either RS-232 or Ethernet). The capabilities provided at this interface depend on what capabilities were configured into the platform when it was built. After MicroMonitor does some initialization of the target, it presents itself as a command line interface to the user, typically through an RS-232 port. (If an Ethernet interface is included in the hardware, the developer also can communicate with MicroMonitor through the User Datagram Protocol (UDP).)

The command set includes basic capabilities like memory display and modification, parallel I/O control, and command line editing/history. MicroMonitor also configures part of the flash memory to be used as a file system (TFS, discussed in Chapter 7). The presence of a file system means that code can access the flash memory as name space instead of address space. Adding a file system opens up a whole new set of a capabilities for the embedded target, and this is what sets MicroMonitor apart from most boot monitors. Among other things, a file system allows the system and its software to be dynamically reconfigured without recompilation. For example, since the file system supports an "auto-bootable" attribute, at boot time, the monitor can look for files with that attribute and automatically run them. These files might be conventional, compiled binary executables, or they might be configuration scripts that configure the target to run Dynamic Host Configuration Protocol (DHCP) or Bootstrap Protocol (BOOTP) or that assign a fixed IP and MAC address to the target.

You can configure multiple files for autoboot, and MicroMonitor automatically runs the files in alphabetical order. Additionally, TFS and MicroMonitor's command line interface (CLI) share the concept of user levels. When the target first starts up, it is running at the highest user level (similar to UNIX superuser or Windows administrator). After control is turned over to the individual TFS files, the user level can be adjusted so that certain portions of the system (both files and commands) are only accessible to certain user levels. User-level access is controlled through scrambled passwords that are stored in a TFS file. If somehow the passwords are lost or inaccessible, there is a "back-door" password that is derived from the MAC address of the target.

In this design, everything except the monitor image itself is a file — even the main application invoked by the monitor is just another file in TFS. When the application is running (as a result of the monitor loading it from TFS flash memory to DRAM), other files can be accessed by the active application. You can therefore build one application binary that configures itself based on a few locally editable ASCII files in TFS. Also, since the application executes out of DRAM (rather than directly out of the flash memory in TFS), a new application can be loaded into flash memory while the current application in DRAM is left running.

As you can see, MicroMonitor is very heavily linked to TFS. As a result, many of the other commands within the CLI's command set assume the existence of a file system. Xmodem and TFTP both interface to the file system so uploads and downloads can all be name-based, instead of address-based. This design makes life a lot easier, and it makes applications that reside on top of the platform a lot easier to manage. MicroMonitor makes an embedded target look a bit like a PC with regard to the basic environment. The PC provides a core set of capabilities that the application can use: a file system, BIOS, and standard I/O. MicroMonitor allows the target to present itself as a platform that provides a similar set of facilities.

Target-Resident Command Set

The following table lists each of the MicroMonitor commands accessible from the CLI. For complete details, refer to the CD-ROM.

argv	Build argv list
arp	Address Resolution Protocol (ARP)
call	Call embedded function
cast	Cast a structure definition across data in memory
cm	Copy memory
dhcp	Issue DHCP/BOOTP discover
dis	Disassemble memory
dm	Display memory
echo	Print string to console
edit	Edit file or buffer
etest	Test to verify operation of exception handling

ether	Ethernet interface operations
exit	Exit a script
flash	Flash memory operations
fm	Fill memory
gosub	Call a subroutine within a script
goto	Branch to script tag
heap	Heap operations
help	Display command set details
history	Display command history
icmp	Internet Control Message Protocol (ICMP) interface operations
idev	Device interface operations
if	Conditional branching within scripts
item	Extract an item from a list
let	Set shell variable equal to result of expression
mstat	Monitor status (target specific)
mt	Memory test
pm	Put to memory
read	Interactive shell variable entry for scripts
reset	Firmware restart (warmstart)
return	Return from subroutine within script
set	Shell variable operations
sleep	Second (or millisecond) delay
sm	Search memory
strace	Stack trace (target specific)
tftp	TFTP client/server operations
tfs	TFS operations
ulvl	Display or modify current user level
unzip	Decompress block of memory to some other block of memory
xmodem	Xmodem file transfer
version	Version information

API Presented to the Application

This section lists each function of the MicroMonitor API accessible to the application. For complete details, refer to the CD-ROM.

`mon_addcommand()`	Add a command to the monitor
`mon_appexit()`	Call this function when the application exits
`mon_com()`	Basic hook between monitor and application
`mon_cprintf()`	Centered small `printf()`
`mon_crc32()`	A `crc32` function
`mon_decompress()`	Decompress a block of data
`mon_docommand()`	Invoke a command in the monitor
`mon_free()`	Return memory to monitor's heap
`mon_getargv()`	Retrieve the current argument list from the monitor
`mon_getbytes()`	Retrieve characters from console port
`mon_getchar()`	Retrieve one character from console port
`mon_getenv()`	Retrieve content of specified shell variable
`mon_getline()`	Retrieve a line of characters from console port
`mon_gotachar()`	Return indication of character presence on console port
`mon_intsoff()`	Turn off interrupts
`mon_intsrestore()`	Restore interrupt state
`mon_malloc()`	Allocate memory from heap managed by monitor
`mon_pioclr()`	Clear state of specified PIO pin
`mon_pioget()`	Retrieve state of specified PIO pin
`mon_pioset()`	Set state of specified PIO pin
`mon_printf()`	Small `printf` (no floating point)
`mon_putchar()`	Send character to console port
`mon_restart()`	Monitor restart point
`mon_setenv()`	Establish a new environment variable
`mon_setUserLevel()`	Establish a new user level in the monitor
`mon_sprintf()`	Small `sprintf` (no floating point)
`mon_tfsadd()`	Add a file to TFS
`mon_tfseof()`	Return end-of-file (EOF) state of opened file
`mon_tfsinit()`	Initialize (erase) flash memory used by TFS

mon_tfsclose()	Similar to standard close() on a TFS file
mon_tfsctrl()	Perform various control functions on TFS file
mon_tfsfstat()	Retrieve a local copy of a file's header
mon_tfsgetline()	Retrieve next line of an opened ASCII file in TFS
mon_tfsipmod()	Perform an in-place modification on a TFS file
mon_tfsnext()	Step through list of file headers in TFS
mon_tfsopen()	Similar to standard open on a TFS file
mon_tfsread()	Similar to standard read on a TFS file
mon_tfsrun()	Run some executable file (script or binary) in TFS
mon_tfsseek()	Similar to standard seek on a TFS file
mon_tfstruncate()	Truncate the size of a file currently opened for writing
mon_tfsunlink()	Remove file from TFS
mon_tfswrite()	Similar to standard write() on a TFS file
mon_xcrc16()	A crc16 function (used internally by Xmodem)

Host-Based Command Set

This section lists each of the commands on the PC that are part of the MicroMonitor package. For complete details, refer to the CD-ROM.

aout	Tool to interface to AOUT format files
bin2srec	Binary to S-record converter
coff	Tool to interface to COFF format files
com	Very basic com port communication tool
defdate	Generate date/time strings for use with monitor version
dhcpsrvr	Single-threaded dhcp/bootp server
elf	Tool to interface to ELF format files
fcmp	File comparison utility
f2mem	Files-to-memory converter
maccrypt	Tool to create a "backdoor" password from a MAC address
moncmd	Interface to monitor's UDP communication interface
monsym	Symbol-table format converter
newmon	Tool to update the boot flash memory
title	Place text on title bar of Win32 console window

ttftp	Single-threaded TFTP client/server
whence	Display path through which an executable is run

Figure 3.1 Applications and MicroMonitor.

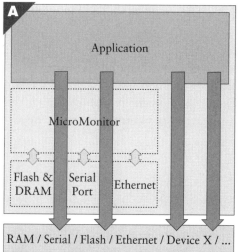
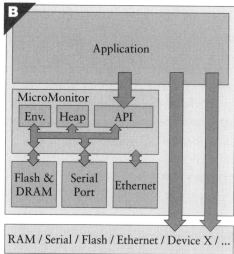
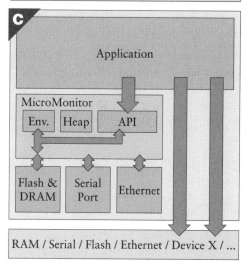

A – The platform exists for quick application download and some debug. It also provides a stable platform to "crash" on when a panic arises.

B – The platform provides all of the previously mentioned features, plus hooks to all of the facilities that its API is aware of (console, TFS, heap, and environment).

C – The platform provides quick application download, some debug, TFS, and shared environment. Other device interfaces are application specific.

Applications running on MicroMonitor can choose to bypass MicroMonitor (A), rely exclusively on MicroMonitor for core services (B), or use only a subset of MicoMonitor's services (C).

A PC that runs DOS by itself doesn't have much value until you put other applications on the PC to run on top of DOS. These applications assume some underlying set of features. The underlying features beneath DOS come from the BIOS. In the case of MicroMonitor, the underlying features come through hooks that allow the application to interface to the monitor directly. MicroMonitor provides the application with some fundamental facilities through its API, but does not prohibit (as a matter of fact, it encourages) the direct connection of the application to the hardware. (Refer to Figure 3.1.) The monitor is not only a standalone program that runs on the target by itself, it is also the basis for other programs that can be downloaded onto the target through facilities provided by the monitor. Think about it: to build the monitor the first time, you have to burn flash memory in some external device just to install the boot code or program. Once the monitor is stable, you can use it to reprogram itself and to download other application programs. No more need for the device programmer!

Summary

The MicroMonitor platform provides an environment onto which a team can develop and deploy a variety of different types of applications. The simplicity of the MicroMonitor implementation makes it very easy to port MicroMonitor from one target to the next. Because MicroMonitor does not inhibit the use of any overlaying RTOS or flash file system (FFS), it offers a common base for development from one project to the next — despite differences in the hardware below or the RTOS above. This common base immediately provides the team with a flash file system, fast application downloads, a convenient field upgrade path, and much more. Like other monitors, MicroMonitor resides in the boot flash memory and provides some target-specific functions that allow you to do things close to the hardware, but MicroMonitor also provides an environment that is valuable to the deployed runtime application.

Chapter 4

Assembly Required

This chapter explains how MicroMonitor handles basic system startup. Here you will learn how the system initializes the execution context, including stack, exception handlers, and important state information.

This startup code is critically important: if it's not right, nothing else will work right. It is also notoriously machine-dependent. To get this part of the monitor right, you must:

- come to terms with the system's memory map;
- identify some means of distinguishing between a power cycle and warm restart;
- master the machine exception handlers;
- learn how to save the entire processor state;
- correctly disable any cache;
- initialize and manipulate a communications port.

Thus, the startup code involves many machine-specific details — and until you get them all correct, you won't have enough working machine to support any code-based debugging. Even so, a great deal of the structure can be coded in relatively machine-independent C. This chapter details the high-level portions of this structure and explains what considerations the lower-level board support code must address. Along the way, I'll point out some of the more important design tradeoffs you'll need to consider to adapt the code to your own projects.

Just After Reset

The code executed immediately out of reset must be written in assembly language. The reset code should be written so that it can be executed either as a result of a real reset or powerup of the hardware or as a result of a firmware-invoked restart. These two types of system startups are commonly referred to as *coldstart* and *warmstart*, respectively, and they perform very similar tasks, with one exception. The goal is that after the execution of code through either entry point, the system looks like it just went through a power cycle or reset. The code at warmstart should do all the same stuff that would intrinsically be done by the CPU as a result of a power cycle and entry into coldstart (see list of initializations later); however, there must be a way for code that runs later to determine which entrypoint was taken. Later code must be able to determine the startup type so that it can decide reliably whether or not to initialize the monitor's global variable space, whether to run some higher-level system startup procedure, and so forth. Following is a list of basic initializations needed at this point in the startup:

- disable interrupts at the CPU level (not peripherals, just CPU);
- disable/flush/invalidate caches appropriately;
- enable the ability to access the boot flash memory at the desired speed and address;
- enable the ability to access the system RAM/DRAM at the desired speed and address;
- initialize a stack pointer.

Listing 4.1 gives a pseudo-code outline of reset.s.

Listing 4.1   Pseudo-Code for reset.s.

```
    .file       "reset.s"


    .extern start, moncom
    .global warmstart, moncomptr


coldstart:
    Initialize "something" to store away a state variable.
    StateOfTarget = INITIIALIZE
    JumpTo continuestart
```

```
moncomptr:
    .long moncom

warmstart:
    Load into StateOfTarget the parameter passed to warmstart
    as if it was the C function:
    warmstart(unsigned long state).

continuestart:
    Disable interrupts
    Flush/invalidate/disable cache
    Adjust boot device access
    Adjust system ram access
    Establish the stack pointer
    JumpTo start()
```

NOTE

In case you aren't comfortable with assembly language conventions:

- Strings ending with a colon (coldstart:, moncomptr:, warmstart:, or continustart:) are *tags*, or symbolically accessible addresses.

- Words that start with a period (.file, .extern, or .global) are *directives* that tell the assembler to do something other than just generate code for some assembler mnemonic. The .extern directive lets the assembler know that the specified symbol is in another file, and the .global directive tells the assembler to make the specified symbol globally accessible (by other functions in other files).

The coldstart tag should be located at the address to which the CPU vectors after a power up or reset. Ignore moncomptr for now (more on moncomptr later). The warmstart tag is seen by the C code as a function. Placing it here gives the C code an easy point to re-start the firmware.

The code at coldstart stores the INITIALIZE value into some location (i.e. StateOfTarget) that will not be corrupted by the reset code; hence, it is retrievable at the beginning of the first C function start(). Retrieving the content of the StateOfTarget variable allows the firmware after start() to decide whether it is executing as part of a complete or partial initialization sequence. A complete startup would initialize all the target's global variable space and all of the target's firmware subsystems. A partial startup (firmware-invoked warmstart) would not reinitialize the global variable space; thus state would be maintained but basic peripherals would be reinitialized.

Note the use of the `StateOfTarget` variable in Listing 4.1. The implementation from system to system may be slightly different depending on what is used to store the state of the target. The state of the target could be stored in memory, in a scratch register on some peripheral device, or perhaps even in a CPU register that will not be corrupted by any code between coldstart in assembly and `start()` in C. It may also be passed as an argument to the `start()` function.

Listing 4.2   `start()`.

```
void
start(void)
{
    int argc;
    register unsigned long state;
    volatile register ulong *ramstart, *ramend;

    /* Copy StateOfTarget to a register prior to the bss
     *   init loop.
     */
    state = StateOfTarget;

    /* Initialize monitor-owned ram... Since this loop initializes
     *   all monitor ram, the code within the loop must NOT use any
     *   ram-based variables (ramstart & ramend are registers). Also,
     *   since the stack gets cleared during this operation, this
     *   function must never return, and cannot expect non-register
     *   local variables to retain their values until after this loop.
     */
    if (state == INITIALIZE) {
        ramstart = (ulong *)&bss_start;
        ramend   = (ulong *)&bss_end;
        while(ramstart < ramend) {
            *ramstart++ = 0;
        }
    }

    /* Now that bss has been initialized, we can store
```

```
 *  StateOfTarget once again in bss space.
 */
StateOfTarget = state;



/* Load bottom of stack with 0xdeaddead for use by stkchk(). */
TargetStack[0] = 0xdeaddead;

/* Initialize vector/exception table. */
vinit();

/* Initialize system devices. */
devInit(19200);

/* Build argument list and go to main(). */
argc = 0;
while(argv[argc] != 0) {
    argc++;
}
main(argc, argv);

/* The function main() should not return, but just in case... */
while(1);
}
```

The very first C function executed by the target is start() (see Listing 4.2). Depending on the environment, you might need to put the first section of this function (the BSS init) at the end of the assembly language code that precedes the call to start(). Putting the BSS init at the end of the assembly language code avoids the potential of the BSS initialization loop stepping on something that is shouldn't. The BSS initialization loop might be a good place to throw a basic memory test, just to verify that the memory the monitor is using is somewhat sane. A simple address in address test (see Listing 4.3) could be inserted just above the ram initialization loop of Listing 4.2.

Listing 4.3   Testing RAM.

```
#if INCLUDE_RAMTEST_AT_STARTUP
      ramstart = (ulong *)&bss_start;
      ramend   = (ulong *)&bss_end;
      while(ramstart < ramend) {
          *ramstart = ramstart;
          ramstart++;
      }

      ramstart = (ulong *)&bss_start;
      ramend   = (ulong *)&bss_end;
      while(ramstart < ramend) {
          if (*ramstart != ramstart)
              error!
          ramstart++;
      }
#endif
```

NOTE

The address-in-address test is a simple pair of loops. The first loop writes 0 to address 0, 4 to address 4, etc. The second loop cycles through all the addresses again, verifying that a read operation will return the location's address. This simple but effective test will detect most common problems affecting either the data bus or the address bus.

In particular, this test is a good way to identify a "stuck" address line. For example, if I "think" I have 64K of RAM, but the upper bit of the address bus is stuck low, when the loop begins writing to the second bank of 32K, it will, instead, overwrite the first bank of 32K. When the address-in-address test attempts to verify the first 32K of memory, the test will fail — and fail in a way that helps identify the source of the problem.

Note the use of bss_start and bss_end in Listing 4.2 and Listing 4.3. The bss_start and bss_end labels must be defined in the link-editor memory map file. Most toolsets have some intrinsic labels that signify the beginning and ending of various significant sections. I have found, however, that the tool-defined labels are not necessarily used consistently; hence, I add my own labels to the link editor file so that I know exactly what the labels mean.

Note that `start()` ends by calling `main()`. Clearly, the system can now support code written in C. Being at C-level doesn't mean you're free and clear. You still need to be aware of the following:

- Stack is limited, or at least it might be. The point is that you are in brand new space here, so don't start writing functions that use much stack. The stack depth and reliability are still somewhat unknown. (Are you sure you initialized the stack pointer properly back in `reset.s`?) As a matter of fact, for the first couple of passes, you should let `start()` be the only function and code everything else as in-line operations using global variables.

- Initialized data is not writable. Remember that one of the MicroMonitor design goals is to be as compiler/CPU/target-independent as possible, and the issue of copying initialized data from ROM to RAM is always a bit different from one toolkit to the next.

- You still don't have a C-level serial port.

I have found it extremely handy to build the first-stage firmware so that there is no need to copy any initialized data to RAM space. This convenience eliminates the hassle of dealing with the different ways that initialization is handled by different tool sets. This approach does, however, require some discipline when coding because there is no compile-time warning if you try to overwrite initialized data (unless you are very careful with the use of `const`).

Also, I found it handy to not use any compiler-supplied libraries for higher-level functions unless absolutely necessary. This philosophy may be a bit conservative, but for a boot platform, I think it is important to have a tight grasp on the code, so MicroMonitor comes with its own `printf()`, `malloc()`, and so forth. Note that I'm not too extreme — I am not suggesting that you write your own math primitives!

I/O Initialization

With `start()` complete, basic initialization completes, and the system is at C-level. The monitor has initialized memory and stack; the next step is to access the peripherals. First, I make sure that all peripherals are settled down. To this end, I reset and disable all I/O[1] and then initialize the UART.

The UART should always be the first device (after memory) to be configured so that the system can use `printf()` to report status to the user. Continuing with the "tiny steps" philosophy, I only tackle one thing at a time. The UART interface is a

---

1. If you have anything to say about it during the hardware design, try to make sure that the microprocessor has the ability to reset each of its peripherals independently, without the need to power-cycle or hard-reset the target. This feature becomes very handy.

polled interface,[2] which allows me to avoid the complexity of interrupt handlers. Remember, I am still somewhat unsure of the footing, so I want to continue taking small and easy steps. I use four functions to interface to the UART: init(), putchar(), getchar(), and gotachar(). The first two functions are the most important. After you can boot your target and actually see a character come out of the serial port, you are almost home. (Not really, but it sure is a good feeling to get to that point!)

The UART functions — putchar(), getchar(), and gotachar() — are written in polled mode. Listing 4.4 is an example implementation for putchar().

Note that the polling loop that waits for the transmit hold buffer to become empty is not an infinite loop. Providing an exit to this loop is especially important when first establishing this function because if you get something wrong in the interface, the error routine lets you know about it (instead of just hanging in the loop).

NOTE

Refer to External Chips by Part Number

If you are writing code that interfaces to some external device in the hardware, refer to that device by its part number, not some generic name or code name. If you are working on code that someone else wrote for hardware with which you are not that familiar, it is very frustrating to see code that says "toggle pin 4 of the scorpion chip" to get the interface to work. What is the "scorpion" chip? The schematics show devices by number, not code names, so use the numbers. Similar confusion can occur if you use generic names instead of part numbers. For example, the code might refer to "the serial port." What if your board has more than one serial device? To the original writer, it might seem obvious that one of the ports is for the console and one is for communication with the external widget. What is obvious to one is lack-of-information to another, so spell out the details in the code comments.

Establish Exception Handlers

The next step is to initialize the CPU vector table. The vector table for the CPU is some block of memory (either at a fixed location or pointed to by a system register) that contains code or pointers to code. When an exception occurs, the running code branches to an entry in the vector table as the result of some system event. The event might be an interrupt, execution of an invalid instruction, a breakpoint trap, or an address alignment error (to name a few). The list of exceptions as well as the implementation of the vector table is different for each CPU.

---

2. Actually, the monitor doesn't even use interrupts, which keeps the porting process from one CPU/target to the next much simpler.

Usually, the exception table takes one of two forms: a table of function pointers or a table of small blocks of code, where the intent of each small block is to perform some very basic task, then jump to some common exception handler. From the monitor's point of view, there are two important things to do: first you must create the table, and second, the code must be prepared to handle the exception. MicroMonitor's exception handlers will log the type of exception that occurred and then store the state of the registers at the time of the exception.

Listing 4.4 **A Polled-Mode** putchar().

```
int
putchar(int c)
{
    int timeout;

    for(timeout=0;timeout<MAX_WAIT;timeout++) {
        if (XMIT_HOLD_EMPTY())
            break;
    }
    if (timeout == MAX_WAIT) {
        ERROR();
    }
    STORE_XMIT_HOLD_REG((char)c);
    return((int)char);
}
```

In general, I am trying to avoid tying the discussion to any one processor; however, here I need to make some assumptions. For this discussion, I will use the PowerPC™ as an example processor. The PPC architecture defines the exception table as blocks of memory, with each block typically (not always) being 256 bytes. For many implementations, the exception table can be placed at alternate locations in memory. The content of a register tells the CPU where in memory to find it. I will assume the exception table is located at physical address 0x0, with the first entry (or block) undefined and each entry after that in address increments of 0x100 (256 decimal) bytes.

Exception Handlers in ROM

The default exception table is typically found in the boot flash memory because the memory space that the boot flash memory covers must be the same space to which the exception table is mapped at reset. Reset is an exception itself; hence, there must be a reset exception handler in the boot flash memory. Immediately out of powerup at least a portion of the exception table is assumed to be in place. The only difference between the code in the exception table and other code in the boot flash memory is that the exception table entries are at fixed locations, not arbitrary locations that the linker resolves. Listing 4.5 is an extension of the pseudo-code shown in Listing 4.1, but now the code includes a portion of the exception table. The code includes some real PPC assembly language mnemonics plus some new directives.

Listing 4.5   Initializing Exception Vectors.

```
    .file       "reset.s"

    .extern start, moncom
    .global warmstart, moncomptr

    .text

    .balign 0x100

coldstart:
    Initialize "something" to store away a state variable.
    StateOfTarget = INITIIALIZE
    JumpTo continuestart

moncomptr:
    .long moncom

    .balign 0x100

vector_type1:
    li  regX, V_TYPE1
    ba  saveregs

    .balign 0x100

vector_type2:
    li  regX, V_TYPE2
```

```
    ba   saveregs

    .balign 0x100

vector_type3:
    li   regX, V_TYPE3
    ba   saveregs

    /* More exception handlers would be here */

warmstart:
    /* Load into StateOfTarget the parameter passed to warmstart
     * as if it was the C function:
     * warmstart(unsigned long state).
     */

continuestart:
    Disable interrupts
    Flush/invalidate/disable cache
    Adjust boot device access
    Adjust system ram access
    Establish the stack pointer
    JumpTo start()
```

The strategy in Listing 4.5 is quite simple. Each offset of 0x100 hexadecimal (established with the `.balign` directive) contains the code that makes the exception handler somewhat unique. The uniqueness is simply that the regX[3] register contains a tag that tells a later function what exception occurred. Each exception handler logs the exception (in `reg X`) and then branches to `saveregs()` to store the context (or register set) of the CPU at the time of the exception. After servicing the exception, the completed monitor either restarts the application or simply returns to the monitor's command line interface (CLI). To keep the register save somewhat generic across multiple target platforms, my implementation constructs an initialized table of register name strings in C, as shown in Listing 4.6.

---

3. Although I am using a PPC as a basic example, I am not using PPC register names.

Listing 4.6   Naming Registers.

```
char  *regnames[] = {
    "RA", "RB", "RC", "RD", "RE", "RF", "RG", "RH",
    "RI", "RJ", "RK", "RL", "RM", "RN", "RO", "RP",
};


#define REGTOT  (sizeof regnames/sizeof(char *))


ulong regtbl[REGTOT];
```

The list of names varies from one CPU to the next. Even within one CPU family, the register sets vary. (I am using a dummy set of register names to stay somewhat general here.) Along with this array of strings, I allocate a table of unsigned long values whose size equals the number of pointers in the regnames[] array just above it, which creates a table of strings and a table of potential values. All that remains is to have the exception handler properly put the content of each register into the appropriate location in the table. For example, register RA would be stored at offset 0, RB would be at offset 1, and so forth. (Note that this code assumes that a register is the size of an unsigned long variable.) Listing 4.7 is the PowerPC assembly language code that uses these tables to save the PowerPC registers.

Listing 4.7   Saving Registers.

```
/* saveregs:
 *  Save register set into regtbl[] array.
 */
saveregs:
    lis     regY,(regtbl)@ha
    addi    regY,regY,(regtbl)@l
    stw     rA,0(regY)
    stw     rB,4(regY)
    stw     rC,8(regY)
    stw     rD,12(regY)
    stw     rE,16(regY)
    stw     rF,20(regY)
    stw     rG,24(regY)
    stw     rH,28(regY)
```

```
stw     rI,32(regY)
stw     rJ,36(regY)
stw     rK,40(regY)
stw     rL,44(regY)
stw     rM,48(regY)
stw     rN,52(regY)
stw     rO,56(regY)
stw     rP,60(regY)


mr      rC,regX     /* parameter to exception (type) */
lis     rP,(exception)@ha
addi    rP,rP,(exception)@l
mtctr   rP
bctr
```

This code uses register regY as a pointer to the regtbl array. As each register is stored, the offset relative to regY is increased by four (the byte size of a 32-bit value). After the registers have been stored, the value of regX is moved to the register that is used by the compiler as the first function parameter register. (For this example, I assume that the first function parameter register is rC.) The next function called (exception) receives the exception type as its argument and, based on that type information, can perform exception-specific things.

Listing 4.8   Exception-Specific Processing Prior to Reset.

```
void
exception(int type)
{
    switch (type) {
        case V_TYPE1
            break;
        case V_TYPE2
            break;
        case V_TYPE3
            break;
        default:
            break;
    }
```

```
    ExceptionType = type;
    ExceptionAddr = getreg("SRR");
    warmstart(EXCEPTION);
}
```

The final stage of the exception handler is to call warmstart() with the EXCEPTION
argument. Recall that the warmstart tag is almost the same as a reset (or coldstart).
The warmstart call causes the target to go back through the startup sequence but
does not cause the BSS space to be reinitialized. The start() function is now called
with the StateOfMonitor set to EXCEPTION. (Note that because the state is not INI-
TIALIZE, the code in start() does not re-initialize BSS space). The function main() is
then called, and the monitor can switch on the exception type to decide what to do
next.

Listing 4.9   MicroMonitor's main().

```
void
main(int argc,char *argv[])
{
    if (StateOfMonitor == INITIALIZE) {
        /* Do some higher level initialization here */
    }

    switch(StateOfMonitor) {
        case INITIALIZE:
            break;
        case APP_EXIT:
            reinit();
            printf("\nApplication Exit Status: %d (0x%x)\n",
            AppExitStatus,AppExitStatus);
            break;
        case EXCEPTION:
            reinit();
            printf("\nEXCEPTION (offset 0x%x) occurred near 0x%lx\n\n",
            ExceptionType,ExceptionAddr);
            showregs();
            exceptionAutoRestart(INITIALIZE);
```

```
            break;
        default:
            printf("Unexpected monitor state: 0x%x\n",StateOfMonitor);
            break;
    }


    /* Enter the endless loop of command processing: */
    CommandLoop();
}
```

In Listing 4.9, the StateOfMonitor variable contains EXCEPTION, so main() can execute based on that. Typically, if the state is anything other than INITIALIZE, the system is only partially restarted; some state is left uninitialized with the assumption that it was initialized already. For example, as you will see later, part of the monitor is a flash file system called tiny file system (TFS). One of the startup procedures when StateOfMonitor is INITIALIZE is to scan through all files in TFS and execute auto-bootable files. These files would not be executed for the EXCEPTION case. The EXCEPTION case does some reinitialization, prints the exception type and the register set, and then automatically restarts the application. The function exceptionAutoRestart() looks at some other environment variables to decide whether it should optionally run a script out of TFS and also optionally restart the application (or just return to the monitor CLI).

One final note regarding this exception handler mechanism. After the registers are stored in the regtbl[] array, the content of that array is coordinated with the content of the regnames[] array. You can, therefore, easily build a function that can retrieve the content of any of the registers based on the register name. The getreg() function (see Listing 4.10) illustrates this mechanism.

Listing 4.10   getreg().

```
int
getreg(char *name, ulong *value)
{
    int     i;
    char    *p;

    p = name;
    while(*p) {
        *p = toupper(*p);
```

```
        p++;
    }
    if (!strcmp(name,"SP")) {
        name="R1";
    }

    for(i=0;i<REGTOT;i++) {
        if (!strcmp(name,regnames[i])) {
            *value = regtbl[i];
            return(0);
        }
    }
    printf("getreg(%s) failed\n",name);
    return(-1);
}
```

The getreg() function, which takes as input a name of a register and an unsigned long pointer, simply steps through the regnames[] table until it finds the requested name. The matching index is used as an offset into the regtbl[] array. The indexed value is returned through the long pointer argument.

Exception Handlers in RAM

This implementation puts all of the exception handlers in ROM, or non-volatile space. This policy is convenient for the reset handler because at reset you need that exception handler to be in place. However, the other handlers are only needed if their corresponding exception occurs. There are many situations where it would be advantageous for these other vectors to be in writable memory space. After the monitor is up and an application is placed on top of it, that application may have other ideas about handling exceptions, so it would be nice if the exception table could be modified. Also, the memory space for the exception handling table can exceed 8K on some CPUs, which might be excessive in flash-limited systems.

If the vector table is to eventually reside in RAM, it must be written as 100% relocatable code, because the vector table is copied from flash memory to RAM.) Converting the vector table to relocatable code is actually quite simple with a minor modification to the previous exception handler (see Listing 4.11).

Notice that now, instead of using a PC-relative branch instruction, this version uses an indirect branch (the equivalent of calling through a pointer to a function). This change makes the branch operation relocatable. So now all I have to do is copy this branch code into the RAM space that will ultimately be the exception table (see Listing 4.12).

Listing 4.11 Installing the Vector Table.

```
/* This function is copied into the vector table DRAM by vinit().
 * Multiple copies of general_vector are made, with the value
 * loaded into regX being modified for each vector.
 */
general_vector:
    li      regX,0x1234     /* '0x1234' is modified by copyGeneralVector(). */
    lis     regZ,(saveregs)@ha
    addi    regZ,regZ,(saveregs)@l
    mtctr   regZ
    bctr
```

Listing 4.12 Copying to RAM.

```
void
copyGeneralVector(ushort *to, ushort vid)
{
    extern  ulong general_vector;

    memcpy((char *)to,(char *)&general_vector,20);
    (to+1) = vid;               /* Modify the vector ID value */
}


void
vinit()
{
    char    *base;
    int offset;

    base = RAM_VTABLE;
    for(offset = 0x00; offset < 0x1000; offset += 0x100) {
        copyGeneralVector((ushort *)(base + offset),offset);
    }

    asm("   sync");         /* Wait for writes to complete */
    putevpr(RAM_VTABLE);    /* Set vector table pointer to RAM */
}
```

The size of the small assemblly language copy function is 20 bytes (five instructions). It simply copies the branch code (as if it were data space) to the new RAM-based vector table. Note that I must be aware of cache configuration at this point. Both instruction and data cache should be disabled. This approach uses only 20 bytes of flash memory to create a vector table that could exceed 8K.

Registers Beware!

Finally, it is very important to be aware of what registers are being used in exception handlers. Each implementation is a bit different but, generally, at least one register is available for exception processing only. You can assume that register is not used by any other portion of the application. In this case, for MicroMonitor, the exception handler's job is simply to log the exception type and store away all registers. The code does assume that a few registers are available for use in the exception handling process. You must investigate this assumption; details vary from one CPU/RTOS/compiler combination to another. Generally, instead of caching registers to a global table, a real exception handler (i.e., one associated with a device driver) pushes all the affected registers onto the stack of the interrupted task.

Summary

While the reset code is technically challenging, it doesn't need to be intimidating. Your initial draft can be quite simple — and should be. As I've stressed before, in these early stages, it's essential that you take baby steps. The modular structure of the code facilitates an incremental approach. Your first implementation of the start–up code should be as primitive as possible. Leave exceptions disabled and stub all the exception handlers with simple traps. Leave the cache and memory management unit in their default, disabled state. Leave all other peripherals, except your communication device, disabled. Use only the simplest communication channel you can — preferably a serial port. Once you get a command prompt from this primitive implementation, then you can pursue more elaborate versions. Again, the modular structure of MicroMonitor helps by suggesting a natural sequence for these revisions.

If you are careful to take small steps, implementing only as much as absolutely necessary at each step, then you should find that building the monitor is a relatively straight-forward process.

5

Chapter 5

Command Line Interface

In the preceding chapter, I built a clean system reset for MicroMonitor with warm-start, exception handlers, and serial interface functions. In this chapter, I will implement a user interface through the console port. Over the last few years, I've probably rewritten this command line interface (CLI) half of a dozen times. I haven't had any need to change it for quite some time now, so maybe this version is a keeper.

The design goal of this CLI is to provide a good amount of flexibility without excess complexity. This CLI provides shell variables and symbols, command line editing and history, command output redirection, user levels, and password protection. If you don't want all of these features, most of this functionality can be optionally removed from the code at build time by setting a few macros in the main MicroMonitor configuration file. To support this configurability without being forced to scatter #ifdefs throughout the code, I have modularized the functionality and accepted a few limitations. The end result is a fairly robust but not very complex CLI handler.

CLI Features

The CLI I develop in this chapter provides MicroMonitor with the following features:

- *Functional Command Execution* — All of the command line processing, except for history and editing, is provided by a single function: `docommand()`. The `docommand()` is passed a string from the command line and a verbosity level. Other modules in MicroMonitor (not just the console connection) can also use `docommand()` to invoke commands from within the code.

- *Command Line Tokenization* — Each command in the system has the standard `cmdfunc(int argc, char *argv[])` prototype. The CLI parses a string of characters into individual white-space delimited tokens to form the argument count (`argc`) and argument list (`argv`), which is then passed to a command-specific function.

- *Shell Variables and Symbols* — The command line processor makes substitutions for shell variables and symbols. Shell variables are seen on the command line as strings prefixed with $. The CLI looks to the string following the dollar sign to see if it matches any of the currently stored shell variable names in MicroMonitor's environment. If the string matches a shell variable name, then a substitution is made; if not, the string is left untouched. A very similar capability is provided for symbols or strings prefixed with %.

- *CLI Editing and History* — As each line is typed, the CLI provides the ability to modify the already-typed characters in a way that is much more efficient than simply backspacing to the point of the error and retyping from that point. History allows the user to retrieve a command string that was entered earlier and either execute it again or modify it to form a new command.

- *Command Output Redirection* — When the CLI passes control to a command function, that function can use `printf()` and `putchar()` to transfer command-specific information to the user. Redirection at the CLI means that all data printed by the command can be redirected to RAM and eventually transferred from RAM to a file in the flash file system.

- *User Levels and Password Protection* — The CLI accesses each command by first determining the current user level of the system and the user level required for the command to execute. If the user level of the system is higher than the required user level for the command, then the command is allowed; otherwise, the command is rejected by the CLI.

- *Fall Through to FFS for Script Execution* — If the command is not found in the command table, then as a last resort, the CLI passes the string to TFS to process as an executable script (if a script with the same name as the command exists).

- *Leading Underscore Processing* — MicroMonitor can have an application running on top of it just as can DOS. The application is likely to have its own command set, but there are times when a command in the monitor is useful to the application (the monitor's API allows the application's CLI to access commands in the monitor's CLI). To support the situation where the application and MicroMonitor both recognize the same command string ("help" is the most common example), the monitor's CLI throws away a leading underscore. Thus the the string _help can be passed to an application where it will fall through to the monitor's CLI and be processed as help.

CLI Data Structure and the Command Table

Each general-purpose command in MicroMonitor has the data structure shown in Listing 5.1. The command data structures are stored in the command table.

Listing 5.1   CLI Data Structure.

```
struct  monCommand {
    char    *name;      /* Name of command seen by user. */
    int     (*func)();  /* Function called when command is invoked. */
    char    **helptxt;  /* Help text. */
};
```

The first member, name, points to the string that must match the first token typed on the command line. The function pointer, func, points to the code that is to be called as a result of the token match, and the helptxt pointer shows the location of the help text for the specific command.

At the base of the command table is a preprocessor #include directive that allows you to add additional, target-specific commands that are independent of the core generic commands.[1] The CLI handler scans a table of these structures looking for a match between the first token on the command line and the name member. Listing 5.2 is a small example of the command table.

---

1.   Remember that we are discussing a boot monitor that supports extensions for various target specific needs. This #include allows the extensions to be added without actually touching the monitor's generic command table.

Listing 5.2   A Section of the Command Table.

```
extern  int    Add(), Echo(), Help(), Version();
extern  char   *AddHelp[], *EchoHelp[], *HelpHelp[];
extern  char   *VersionHelp[];

struct monCommand cmdlist[] = {
    { "add",        Add,        AddHelp, },
    { "echo",       Echo,       EchoHelp, },
    { "help",       Help,       HelpHelp, },
    { "?",          Help,       HelpHelp, },
    { "version",    Version,    VersionHelp, },
#include "xcmdtbl.h"
    { 0,0,0, },
};
```

CLI Processing

The front end of the command-line processor, called docommand(), takes as its arguments the command-line string and a verbosity level. MicroMonitor uses the verbosity levels for debugging scripts. There are three levels of verbosity:

- zero verbosity
- print the incoming line as it is fed to docommand()
- print the line after shell variables and symbols have been converted

All of the command-line processing is handled in the docommand() function prior to passing control to the command-specific function. This processing includes:

- making a copy of the incoming command-line string
- expanding shell variables and symbols
- breaking up the string into its individual white-space delimited tokens
- preparing for command-line redirection
- verifying that the first token is a valid command in the command list
- providing user-level verification

The Functions Beneath the Command Name

Thus, `docommand()` is responsible for tokenization, shell variables, and symbols. It parses the command line, converting it to a list of tokens that is then passed to the command function for command-specific processing. Each command function receives this token or argument list through standard `int argc, char *argv[]`, parameters just like `main()` in a standalone program. Each command function is assumed to return some integer value representing the type of success it had in dealing with the command line. This CLI defines three different return values:

`CMD_SUCCESS`	Tells `docommand()` that the command-specific function completed successfully.
`CMD_FAILURE`	Tells `docommand()` that the command-specific function did not succeed but that there is no need for `docommand()` to print any error message, because the command-specific function has already printed any necessary messages.
`CMD_PARAM_ERROR`	Tells `docommand()` that the command-specific function did not receive a valid set of arguments, and the generic syntax error message can be output by `docommand()`.

If the command function returns `CMD_SUCCESS` or `CMD_FAILURE`, there is nothing else to do except possibly log the fact that the command failed. If the command function returns `CMD_PARAM_ERROR`, then `docommand()` prints out a generic syntax error message. In this case, `docommand()` assumes that the second string in the table of strings within the command-specific help text is a usage message and prints it. (See `Add_Help[]` array in Listing 5.3.) The usage message gives the user some idea of the correct syntax for the attempted command.

This arrangement requires that each command's help strings conform to a certain syntax. The first string in the list is a brief description of the command. The second is the usage message, which follows the common format of braces {} indicating required arguments and brackets [] indicating optional arguments. The remaining lines are command specific. A `NULL` pointer terminates the list.

This design supports several different help-related functions — some provided by `docommand()` and some provided by the `help` command. By stepping through the command table, the `help` command can list each command in a tabulated format. Alternatively each command can be printed with the one-line description provided by the command's help-text array. Finally, when given a command name, `help` can print the entire block of help text for the specified command. All this command-specific `help` is generated in a generic way without the involvement of any of the individual command functions. The only requirement is that the first two strings in the `help` text table have special meaning and that the list of strings be `NULL`-terminated.

Listing 5.3 is help text and function code for a simple command called add. This command accepts two arguments and prints the result. For the sake of this discussion, I add a requirement that both numbers must be greater than zero. If invoked with a -v option, the result is placed in a shell variable and not printed.

Listing 5.3   Help Text and Function Code for the add Command.

```
char *Add_Help[] =
{
    "Add two numbers together",
    "-[v:] {num1} {num2}",
    "Options:",
    " -v {varname}    put result in shell var 'varname'",
    (char *)0,
};

int
Add(int argc, char *argv[])
{
    char *varname;
    int opt, val1, val2, result;

    varname = (char *)0;
    while((opt = getopt(argc,argv,"v:")) != -1)
    {
        switch(opt)
        {
        case 'v':
            varname = optarg;
            break;
        default:
            return(CMD_FAILURE);
        }
    }

    if (argc != optind+2)
    {
```

```
            return(CMD_PARAM_ERROR);
    }


    val1 = atoi(argv[optind]);
    val2 = atoi(argv[optind+1]);


    if ((val1 <= 0) || (val2 <= 0))
    {
        printf("Argument out of range\n");
        return(CMD_FAILURE);
    }


    result = val1 + val2;
    if (varname != (char *)0)
        shell_sprintf(varname,"%d",result);
    else
        printf("%d + %d = %d\n",val1,val2,result);


    return(CMD_SUCCESS);
}
```

Notice that add can return any of the three different return values. If the return value from getopt()[2] falls through to the default case of the switch statement (indicating that an unexpected option was entered), the return is CMD_FAILURE. This occurs because the getopt() function prints out an error message itself, so there is no need for any additional error message. If there aren't exactly two arguments after option processing, the CMD_PARAM_ERROR is returned, and docommand() prints out a syntax error message plus the usage text in the Add_Help[] array. CMD_FAILURE is also returned when the two values are checked for being greater than zero. Because this function prints out a specific message letting the user know that something is wrong, docommand() should not print anything but must still be aware that something went wrong. Finally, if the command completes successfully, the function returns CMD_SUCCESS, and no further action is taken by docommand(). The command function itself does not need to do any of the generic error message printing; it is handled by the command processor code in docommand().

---

2. The getopt() (get options) function is commonly used in UNIX programs to provide a common way to deal with command line options (optional single-character arguments that are assumed to be preceded with a dash and may require arguments of their own).

Also notice that getopt() is a very handy way to allow a command-line syntax to be somewhat variable. The value of optind after the getopt() loop will be the index into the argument list just after the last option processed on the command line; hence, all options are assumed to precede arguments in this case. Commands within MicroMontior can use getopt() not just to process command options that override some defaults but also to redefine what the argument list is in some cases. Because getopt() uses static variables to keep track of how much of the current command line has been processed, docommand() must re-initialize these variables prior to passing control to the command function.

Listing 5.4 shows the portion of docommand() that parses the command table and demonstrates how docommand() uses the help array format.

Listing 5.4   Parsing the Command Table.

```
int
docommand(char *cmdline, int verbose)
{
    int ret, argc;
    char *argv[ARGCNT];
    struct monCommand *cmdptr;


        ...


    /* Step through the command table looking for a match between
     * the first token of the command line and a command name.
     */
    cmdptr = cmdlist;
    while(cmdptr->name) {
        if (strcmp(argv[0],cmdptr->name) == 0)
            break;
        cmdptr++;
    }
    if (cmdptr->name) {
        ret = cmdptr->func(argc,argv);

        /* If command returns parameter error, then print the second
         * string in that commands help text as the usage text.  If
         * the second string is an empty string, then print a generic
```

```
        * "no arguments" string as the usage message.
        */
      if (ret == CMD_PARAM_ERROR) {
         char *usage;

         usage = cmdptr->helptxt[1];
         printf("Command line error...\n");
            printf("Usage: %s %s\n",
                  cmdptr->name,*usage ? usage : "(no args/opts)");
      }
      return(ret);
   }
   /* If command is not in command table, then see if it is in
    * the file system.
    */
   if (tfsstat(argv[0])) {
      int err;
      err = tfsrun(argv,verbose);
      if (err != TFS_OKAY) {
         printf("%s: %s\n",argv[0], (char *)tfsctrl(TFS_ERRMSG,err,0));
      }
      return(CMD_SUCCESS);
   }
   else
      printf("Command not found: %s\n",argv[0]);

   return(CMD_NOT_FOUND);
}
```

Listing 5.4 is only a portion of the docommand() function but an adequate chunk for the sake of this discussion. The code assumes that the command line has been turned into a list of white-space delimited tokens in a char *argv[] type of list. The content of argv[0] is the command name and is used to find a match in the command table. If the end of the command table is reached, the name pointer will be NULL, indicating that the input command is invalid. If name is not NULL, the code can safely assume that the loop through the command list has found a match between a command in the table and the first argument of the command. This results in a call to the function that corresponds to the command string entered. The return value from this function is then used to determine if docommand() needs to print any additional error message. Note, once again, that the command-specific code is not required to deal with any of the generic error messaging; the code simply returns CMD_PARAM_ERROR to docommand(), and a standard message is printed.

NOTE

At the point where the program determines there is no match between argv[0] and a command in the table, one more test is done to see if argv[0] is a script in the flash file system. I'll say more on scripts and the flash file system in Chapters 6, 7, and 8.

Shell Variable and Symbol Processing

The MicroMonitor CLI provides for two similar types of token substitution: shell variables and symbols. Shell variables (strings preceded by $) get their substitution data from the MicroMonitor environment in RAM. Symbols (strings preceded by %) get their substitution data from a file. From the parsing point of view, both symbols and shell variables are handled exactly the same way except that, at the time of substitution, MicroMonitor searches a file for symbols and the environment for shell variables. Shell variables are convenient and do not require a file system; however, storage of a large number of shell variables is a bit impractical because of the RAM space needed and the volatility of the RAM. On the other hand, if TFS is included in the monitor build, then a symbol table file can be downloaded to TFS, and the system can process a large number of symbols because the data is stored in flash memory. I typically use the symbol table feature of MicroMonitor for storage of the application's actual symbol-to-address list. Putting the symbol-to-address list in a symbol table makes debugging more convenient when I am not attached to a symbolic debugger.

Listing 5.5 shows the code in the docommand() function that initiates the substitution.

The workhorse for this functionality is the expandshellvars() function (see Listing 5.6). The expandshellvars() function is passed a string that is to be expanded with all shell variables converted. It supports variables of type $VARNAME and ${VARNAME}. The expandshellvars() function also supports the ability to have shell variables embedded within shell variables. For example... ${VAR${NAME}} causes a two-pass expansion in which ${NAME} is evaluated and then ${VARXXX} is evaluated (where XXX is whatever was in the variable ${NAME}).

Listing 5.5   Expanding Shell Variables and Symbols.

```
/* If there are any instances of a dollar or percent sign within the
 * command line, then expand any shell variables (or symbols) that may
 * be present.
 */
if (strpbrk(cmdcpy,"$%")) {
    if (expandshellvars(cmdcpy) < 0) {
        return(CMD_LINE_ERROR);
    }
}
```

Listing 5.6   expandshellvars().

```
int
expandshellvars(char *newstring)
{
    char    *cp;
    int     result, cno, ndp;

    /* Verify that there is a balanced set of braces in the incoming
     * string...
     */
    ndp = 0;

    if (braceimbalance(newstring,&cno,&ndp)) {
        printf("Brace imbalance @ %d%s.\n",
            cno,ndp ? " ({ missing $ or %)" : "");
        return(-1);
    }

    /* Process the variable names within braces... */
    while((result = processbraces(newstring)) == 1);
    if (result == -1)
        return(-1);

    /* Process dollar signs (left-most first)...    */
```

```
    while((result = processprefixes(newstring)) == 1);
    if (result == -1)
        return(-1);

    /* Cleanup any remaining "\{", "\}" or "\$" strings... */
    cp = newstring+1;
    while(*cp) {
        if (*cp == '{' || *cp == '}' || *cp == '$' || *cp == '%') {
            if (*(cp-1) == '\\') {
                strcpy(cp-1,cp);
                cp -= 2;
            }
        }
        cp++;
    }
    return(0);
}
```

The function `braceimbalance()` in Listing 5.6 does some preprocessing to verify the basic sanity of the command line. The `braceimbalance()` function returns zero if there is an even number of braces on the command line. It takes into account backslash processing (meaning that a \} or \{ is taken as a literal brace instead of a brace enclosing a shell variable). If `braceimbalance()` returns non-zero, an error message is printed, and an error (-1) is returned. If `braceimbalance()` completes successfully, then the rest of the code can at least assume basic brace sanity in the line. If the braces balance, `expandshellvars()` calls `processbraces()`. This function looks into the incoming string for the deepest set of braces and replaces those braces and the enclosed variable name with the value stored in the corresponding shell variable. The function returns 1 if a set of braces was processed, and 0 if all braces have been processed. Also, `processbraces()` returns -1 if some kind of processing error occurs.

The `processprefixes()` function conducts a similiar looping process. It processes the $ for shell variables and the % for symbols. The `processprefixes()` function looks for the last $ (or %) in the incoming string and attempts to make a shell variable (or symbol) substitution. If no prefix ($ or %) is found, `processprefixes()` returns 0.

The bottom `while` loop in Listing 5.6 removes any backslashes that may have been present to provide immunity to the previous special-case character processing. The complete code for each of these functions is on the CD. Because of the nitty-gritty detail involved in parsing each line, only the top-level details have been repeated here.

Command-Line Redirection

MicroMonitor also includes support for command-line redirection. Command-line redirection is handy, for example, to log the output of a command to a file. My primary motivation for adding command-line redirection is to support the ability to dump a stack trace output to a file.

I discussed exception handling earlier. In the next few chapters, I will describe a flash file system and show how to dump an application stack. Consider the case where your system is in the field and taking a strange exception every other blue moon. How do you find the cause for the strange exception without camping out at the customer site? If the exception handler has the optional ability to execute a specified script (from the file system), then that script, among other things, can issue a stack trace command (strace) and redirect the output to a file. If this script has been activated, when the customer calls saying that something appears to have crashed and restarted, you can query the file system for the trace output file and see what caused the exception.

By default all printf output passes through putchar(), which sends each character to the console port. If putchar has some additional smarts and can place its incoming character into a buffer of some known size, then the output will be logged to RAM. To convert this internal logging to output redirection, I need only provide a mechanism to tell MicroMonitor to transfer the buffer to a file. Traditionally, CLI redirection syntax is

```
echo hey you >filename
```

This syntax isn't good for MicroMonitor's command-line redirection because I want the output to go to RAM first. So I deviate slightly with two different forms:

1. `echo hey you > buffer, buffer_size[, filename]`
   This format consists of single right arrow with a one- or two-comma delimited string containing a buffer address followed by the size of the buffer and an optional filename. If the filename is specified, the output of the command is copied to the buffer (truncated at buffer_size if necessary) and then transferred to TFS as filename. The running buffer pointer is reset back to the base address of buffer. If a filename is omitted, the output of the command is copied to the buffer, and the pointer into the buffer is left at the position following the data (assuming buffer_size is not reached).

2. `echo hey you again >>[filename]`

This syntax is used to append the output of the command to the buffer that was created by the > syntax described above. If a filename is included, the content of the buffer is transferred to TFS under the specified name (in this example), and the running buffer pointer is reset to the base address of the buffer. If a filename is not specified, there is no transfer to a file, and the running pointer is incremented by one to the position just after the data copied (once again, assuming `buffer_size` is not reached).

To implement this feature, the function `putchar()` needs an additional call at the top (see Listing 5.7).

Listing 5.7   Adding Redirection to `putchar()`.

```
int
putchar(uchar c)
{
    RedirectCharacter(c);
    if (c == '\n')
        rputchar('\r');
    rputchar(c);
    return((int)c);
}
```

The `RedirectCharacter()` function (see Listing 5.8) looks at a state to determine if it does anything at all. The `RedirectCharacter()` function either does nothing or, after checking to see that the running buffer pointer has not reached the end of the buffer, copies the character to the buffer space and increments the pointer by one.

Listing 5.8   `RedirectCharacter()`.

```
void
RedirectCharacter(char c)
{
    if (RedirectState == REDIRECT_ACTIVE) {
        if (RedirectPtr < RedirectEnd)
            *RedirectPtr++ = c;
    }
}
```

I must also modify docommand() so it can recognize the redirection syntax (set RedirectState to REDIRECT_ACTIVE) and, when appropriate, notify the redirection code that the command has completed (set RedirectState back to REDIRECT_IDLE). So I must add a few lines to docommand().

```
if (RedirectionCheck(cmdcpy) == -1)
    return(CMD_LINE_ERROR);
```

I insert the preceding code into docommand() just *after* the shell variable processing. Placing the modification after shell variable processing allows the user to do something like

```
echo hi >$APPRAMBASE,100
```

and know that when RedirectionCheck() is called, the content of $APPRAMBASE has already been converted to a physical address by the CLI shell-variable processor described previously. At the bottom of docommand(), I add another call to indicate command completion. This call is simply a call to RedirectionDone() prior to returning from docommand().

The RedirectionCheck() function (see Listing 5.9) starts by looking through the line for the redirection symbol. If, at the end of the line, RedirectionCheck() hasn't found a right arrow (>), it simply returns. If it finds a second arrow, then RedirectState should already be REDIRECT_ACTIVE; any other state indicates an error. If RedirectState is correct, then RedirectionCheck() looks for a filename and stores it away for use later. Finally, when RedirectionCheck() does not find a second arrow, it processes the comma-delimited string after the arrow and establishes pointers and counters appropriately.

Listing 5.9   Parsing Redirection Commands.

```
#define REDIRECT_UNINITIALIZED  0
#define REDIRECT_ACTIVE         0x12345678
#define REDIRECT_IDLE           0x87654321


static int  RedirectSize, RedirectState;
static char *RedirectBase, *RedirectPtr, *RedirectEnd;
static char RedirectFile[TFSNAMESIZE];


int
RedirectionCheck(char *cmdcpy)
{
```

```
int inquote;
char *arrow, *base, *comma, *space;


base = cmdcpy;
arrow = (char *)0;


/* Parse the incoming command line looking for a right arrow.
 * This parsing assumes that there will be no negated arrows
 * (preceding backslash) after a non-negated arrow is detected.
 * Note that a redirection arrow within a double-quote set is
 * ignored.  This allows a shell variable that contains a right arrow
 * to be printed properly if put in double quotes.
 *  For example...
 *  set PROMPT "maint> "
 *  echo $PROMPT    # This will generate a redirection syntax error
 *      echo "$PROMPT"  # This won't.
 */
inquote = 0;

while(*cmdcpy) {
    if ((*cmdcpy == '"') && ((cmdcpy == base) || (*(cmdcpy-1) != '\\'))) {
        inquote = inquote == 1 ? 0 : 1;
        cmdcpy++;
        continue;
    }
    if (inquote == 1) {
        cmdcpy++;
        continue;
    }
    if (*cmdcpy == '>') {
        arrow = cmdcpy;
        if (*(arrow-1) == '\\') {
            strcpy(arrow-1,arrow);
            cmdcpy = arrow+1;
            arrow = (char *)0;
            continue;
        }
```

```
            break;
        }
        cmdcpy++;
    }


    if (arrow == (char *)0)
        return(0);


    /* Remove the remaining text from the command line because it is to
     * be used only by the redirection mechanism.
     */
    *arrow = 0;


    /* Now parse the text after the first non-negated arrow. */
    if (*(arrow+1) == '>') {
        if (RedirectState == REDIRECT_UNINITIALIZED) {
            printf("Redirection not initialized\n");
            return(-1);
        }
        arrow += 2;
        while(isspace(*arrow))
            arrow++;
        if (*arrow != 0)
            strncpy(RedirectFile,arrow,TFSNAMESIZE);
    }
    else {
        RedirectPtr = RedirectBase = (char *)strtoul(arrow+1,&comma,0);
        if (*comma == ',') {
            RedirectSize = (int)strtol(comma+1,&comma,0);
            if (RedirectSize <= 0) {
                printf("Redirection size error: %d\n",RedirectSize);
                return(-1);
            }
            RedirectEnd = RedirectBase + RedirectSize;
            if (*comma == ',') {
                space = strpbrk(comma," \t\r\n");
                if (space)
```

```
                    *space = 0;
                strncpy(RedirectFile,comma+1,TFSNAMESIZE);
            }
            else
                RedirectFile[0] = 0;
        }
        else {
            printf("Redirection syntax error\n");
            return(-1);
        }
    }
    RedirectState = REDIRECT_ACTIVE;
    return(0);
}
```

Finally, docommand() informs the redirection code that the command completed by calling RedirectionCmdDone() (see Listing 5.10).

Listing 5.10   RedirectionCmdDone().

```
void
RedirectionCmdDone(void)
{
    if (RedirectState != REDIRECT_UNINITIALIZED) {
        RedirectState = REDIRECT_IDLE;
        if (RedirectFile[0]) {
            tfsadd(RedirectFile,0,0,(uchar *)RedirectBase,
                (int)(RedirectPtr-RedirectBase));
            RedirectFile[0] = 0;
            RedirectPtr = RedirectBase;
        }
    }
}
```

If the state has been previously initialized (by RedirectionCheck()) this function checks for the presence of the redirection filename. The redirection filename is only present if the filename was specified as part of the command. Assuming the redirection filename is set, the buffer is transferred to a file using the flash file system call tfsadd(), which simply transfers a block of memory to a file in the flash file system.

Although in some implementations redirection can be a complicated add-on, here the whole facility is really trivial to incorporate into the CLI. Notice that the only complexity added to `docommand()` are calls to `RedirectionCheck()` and `Redirection-CmdDone()`. This implementation of command-line redirection is a good example of modular functionality. Complexity for the feature is limited to the function responsible for the complexity; the complexity is not distributed throughout other components.

Command Line Editing and History

CLI history is a feature that lets you retrieve previously typed commands for reuse. *CLI editing* is the ability to modify a command line through some set of escape or control keystrokes. Combine CLI history and CLI editing, and you have a very handy mechanism for command-line recycling. Command-line recycling becomes very useful when you are doing a lot of long, repetitive commands that each differ slightly.

Command-line recycling is a wonderful tool that allows us geeky computer types to look like we can type really fast. In reality, we're spending the majority of our time using the control or escape sequences in the command line editor to undo all our typing mistakes, instead of retyping the whole line. When you are doing a lot of commands like `DM 0x14280040 0x40` followed by `DM 0x14290040 0x40`, command-line recycling is a big help.

Like terminal-based file editors, command-line editors come in two major types: modal and modeless. Modal means that you type some escape character to enter a "mode" that redefines the use of some of the keystrokes; then you type some other character to terminate the "mode" and return to normal character entry. Modeless means that certain control sequences are dedicated to certain features of the editor, and these control sequences can be used without entering any alternate "mode."

For this implementation, I chose to implement a modal CLI editor that is a subset of the `vi`-like editing capability provided by many other shells. When I wrote this editor years ago, I chose a `vi`-style interface because that's what I was familiar with on UNIX. Over time, I have incorporated this editor into a few different tools, and I have gotten some flack over not supporting a modeless emacs-like version. I stuck to the modal approach because it was more easily isolated from the rest of the character retrieval process.

As implemented here, the function that retrieves a command line only needs to look for one escape character. After receiving that character, it passes control to the line editor. The line-editing code is therefore isolated from the rest of the system, which makes it very easy to include or exclude line-editing from the package. The following code is the only necessary addition to the general character retrieval function[3] that passes a command line to docommand()

```
#define ESC 0x1b


...


#if INCLUDE_LINEEDIT
    if (inchar == ESC) {
        (void)line_edit(inbuf);
        break;
    }
    else
#endif
```

Whenever inchar contains an escape character, control passes to the function line_edit(), which switches command line input into the editing mode. The line_edit() function takes a pointer to the current input buffer. The remainder of that line's content is built through interaction with the user and the editing mode features provided by line_edit(). The line_edit() function itself gets quite messy because of all of the character overwriting performed while editing a line. This complexity, however, is all isolated from the generic retrieval of a command line.

After accessing the line_edit() function, the monitor is in the editing mode. Within that function though, there are several sub-modes that must be handled while editing the line. The user may be inserting characters, deleting characters, replacing characters, moving to a different location on the line, or just stepping through the list of commands currently in the history buffer of the editor. Also, the function must always know where it is on the command line so that it can move the cursor right or left. Unfortunately, you can't take advantage of any convenient terminal modes without limiting the function to work only with those terminals. Although use of the arrow keys might seem like the obvious set of keystrokes for moving right/left across the line and up/down through the command list, using the arrows might not be practical because many terminals (or terminal emulators) do not map the arrow keys to serial port characters.

Listing 5.11 shows part of the code for linedit.c. (Please refer to the CD, file linedit.c for the complete implementation. A full discussion of the line editor code

---

3. On the CD, this is in the function _getline() (part of chario.c).

is beyond the scope of this text. I'll introduce the implementation but leave the nitty-gritty details for the reader to review in the CD source code.) The function `lineeditor()` is called by `line_edit()` with a type that lets it know that it is being asked to edit a command line.[4] At this point, the editor has just started and is in the command (CMD) mode. The function sets the current position pointer to the location where the escape character was just entered on the line. Some additional pointers and state variables are established, and the code enters a loop to process incoming characters. The first character processed is the escape character. Depending on the current mode, the escape character either terminates the line editing entirely, or it terminates one of the sub-modes and returns the editor to command mode. Any character other than an escape is processed based on the mode.

Listing 5.11   `linedit.c`.

```
static int       stridx;        /* history storage index */
static int       shwidx;        /* history display index */
static int       srchidx;
static int       lastsize;      /* size of last command */
static char      curChar;       /* latest input character */
static char      *curPos;       /* current position on command line */
static char      *startOfLine;  /* start of command line */
static int       lineLen;       /* length of line */
static int       lMode;         /* present mode of entry */


static char *
lineeditor(char *line_to_edit,int type)
{
    lMode = CMD;
    startOfLine = line_to_edit;
    curPos = line_to_edit;
    while(*curPos != ESC)
        curPos++;
    *curPos = 0;                 /* Remove the escape char from the line */
    lineLen = (ulong)curPos - (ulong)startOfLine;
    if (lineLen > 0) {
```

---

4. This line editor is also used by a flash file editor, and, for that case, there are a few different rules applied.

```
            curPos--;
        pwrite(1," \b\b",3);
    }
    else
        pwrite(1," \b",2);
    lastsize = 0;
    shwidx = stridx;
    srchidx = stridx;

    while(1) {
        curChar = (char)getchar();
        switch(curChar) {
            case ESC:
                if (lMode != CMD) {
                    lMode = CMD;
                    continue;
                }
                else {
                    putchar('\n');
                    return((char *)0);
                }
            case '\r':
            case '\n':
                putchar('\n');
                if (lineLen == 0)
                    return((char *)0);
                *(char *)(startOfLine + lineLen) = '\0';
                return(startOfLine);
        }
        switch(lMode) {
            case CMD:
                lcmd(type);
                if (lMode == NEITHER)
                    return((char *)0);
                break;
            case INSERT:
                linsert();
```

```
                        break;
                case EDIT1:
                case EDIT:
                        ledit();
                        break;
        }
        if (lineLen >= MAXLINESIZE) {
                printf("line overflow\n");
                        return((char *)0);
        }
    }
}
```

This command-line editor supports three different sub-modes: INSERT, EDIT, and CMD. INSERT mode means that the user is inserting characters somewhere into the current command line. Characters are entered into the command line using the linsert() function. EDIT mode means that the user is modifying characters that are already in the command line (the ledit() function). CMD mode expects incoming characters to perform some action on the command line, put the editor into one of the other modes, or both.

If the system is in CMD mode, the lcmd() function (see Listing 5.12) processes different characters as different commands based on a subset of the vi-like command-line editing rules. A zero tells the editor to put the cursor at the beginning of the line, an A tells the editor to enter INSERT mode with the cursor positioned just *after* the last character of the current line. The i, r, and R commands simply transition to either EDIT or INSERT mode. The l and h commands move the cursor to the right or left, and the j and k commands tell the editor to step up or down through the command-line history list.

Listing 5.12   lcmd().

```
static void
lcmd(int type)
{
    switch(curChar) {
        case '0':
                gotobegin();
                return;
        case 'A':
```

```
        gotoend();
        putchar(*curPos);
        curPos++;
        lMode = INSERT;
        return;
    case 'i':
        lMode = INSERT;
        return;
    case 'x':
        ldelete();
        return;
    case ' ':
    case 'l':
        if (curPos < startOfLine+lineLen-1) {
            putchar(*curPos);
            curPos++;
        }
        return;
    case '\b':
    case 'h':
        if (curPos > startOfLine) {
            putchar('\b');
            curPos--;
        }
        return;
    case 'r':
        lMode = EDIT1;
        return;
    case 'R':
        lMode = EDIT;
        return;
    case '/':
        putchar('/');
        historysearch();
        return;
    case '+':
    case 'j':
```

```
        shownext();
        return;
    case '-':
    case 'k':
        showprev();
        return;
    }

    /* Beep to indicate an error. */
    putchar('\007');
}
```

For further detail on command-line editing, refer to the `lineedit.c` source code on the CD.

User Levels

As discussed earlier, MicroMonitor's CLI could also be accessible to the user interface of the application which is good and bad. Making the CLI accessible to applications is good because it keeps MicroMonitor accessible when the application is up. Developers can therefore do some "bare metal" stuff at the application command line without having to build additional features into the application. However, making the MicroMonitor CLI accessible to the application also makes it accessible to an end user. This means that the end user could modify RAM, erase flash memory, edit/remove files from TFS, and take other drastic actions that can have a permanent effect on the system. If you are worried about a user getting control of the system, the easiest solution is to just not enable the hook that allows the MicroMonitor commands to be accessible through the application; however, this eliminates the ability to use the monitor CLI from application space.

To mitigate some of these risks, MicroMonitor supports user levels, allowing each command to be configured so that it can only be run at or above a particular user level. If the application is running at a user level below the level required to access a MicroMonitor command, the user cannot access the command through the application. User-level functionality provides flexibility and is simple to add to the CLI.

Implementing user-level security requires some way to store a configurable user level for each command, plus a password facility. I chose to store the user level for each command in an array that parallels the command table array. Note that this array is separate from the command table because the command table array in ROM and this array must be in RAM, and, in MicroMonitor, I assume there is no writable initialized data. The declaration looks like this

```
char cmdUlvl[(sizeof(cmdlist)/sizeof(struct monCommand))];
```

The number of entries in this table matches the number of entries in the command table, so this and the command table can be indexed similarly. If the third command in the cmdlist[] table is add, the required user level to execute the add command is stored in the third element of the cmdUlvl table. I can include user-level functionality with the command line processor by adding a few more lines to the docommand() function (see Listing 5.13). The getUsrLvl() function simply returns the current user level of the system. Pointer arithmetic is used to determine what the index into the cmdUlvl[] array needs to be, and that index value is compared to the return value of getUsrLvl().

Listing 5.13   Adding User Levels to docommand().

```
    ...

    cmdptr = cmdlist;
    while(cmdptr->name) {
        if (strcmp(argv[0],cmdptr->name) == 0)
            break;
        cmdptr++;
    }
    if (cmdptr->name) {
        if (cmdUlvl[cmdptr-cmdlist] > getUsrLvl()) {
            printf("User-level access denied.\n");
            return(CMD_ULVL_DENIED);
        }
        ret = cmdptr->func(argc,argv);
    }

    ...
```

By default, the user level for each command is set to zero, and MicroMonitor itself runs at level three. A higher user level means more privileges, so the default behavior is for all commands to be accessible. A MicroMonitor command, ulvl, allows the user to re-configure both the monitor's running user level and the user level required to access each of the commands. Stepping down to a lower user level is granted without challenge. Stepping up to a higher user level requires a password. Because the monitor has four user levels, the system needs three passwords. (Level 0 does not require a password.) The ulvl command handles administration of the password file. The password file is always stored at the highest user level, so the password file is inaccessible to all user levels below user level three. Files in the flash file system can also be stored with a password based on user level. (See "User Levels" on page 140 of Chapter 7.)

Listing 5.14 shows the code used to set up a command's user level. The input is a comma-delimited string containing the command name followed by the requested user level.

Listing 5.14   Setting Up the User Level for a Command.

```
int
setCmdUlvl(char *cmdandlevel, int verbose)
{
    struct monCommand *cptr;
    int newlevel, idx;
    char *comma;

    /* First verify that the comma is in the string... */
    comma = strchr(cmdandlevel,',');
    if (!comma)
        goto showerr;

    /* Retrieve and verify the new level to be assigned... */
    newlevel = atoi(comma+1);
    if ((newlevel < MINUSRLEVEL) || (newlevel > MAXUSRLEVEL))
        goto showerr;

    *comma = 0;

    /* Don't allow adjustment of the ulvl command itself.
     *  It must be able to run as user level 0 all the time...
     */
    if (!strcmp(cmdandlevel, ULVLCMD))
    {
        printf("Can't adjust '%s' user level.\n", ULVLCMD);
        return(-1);
```

```
        }

        /* Find the command in the table that is to be adjusted...
         */
        for(idx=0,cptr=cmdlist;cptr->name;cptr++,idx++)
        {
            if (!strcmp(cmdandlevel, cptr->name))
            {
                /* If the command's user level is to be lowered, then
                 * the current monitor user level must be at least as
                 * high as the command's current user level...
                 */
                if ((newlevel < cmdUlvl[idx]) &&
                    (getUsrLvl() < cmdUlvl[idx]))
                {
                    if (verbose)
                        printf("Ulvl failed: %s\n", cmdandlevel);
                    return(1);
                }
                cmdUlvl[idx] = newlevel;
                return(0);
            }
        }
    }
showerr:
    if (verbose)
        printf("Input error: %s\n", cmdandlevel);
    return(-1);
}
```

Notice that the ulvl command itself cannot have its user level changed. It must always be accessible without the need for a password. Otherwise you could trap yourself by making the ulvl command a level three command, then lowering the user level to two. After the levels were changed, there would be no way to get to level three again, because you must *already* be at level three to use the ulvl command. Forcing the ulvl command to stay at level zero eliminates this catch-22.

Password Protection

The passwords for the different user levels are stored in a file. The file is set to require user level three and is only readable when MicroMonitor is at user level three. To secure the passwords, they are stored in scrambled form. The same scrambling algorithm can be used when someone enters a password. The scrambled version of what the user enters is compared to what is in the password file. Listing 5.15 is a very simple example of a scrambling function.

Listing 5.15   A Scrambling Function.

```
static unsigned char *datatbl =
"This_should_be_an_initialized_table_of_256_bytes_of_printable_ascii_characters
.";


char *
scrambler(char *string, char *setting, char *result)
{
    int offset, csum;
    char *rp, *sp;

    csum = 0;
    sp = string;
    while(*sp)
        csum += *sp++;
    rp = result;

    /* Set up an offset into the data table that is based on the
     * checksum of the incoming string plus the sum of the two
     * setting characters...
     */
    offset = (csum + setting[0] + setting[1]) % 255;

    /* For each character in the incoming string, replace it with a
     * character in the data table.  If the incoming character has the
     * 00001000 bit set, then use that character twice.
     */
    while(*string)
```

```
{
        offset += (int)*string;
        offset = offset % 255;
        *rp = datatbl[offset];
        if (*string & 8)
        {
            rp++;
            offset += (int)*string;
            offset = offset % 255;
            *rp = datatbl[offset];
        }
        string++;
        rp++;
    }
    *rp = 0;
    return(result);
}
```

The `ulvl` command uses these two functions (`setCmdUlvl()` and `scrambler()`) for maintenance of the password file and for updating a command's user level.

When the system is first booted, the `monrc` file could contain all of the `ulvl` commands needed to adjust the current MicroMonitor user level and to configure the user level required to access certain commands. The `monrc` file is a file that is automatically executed by the monitor when booted (see Chapter 7).

Summary

While relatively simple, the CLI developed here is powerful, extensible, and highly modular. The CLI is worth careful attention, as it constitutes a central component of the monitor. The CLI is the "big hook" on which almost everything else in the monitor hangs. It is the interface to debugging commands. It is the executive that launches applications. It is the interpreter that processes configuration scripts.

Despite this critical and central role, the CLI remains highly configurable. You can configure a particular implementation with as many or as few of the advanced features as you like.

6

Chapter 6

Interfacing to Flash Memory

Flash memory is quickly becoming the standard non-volatile memory choice in embedded systems. Flash memory's versatility, price per byte, and density fall in the right range to make it a very good choice for most new embedded systems projects. Flash memory is non-volatile and in-system-writable memory. In other words, the content of the device remains intact even after power is removed. There are mechanisms, however, available to the firmware that support the ability to write and re-write data to the flash memory device.

Interfacing to flash devices comes with its share of headaches. Reading from flash memory is the same as reading from regular memory, but that's where the similarity ends. Flash devices vary in size from about 64KB to 8MB and densities increase regularly. Flash devices are broken up into sectors or blocks of memory space. Each sector is an erasable unit. When a sector is erased, the bits of data within that sector are all set to 1 (bytes = 0xff). Writing to the flash device (after it has been erased) is the process of changing a bit that is currently a 1 to a 0. After the bit is 0, the only way it can be set back to 1 is by erasing the entire sector that contains the byte. Both the erase and write operations involve a complicated handshake between the processor and the memory device.

On top of all of this, for most flash devices, while an operation (write or erase) is being performed on the device, the CPU cannot access the device for anything else; hence, you can't be executing out of the same flash device on which you are operating. Just in case you're still not up to your ears in complexity, these devices eventually wear out. Typically, a sector on the device is guaranteed to last for 100,000 to 1,000,000 erase cycles — not very large numbers for an embedded microprocessor system.

This chapter describes how to provide support for multiple flash devices in varying widths and not necessarily in contiguous memory space. I will step through the MicroMonitor's flash command and discuss the functions that underlie MicroMonitor's flash memory features. This discussion continues in Chapter 7, which describes a flash file system.

The Interface Functions

There are five major flash memory interface functions. These functions provide initialization of control structures, retrieval of the device ID, and ability to write to and erase the device.

- FlashInit() — Initializes the data structures used by the flash driver to work with the device(s) on board.
- Flashid() — Returns some indication of the type of flash device that is populated on the system board. This function is useful because it provides a sanity check that the flash memory is writable. (In most cases, you must write to the flash memory to read back its ID properly.) Also, this function allows the firmware to support the possibility of different types of devices installed in the system.
- Flasherase() — Takes a sector number as input and properly erases that sector (or all sectors).
- FlashWrite() — Takes a source pointer, a destination pointer, and a size and writes the source data to the destination address. This function assumes that the destination is flash memory and that it has been erased.
- FlashEwrite() — Combines Flasherase() and FlashWrite(). This function takes the same arguments as FlashWrite() but erases the affected sectors prior to the write. This function is used to re-write a new monitor in place.

Flash Banks

The flash driver supports multiple banks of devices not necessarily in contiguous memory space. A *bank* in this context is one or more devices that are accessed as a unit. For example, if one 8-bit device is accessible to the CPU, then that device is considered a single bank.

As shown in Figure 6.1, if a second device is wired above the first device — providing double the memory — but each device is accessed individually as 8-bit data space (note the two distinct chip-selects), the system would be said to contain two banks because at any given time only one device can be accessed.

Figure 6.1   Two Flash Devices, Two Separate Banks.

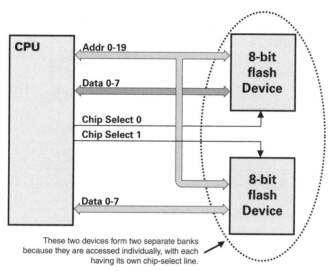

These two devices form two separate banks because they are accessed individually, with each having its own chip-select line.

It is common in small systems for each memory chip to be treated as a separate bank. In larger systems, separate banks might consist of multiple paralleled chips (see Figure 6.2.) In this example, the processor chip select lines are used to activate the appropriate bank.

If the second device is wired so that the CPU can access both devices as a 16-bit block (see Figure 6.2 — note only one chip select), then the result would be a single, two-device bank. Similarly four 8-bit devices or two 16-bit devices wired in parallel to present a 32-bit block of flash memory to the CPU would also be a single bank of flash memory.

Figure 6.2 Two Flash Devices, One Single Bank.

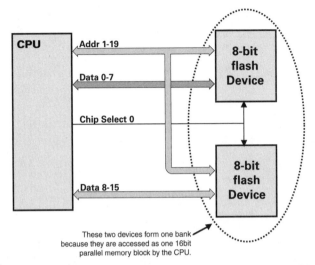

These two devices form one bank
because they are accessed as one 16bit
parallel memory block by the CPU.

In this example, two 8-bit memory chips are connected in parallel to create a single 16-bit wide memory bank. Note that the chip select line activates the entire bank as a unit.

Operations on flash memory take time. Usually the controlling firmware must poll the device and wait for completion of some internal operation. Depending on design goals and requirements, it is wise to consider putting more devices in parallel to build up to a specified flash density. Many flash devices can be configured to run in 8- or 16-bit mode. If your design calls for an amount of flash memory that requires four of these devices, it is more efficient (from the programming time point of view) to put all four devices in 8-bit mode to form one 32-bit bank instead of building two banks with each device in 16-bit mode. Putting four devices in parallel allows all four to perform internal operations simultaneously; hence, the programming time-per-byte is reduced.

Relocating Flash Operation Functions to RAM

One of the challenges of writing flash interface functions is that the flash interface function must be executed out of memory space that is not located on the flash device you are manipulating. Some newer devices allow you to get fancy and execute from one section of the device while operating on another, but I assume you're not using these special devices.

The idea behind the flash interface function is to create the function in flash memory, then copy the function to RAM and load a function pointer with the address of that copy space. The function pointer is then used to access the RAM-based copy of the function. The code within the function must be entirely self-relative (i.e., relocatable).

In general, code within a function is almost always self-relative anyway, as long as there are no calls to other functions. Some compilers, however, use intrinsic functions for doing basic math operations, such as multiply and divide; you won't see the call, but it's still there. Most tool sets support the ability to write position-independent code. Position-independent code simply means that branches to other functions (from within a function) are not done through PC-relative branching. Instead, the entire address of the function is loaded into a register, and the branch is taken using that register. This approach still doesn't help in the case of a flash interface function because if the function you call is in flash memory, you're executing out of the very same flash memory you are trying to avoid. The point of all of this information is that the flash operation functions that are relocated to RAM should be kept simple and to the point. Just be disciplined and don't put any function calls within this code.

The system should copy the flash code to RAM prior to enabling any of the CPU's caching (because the RAM copy uses data accesses to populate instruction space and you don't want to have to worry about the fact that instructions might be in the data cache). The following is a very basic example of how to copy a function into RAM. Note that the buffer is 32-bit aligned using an array of longs instead of chars. Using longs guarantees that the buffer starts on a modulo-4 address.[1] It assumes that the linker is placing functions within a file in contiguous memory space and that the function fits in the specified buffer.

Listing 6.1   Copying a Flash Function to RAM.

```
int (*RamFlashWrite)();
unsigned long RamFlashWriteBuf[1000];

int
FlashWrite()
```

---

1. Some processors require each instruction to be on a 32-bit boundary, so this satisfies that requirement but does not hurt anything for those CPUs that do not have this requirement.

```
{
    /* code to write to flash goes here */
}

int
EndFlashWrite()
{
    return(1);
}

...

/* Copy from flash space to RAM space: */
memcpy((char *)RAMFlashWriteBuf,(char *)FlashWrite,
(int)((ulong)EndFlashWrite-(ulong)FlashWrite));

/* Establish a function pointer into the RAM buffer: */
RamFlashWrite = (int(*)())RamFlashWriteBuf;
```

After this code completes, the function pointer RamFlashWrite can be used to access the RAM-based version of the FlashWrite() function. The RAM-based function uses the same API as the flash-based version; the only difference is that the CPU fetches it out of RAM instead of flash memory.

Flash Control Structure Initialization

To allow the same API to work across several different devices, making the device type insignificant to the code, I use a few data structures to keep track of device-specific information. The main structure is flashinfo (see Listing 6.2). The flashinfo structure contains a set of function pointers that are initialized to point to the RAM space that contains the flash operation functions. To allow one driver to support several different devices within a family, the ID of the device is retrieved, and, based on the ID, additional sector-specific information about the device can be loaded. This sector-specific information is stored in the sectorinfo structure. There is one sectorinfo structure per sector. The pointer to the sectorinfo structure within the flashinfo structure points to a table of sectorinfo structures whose size is equal to the number of sectors in the device. The table pointed to by the sectors pointer within the flashinfo structure is established in the FlashInit() function (see Listing 6.4).

Listing 6.2   Flash Device Descriptors.

```
struct  sectorinfo {
    long    size;          /* size of sector */
    int snum;              /* number of sector (amongst possibly */
                           /* several devices) */
    int protected;         /* if set, sector is protected by window */
    unsigned char *begin;  /* base address of sector */
    unsigned char *end;    /* end address of sector */
};


struct  flashinfo {
    unsigned long   id;    /* manufacturer & device id */
    unsigned char   *base; /* base address of bank */
    unsigned char   *end;  /* end address of bank */
    int     sectorcnt;     /* number of sectors */
    int     width;         /* 1, 2, or 4 */
    int     (*fltype)();
    int     (*flerase)();
    int     (*flwrite)();
    int     (*flewrite)();
    struct sectorinfo *sectors;
};
```

Flash Operations for the 29F040 Family

Breaking from the book's general, device-independent philosophy, I will now step through a device-specific example. The 29F040 family of devices has been around for a while, comes in a few different package types, and is manufactured by more than just one silicon vendor.

First, I create several RAM arrays (see Listing 6.3) that are used to store the flash operation functions — one for each of the operations: TYPE, ERASE, WRITE, and ERASEandWRITE. Next I define a table of flashinfo structures. The size of the table (FLASHBANKS) should equal the number of banks in the system. For this example, the size is just one. The last piece of data is the table of sectorinfo structures. Because the 29F040 and 29F010 both have eight sectors, the same table can be used for either device.

Listing 6.3   RAM Arrays.

```
ulong    FlashTypeFbuf[FLASHFUNCSIZE];
ulong    FlashEraseFbuf[FLASHFUNCSIZE];
ulong    FlashWriteFbuf[FLASHFUNCSIZE];
ulong    FlashEwriteFbuf[FLASHFUNCSIZE];


struct   flashinfo FlashBank[FLASHBANKS];


struct   sectorinfo sinfo040[8];
```

The FlashInit() function (see Listing 6.4) is called at system startup. The calls to flashopload() (not shown) copy the flash operation functions from flash memory to RAM. If for any reason the copy fails, flashopload() returns −1 and FlashInit() aborts. Remember that it is important to copy the flash operation to RAM while the system cache is disabled to avoid the confusion that is created by the fact that the memory copy can leave some of the instructions in the data cache.[2] The flashopload() function is basically a fancy memcpy(). The flashopload() function verifies that the flash operation's function fits in the buffer and then verifies that the writes were successful (by reading all that is written during the copy). Next, the flashinfo structure in the FlashBank[] table is initialized. The base and width of the device is recorded, and each function pointer is loaded with the location of the corresponding RAM array that now contains the flash operation code.

Listing 6.4   Initializing Flash-Related Structures.

```
int
FlashInit(void)
{
    int     snum;
    struct  flashinfo *fbnk;

    snum = 0;
```

---

2.   Optionally, we could just flush/invalidate the caches at the end of this function, but because this process is done early on in the system initialization, it is reasonable to just do this prior to enabling cache.

```
    if (flashopload((ulong *)FlashType040,(ulong *)EndFlashType040,
        FlashTypeFbuf,sizeof(FlashTypeFbuf)) < 0)
        return(-1);
    if (flashopload((ulong *)FlashErase040,(ulong *)EndFlashErase040,
        FlashEraseFbuf,sizeof(FlashEraseFbuf)) < 0)
        return(-1);
    if (flashopload((ulong *)FlashEwrite040,(ulong *)EndFlashEwrite040,
        FlashEwriteFbuf,sizeof(FlashEwriteFbuf)) < 0)
        return(-1);
    if (flashopload((ulong *)FlashWrite040,(ulong *)EndFlashWrite040,
        FlashWriteFbuf,sizeof(FlashWriteFbuf)) < 0)
        return(-1);

    fbnk = &FlashBank[0];
    fbnk->base = (unsigned char *)FLASH_BANK0_BASE_ADDR;
    fbnk->width = FLASH_BANK0_WIDTH;
    fbnk->fltype = (int(*)())FlashTypeFbuf;
    fbnk->flerase = (int(*)())FlashEraseFbuf;
    fbnk->flwrite = (int(*)())FlashWriteFbuf;
    fbnk->flewrite = (int(*)())FlashEwriteFbuf;
    fbnk->sectors = sinfo040;
    snum += FlashBankInit(fbnk,snum);
    sectorProtect(FLASH_PROTECT_RANGE,1);
    return(0);
}
```

To determine the type of device, the flash initialization routine calls FlashBankInit() (see Listing 6.5). The FlashBankInit() function calls the function flashtype(), which is simply a wrapper around the fbnk->fltype function pointer (which points to the RAM array that contains the flash TYPE operation code — thanks to flashopload()). The ID of the device is retrieved, and, depending on whether the installed device is AMD20F040 or AMD29F010, the sector information structures are configured appropriately (the sector size for the '040 is 64K, for the '010, it's 16K). The loop at the bottom of FlashBankInit() initializes each of the sectorinfo entries based on characteristics established from the device type.

Listing 6.5   Initializing the Flash Descriptors.

```c
int
FlashBankInit(struct flashinfo *fbnk, int snum)
{
    int i, ssize;


    flashtype(fbnk);
    switch(fbnk->id) {
        case AMD29LV040:
        case SGS29LV040:
        case SGS29F040:
        case AMD29F040:
            fbnk->sectorcnt = 8;
            ssize = 0x10000 * fbnk->width;
            fbnk->end = fbnk->base + (0x80000 * fbnk->width) - 1;
            break;
        case AMD29F010:
            fbnk->sectorcnt = 8;
            ssize = 0x4000 * fbnk->width;
            fbnk->end = fbnk->base + (0x20000 * fbnk->width) - 1;
            break;
        default:
            printf("Flash device id 0x%lx unknown\n", fbnk->id);
            return(-1);
    }
    for(i=0;i<fbnk->sectorcnt;i++) {
        fbnk->sectors[i].snum = snum+i;
        fbnk->sectors[i].size = ssize;
        fbnk->sectors[i].begin = fbnk->base + (i*ssize);
        fbnk->sectors[i].end = fbnk->sectors[i].begin + ssize - 1;
        fbnk->sectors[i].protected = 0;
    }
    return(0);
}
```

The final call in `FlashInit()` (refer to Listing 6.4) is to `sectorProtect()`. The `sectorProtect()` function establishes certain sectors as protected. In this case, the term protected means "software" protected. The flash operations that perform erase or write on the device must first look to see if the affected sector is protected. If the sector is protected, the flash operation is aborted. Note that this methodology offers only a software level of protection. In this case, the protection is quite adequate because two different functions must be called sequentially to bypass it accidentally — first unprotect the sector and then perform the operation. Because the "unprotect" is performed through the MicroMonitor CLI, the two necessary steps are not in any one function; this makes it extremely unlikely that an accidental erase or write of a protected sector will occur.

Now that I've explained how the flash functions get copied to RAM, I'll explain how the flash interface works, beginning with the details of the flash write operation.

The 29F040 has eight 64K sectors, each of which can be erased at least 100,000 times. Unlike RAM and DRAM, which allow you to write as you please, the actual write operation for flash memory requires you to notify the device to which you intend to write. A typical write operation consists of writing some chunk of data to some chunk of space within the flash device. Then the actual unit of data is written. The algorithm then waits for the internal machine of the flash device to indicate write completion. Finally the device is told to go back to standard read mode.

Listing 6.6 shows the code for a flash write operation on the 29F040. The function takes a pointer to a `flashinfo` structure along with source, destination, and size. Note the three `WRITE` macros prior to each `FWRITE` macro. The three-write sequence prepares the device for the actual data write, which is performed by the `FWRITE` macro. After `FWRITE` transfers the data, a wait loop polls the device to determine when the operation completes. When the operation completes, another sequence is written to the device to put the device back into standard read mode so that the device is available for read operations.

Listing 6.6   The Flash Write Operation.

```
/* Macros used for flash operations: */

#define ftype              volatile unsigned char
#define WRITE_AA_TO_5555()  (*(ftype *)(fdev->base + (0x5555<<0)) = 0xaa)
#define WRITE_55_TO_2AAA()  (*(ftype *)(fdev->base + (0x2aaa<<0)) = 0x55)
#define WRITE_80_TO_5555()  (*(ftype *)(fdev->base + (0x5555<<0)) = 0x80)
#define WRITE_A0_TO_5555()  (*(ftype *)(fdev->base + (0x5555<<0)) = 0xa0)
#define WRITE_F0_TO_5555()  (*(ftype *)(fdev->base + (0x5555<<0)) = 0xf0)
```

```
#define WRITE_90_TO_5555()   (*(ftype *)(fdev->base + (0x5555<<0)) = 0x90)
#define WRITE_30_TO_(add)    (*(ftype *)add = 0x30)
#define READ_0000()          (*(ftype *)(fdev->base + 0x0000<<0)))
#define READ_0001()          (*(ftype *)(fdev->base + (0x0001<<0)))
#define READ_5555()          (*(ftype *)(fdev->base + (0x5555<<0)))
#define IS_FF(add)           (*(ftype *)add == 0xff)
#define IS_NOT_FF(add)       (*(ftype *)add != 0xff)
#define D5_TIMEOUT(add)      ((*(ftype *)add & 0xdf) == 0x20)
#define FWRITE(to,frm)       (*(ftype *)to = *(ftype *)frm)
#define IS_EQUAL(p1,p2)      (*(ftype *)p1 == *(ftype *)p2)
#define IS_NOT_EQUAL(p1,p2)  (*(ftype *)p1 != *(ftype *)p2)


int
FlashWrite040(struct flashinfo *fdev, ftype *dest,ftype *src,long bytecnt)
{
    int i, ret;
    ftype  val;

    /* Each pass through this loop writes 'fdev->width' bytes... */
    ret = 0;
    for (i=0;i<bytecnt;i++) {

        /* Flash write command */
        WRITE_AA_TO_5555();
        WRITE_55_TO_2AAA();
        WRITE_A0_TO_5555();

        /* Write the value */
        FWRITE(dest,src);

        /* Wait for write to complete or timeout. */
        while(1) {
            if (IS_EQUAL(dest,src)) {
                if (IS_EQUAL(dest,src))
                    break;
            }
            /* Check D5 for timeout... */
```

```
                if (D5_TIMEOUT(dest)) {
                    if (IS_NOT_EQUAL(dest,src))
                        ret = -1;
                    goto done;
                }
            }
        dest++; src++;
    }
done:
    /* Read/reset command: */
    WRITE_AA_TO_5555();
    WRITE_55_TO_2AAA();
    WRITE_F0_TO_5555();
    val = READ_5555();
    return(ret);
}


/* EndFlashwrite():
 *  Function place holder to determine the "end" of the
 *  Flashwrite() function.
 */
void
EndFlashWrite040()
{}
```

The `Flasherase()` function (see Listing 6.7) is very similar to `FlashWrite()`. A sequence of writes notifies the device of the impending erase operation. Next, the command that initiates the sector-specific erasure is completed. The polling loop then waits for completion, and, finally, a sequence of writes tells the device to go back to standard read mode.

Listing 6.7   `Flasherase()`.

```
/* Flasherase():
 * Based on the 'snum' value, erase the appropriate sector(s).
 * Return 0 if success, else -1.
 */
int
```

```
FlashErase040(struct flashinfo *fdev,int snum)
{
    ftype         val;
    unsigned long add;
    int           ret, sector;

    ret = 0;
    add = (unsigned long)(fdev->base);

    /* Erase the request sector(s): */
    for (sector=0;sector<fdev->sectorcnt;sector++) {
        if (((!FlashProtectWindow) &&
            (fdev->sectors[sector].protected)) {
            add += fdev->sectors[sector].size;
            continue;
        }
        if ((snum == ALL_SECTORS) || (snum == sector)) {
            /* Issue the sector erase command sequence: */
            WRITE_AA_TO_5555();
            WRITE_55_TO_2AAA();
            WRITE_80_TO_5555();
            WRITE_AA_TO_5555();
            WRITE_55_TO_2AAA();

            WRITE_30_TO_(add);

            /* Wait for sector erase to complete or timeout..
             * DQ7 polling: wait for D7 to be 1.
             * DQ6 toggling: wait for D6 to not toggle.
             * DQ5 timeout: if DQ7 = 0, and DQ5 = 1, timeout.
             */
            while(1) {
                if (IS_FF(add)) {
                    if (IS_FF(add))
                        break;
                }
                if (D5_TIMEOUT(add)) {
```

```
                if (IS_NOT_FF(add))
                    ret = -1;
                break;
            }
        }
    }
    add += fdev->sectors[sector].size;
}

WRITE_AA_TO_5555();
WRITE_55_TO_2AAA();
WRITE_F0_TO_5555();
val = READ_5555();
return(ret);
}


/* EndFlasherase():
 * Function place holder to determine the "end" of the
 * sectorerase() function.
 */
void
EndFlashErase040()
{}
```

At the top of the Flasherase() function, the global variable FlashProtectWindow is tested against the protected member of the sectorinfo structure. The Flash-ProtectWindow variable can only be set by the CLI command flash opw (open flash protection window), and, as a result of the flash opw command, the variable is set to 2. At the completion of each CLI command, this variable is tested for non-zero state and, if positive, is decremented by one. Upon completion of the flash opw command itself, the variable is decremented to 1. The window of time for which the variable is non-zero is, therefore, one CLI command, which provides the "soft" protection mentioned earlier.

Dealing with 16- and 32-bit Banks

At the start of this flash driver section, I mentioned that the devices can be in banks, and any given bank can be 8, 16, or 32 bits. The example code then elaborated on an 8-bit device interface. This approach is fine for demonstrating just how to deal with the flash device, but I must still mention one more sticky issue. If you have multiple devices in parallel forming a 32-bit bank, the call to FlashWrite() must deal with the possibility that the starting address of the write may not be 32-bit aligned. The model of banks requires that the banks are in units of the same width, so if you want to start the flash write on some odd address, you need to back up to the preceding 32-bit aligned address and include some of the data already in flash memory as part of the first unit write. Refer to Figure 6.3.

Figure 6.3   Adjusting Start Address to 32-bit Alignment.

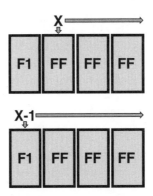

To write 0x112233 **starting at the address X, we convert the 3-byte write on the top to the 4-byte write on the bottom. This process is done by backing up the destination address by one and making that byte be part of the 4-byte write to the memory space. So we write** 0xF1112233 **at address X-1.**

The same principle applies to a write that does not end on a 32-bit alignment. You might have to read ahead a few bytes and include that read data in the final 32-bit write.

Flash Driver Front End

At this point, the portions of the flash device driver that directly touch the flash are copied to RAM so that the system can still execute out of the 29F040 while performing flash operations. However, the lowest level functions, FlashWrite040() and FlashErase040(), are device-dependent. I need to add another layer before I start allowing the rest of the system to use this functionality. I need a front end that allows me to write to any flash device using an interface similar to memcpy() (i.e., source and destination plus a size). For erasure, I need the ability to call a function and specify the sector I wish to erase. This function eliminates the need for the higher-level code to know about the specific flash device.

At the command line, flash memory is manipulated with the flash command. This section explains how this command can manipulate the flash memory without knowing any device specifics.

Listing 6.8   The flash Command.

```
int
FlashCmd(int argc,char *argv[])
{
    int ret;
    ulong   dest, src, oints;
    long    bytecnt, rslt;
    struct  flashinfo *fbnk;

    fbnk = &FlashBank[FlashCurrentBank];
    ret = CMD_SUCCESS;

    if (strcmp(argv[1],"bank") == 0)  {
        int tmpbank;
        if (argc == 3) {
            tmpbank = atoi(argv[2]);
            if (tmpbank < FLASHBANKS)
                FlashCurrentBank = tmpbank;
                printf("Subsequent flash ops apply to bank %d\n",
                    FlashCurrentBank);
        }
        else
            printf("Current flash bank: %d\n",FlashCurrentBank);
    }
    else if (!strcmp(argv[1],"write")) {
        if (argc == 5) {
            dest = strtoul(argv[2],(char **)0,0);
            src = strtoul(argv[3],(char **)0,0);
```

```
            bytecnt = (long)strtoul(argv[4],(char **)0,0);
            rslt = AppFlashWrite((ulong *)dest,(ulong *)src,bytecnt);
            if (rslt == -1)
                printf("Write failed\n");
        }
        else
            ret = CMD_PARAM_ERROR;
    }
    else if (!strcmp(argv[1],"opw")) {
        FlashProtectWindow = 2;
    }
    else {
        ret = CMD_PARAM_ERROR;
    }

    return(ret);
}
```

The format for the `flash` command is

```
    flash {command} [args based on command]
```

For example

```
    flash write 0x1000 0xfff80000 128
```

copies 128 bytes from `0xfff80000` to the flash destination of `0x1000`. There's nothing fancy here. This command doesn't take any options (see Listing 6.8), so `getopt()` is not used. The content of `FlashCurrentBank` points to the appropriate bank. Based on the earlier discussion, we know the 29F040-based target has only one bank, but multiples can be supported by increasing the size of the `FlashBank[]` array to the number of banks in the system. Listing 6.8 also shows how the `FlashProtectWindow` variable gets set so that the other flash operations that might be software protected can run. The most important thing to notice in `FlashCMD()` is the call to `AppFlashWrite()`.

The `AppFlashWrite()` function (in Listing 6.9) is used to abstract the characteristics of the flash memory. Notice that no device-specific information is passed to this function; hence, the caller is unaware of the underlying flash device characteristics.

Listing 6.9   **Abstracting Flash Memory Characteristics.**

```
int
AppFlashWrite(uchar *dest,uchar *src, long bytecnt)
{
    struct  flashinfo *fbnk;
    int     ret;
    long    tmpcnt;

    ret = 0;
    while(bytecnt > 0) {
        fbnk = addrtobank(dest);
        if (!fbnk)
            return(-1);

        if (((int)dest + bytecnt) <= (int)(fbnk->end))
            tmpcnt = bytecnt;
        else
            tmpcnt = ((int)(fbnk->end) - (int)dest) + 1;

        ret = fdev->flwrite(fbnk,dest,src,tmpcnt);
        if (ret < 0) {
            printf("AppFlashWrite(0x%lx,0x%lx,%ld) failed\n",
                (ulong)dest,(ulong)src,bytecnt);
            break;
        }
        dest += tmpcnt;
        src += tmpcnt;
        bytecnt -= tmpcnt;
    }
    return(ret);
}

struct flashinfo *
addrtobank(uchar *addr)
{
    struct  flashinfo *fbnk;
    int     dev;
```

```
    for(dev=0;dev<FLASHBANKS;dev++) {
        fbnk = &FlashBank[dev];
        if ((addr >= fbnk->base) && (addr <= fbnk->end))
            return(fbnk);
    }
    printf("addrtobank(0x%lx) failed\n",(ulong)addr);
    return(0);
}
```

A few neat things occur in AppFlashWrite(). Notice that addrtobank() converts the destination address into a corresponding flashinfo structure pointer. Then the destination address is compared to the end address of the bank. If the destination + bytecount passes the end of the bank, the byte count shrinks to a value that ends at the last address in the bank. Then on the next pass through the loop, addrtobank() is called again, and the new flashinfo pointer is returned for the next block write. Finally, notice that the flashinfo structure is once again used to call the flash write function (through the function pointer fdev->flwrite that corresponds to the bank of flash memory that overlaps the destination address). This is only applicable to systems that have more than one flash bank.

Summary

That's about all there is to a flash interface. The implementation discussed here has a front end that you can reuse across virtually any bus-based flash device configuration. The API and commands provide an interface between the user and flash device that requires the user to realize that the address space dedicated to flash memory is written and erased through an API. As long as the API is followed, the writes and erases will succeed, regardless of the underlying device.

At the application level, the flash interface discussed in this chapter is a convenience. At the driver level, someone still must write the protocol necessary to interface to the device (similar to what we just went through with the 29F040 device). Recall that the 29F040 is one of a family of devices that are similar in their architecture and interface. This family implements a device ID feature, allowing firmware to self-configure for whatever device is actually soldered on the board. Because the device is self-identifying, you can build target hardware with one of several different devices of the same family without making any changes to the firmware. This solution is adequate for simple environments in which the device is soldered on the target board, and for which, at most, one or two different device types are supported.

Chapter 7

A Flash File System

At this point, the monitor design has enough features to complete a basic shell around the hardware. I have the boot-up, serial port, and flash drivers and a solid command-line interface. The next few chapters put icing on the cake. In this chaper, I will start work on a flash file system, called Tiny File System (TFS). Flash file systems in embedded systems are still a bit sparse, but as we see more and more use of higher-density flash parts and removable flash media, we will surely see more and more appearances of flash file systems. A flash file system is usually considered a frivolous luxury; hence, programmers must often interface their application to the flash device using some home grown set of primitives. A flash file system certainly makes the embedded system easier to manage, but writing one from scratch is likely to be more complicated than you first expected.

This chapter presents a mechanism that allows the programmer to treat the memory space allocated to flash as namespace instead of address space. TFS solves some of the basic problems of interfacing to flash. For instance, TFS provides an API that is independent of the underlying flash device yet does not inhibit the program from directly accessing the raw memory if necessary. TFS offers an efficient alternative for applications that need a flash file system but don't require a sophisticated implementation with wear-leveling, directory hierarchy, and DOS-file-format compatibility. TFS provides an API accessible to both MicroMonitor and the application loaded by MicroMonitor. The TFS API provides an interface for operations that let you read, write, open, close, seek, and assemble statistical information. MicroMonitor's TFS command lets you list, delete, create, display, copy, decompress, load, execute, and clean up files on the flash device. TFS lets you automatically boot one or more application files and allows other portions of the boot platform to assume the existence of a flash file system.

The Role of TFS in the Platform

The platform I am constructing depends heavily on the presence of the TFS file system. Even the basic boot of MicroMonitor depends upon obtaining certain configuration parameters from a file. Execution of a monitor run control file monrc allows a file in TFS to configure various other parameters in the platform. Things like the IP and MAC addresses are established in this script file that automatically runs at startup. In the next chapter, I will show how TFS allows files to be scripts (similar to DOS batch files). The communication interfaces (Xmodem and TFTP) both interface with TFS for file transfer, and, after an application is transferred into TFS, it can be loaded from flash into RAM automatically by TFS autoboot at system startup. Then, when the application is running, it can access the TFS API to access files in flash. TFS is not just another interface; it is a major portion of the platform.

The TFS Design Criteria

The initial goal of TFS was to provide my firmware with the ability to treat system flash as namespace instead of address space. This approach eliminates the need for each new application to deal with the flash memory in some unfamiliar or clumsy way. At the same time, I didn't want to eliminate the ability to access the data within the file as simple memory; hence, I needed an API to support the namespace model, but I wanted a hook into the raw flash to support the basic address/data model. To support both access methods, TFS must guarantee that the data for any one file is in contiguous address space in flash.

Another goal of the design was to make TFS somewhat device- and RTOS–independent. To avoid potential real-time conflicts, TFS is designed to operate without requiring system interrupts. TFS works with a wide range of flash devices. The only restriction on the underlying flash device is that its sector size must be larger than the TFS header size (currently 92 bytes). As a consequence of these choices, TFS can support a high-level application that wants a file system model (i.e., access to files and data through an open/close/read/write API), as well as a real-time application that needs quick memory access (access file by name, access data within the file by address).

TFS is a linear file system that gives a typical embedded systems project all of the file-system-like capabilities it will ever need. TFS does not support any sophisticated wear-leveling algorithm, it doesn't have a directory hierarchy, and it is not compatible with any other file system. I have yet to work on a project that was accessing the flash frequently enough to need wear leveling, and DOS compatibility is not necessary if the media is not removable. TFS is independent of the RTOS (it doesn't need an RTOS), and it is easily hooked into an application.

File Attributes

TFS supports file attributes. Each attribute (or flag) simply describes the file to TFS. An attribute in the file header is simply a bit setting. At the command line, each attribute is identified by a single letter. The following is a list of all the file attributes, including a brief description of each:

Attribute	Abbreviation	Description
executable script	e	ASCII file executed as a script
executable binary	E	binary file loaded and run based on format
autoboot	b	file is executed at startup
autoboot with query	B	file is executed at startup if user query passes
compressed	c	file is compressed
in-place-modifiable	I	file is in-place-modifiable
unreadable	u	file cannot be read at lower user level
user level	0-3	file can only be written at or above its user level

Currently, the executable binary file formats supported are AOUT (old Unix file format), COFF (common object file format), and ELF (executable and linking format). New formats can easily be incorporated into TFS.

Autobootable Files

At some point in the startup process, MicroMonitor looks to TFS for autobootable files. MicroMonitor supports three types of autobootable files: two file types designated by the attributes assigned to the file and one special case (the monrc file). For the monrc file to run automatically, it must exist and have the e attribute (executable script) set. The monrc file runs prior to any other autobootable file in TFS and prior to MicroMonitor completing its own initialization. MicroMonitor can therefore configure itself using parameters established in the `monrc` executable. Remaining autobootable files are run after MicroMonitor has completed initialization. The files are run in alphabetical order, so the order in which they are placed in TFS doesn't matter. The order in which they are listed via the command `tfs ls` is the order in which they execute.

Listing 7.1   Output of the Command `tfs ls`.

Name	Size	Location	Flags
bkgd.jpg	5976	0x80047a6c	
cardtilt.gif	6099	0x80040c1c	
boot_diag	109358	0x8004921c	BE
construction.gif	20222	0x8004243c	
form.html	466	0x8004004c	
my_app	792080	0x80155a7c	BE
index.html	442	0x8004026c	
info1.html	1053	0x8004047c	
info2.html	734	0x800408ec	
lucentlogo.gif	1680	0x8004738c	
monrc	823	0x80154d2c	e

The order of autoboot execution for the files given in Listing 7.1 is:

1. `monrc`
2. `boot_diag`
3. `my_app`

All other files listed are data files used by the application. The two autobootable attributes supported are B and b, both of which run at startup. The B type queries the user at the console port, providing an opportunity to abort the autoboot of that file. If the query times out (about two seconds) before the user responds, the file executes. You can configure both scripts and binary executables with the autoboot attribute.

User Levels

MicroMonitor supports the concept of user levels. One user level is considered active at any given time. TFS supports the ability to store a file at a particular user level then limit access to that file based on the user level at the time of the access. Individual files can be marked read-only or not-even-readable. Because each user level is attainable only via password, a system can be built at user level 3 and then lowered to user level 2, 1, or 0 to provide varying degrees of protection from unauthorized access.

High-Level Details

The following details assume a basic system: CPU, I/O, RAM, and one flash device. The system flash memory includes three defined sections: flash space used by the MicroMonitor code itself, the flash space used to store the files, and the space dedicated to interruptible defragmentation (the "spare sector"). The flash memory used by TFS for file storage begins on a sector boundary, and the spare sector is located immediately after the last sector in which files are stored. The spare sector must be at least as large as any other sector in the device, and the sector prior to the spare is assumed to be of equal size (refer to Figure 7.1).

Figure 7.1   TFS Overlayed on a Flash Device.

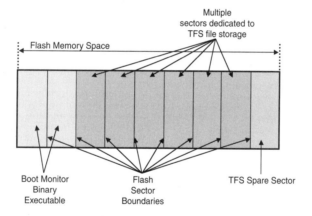

TFS organizes the files within the flash memory in a contiguous, one-way linked list. The initial portion of the file is a file header (see Figure 7.2), which contains information about the file, a pointer to the next file, and a 32-bit cyclic redundancy check (CRC) of the header and data portion of the file. Maintaining unique CRC checks for header and data allows TFS to detect corruption. File size is limited only by the amount of flash memory allocated to TFS. There is no restriction with regard to sector boundaries. The header structure is shown in Listing 7.2.

Listing 7.2   TFS Header Structure.

```
struct tfshdr {
    ushort  hdrsize;                    /* Size of this header.            */
    ushort  hdrvrsn;                    /* Header version #.               */
    long    filsize;                    /* Size of the file.               */
    long    flags;                      /* Flags describing the file.      */
    ulong   filcrc;                     /* 32 bit CRC of file.             */
    ulong   hdrcrc;                     /* 32 bit CRC of the header.       */
    ulong   modtime;                    /* Time when file was last modified. */
    struct  tfshdr  *next;              /* Pointer to next file in list.   */
    char    name[TFSNAMESIZE+1];        /* Name of file.                   */
    char    info[TFSINFOSIZE+1];        /* Miscellaneous info field.       */
#if TFS_RESERVED
    ulong   rsvd[TFS_RESERVED];
#endif
};
```

Figure 7.2   Files (Data and Header) Within Flash Space.

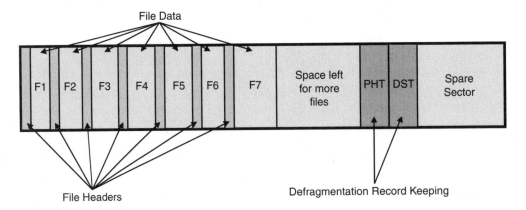

TFS must be initialized when the system is first built. The flash space allocated to TFS must therefore be erased. From that point on, as a file is created it is appended to the end of the linked list of files. If a file is deleted from the list, the file is simply marked as deleted. At some point, after several files have been deleted, it becomes necessary to clean up the TFS flash space by running a defragmentation process. This defragmentation process requires a spare sector plus some space that grows downward from the top of the last TFS sector and whose size is dependent on the number of active files.

Note that the spare sector cannot reside within the space used by TFS. The spare sector must be at the end of the space because TFS assumes that all files are contiguous within the flash space. Contiguous data is a very nice feature for extremely time-critical applications. You can store a data file in flash and access the file by name to retrieve the starting point of the data. From that point on, you can use simple (and more efficient) memory accesses to read data from the memory space.

Flash Space Overhead Required by TFS

Overlaying TFS onto a flash device is not free. TFS imposes a certain amount of overhead. Some of the extra space is fixed; some depends on the number of files stored. Referring to Figure 7.2, five portions of overhead must be considered:

- *TFS Header*— a per file overhead of 92 bytes. The value of 92 assumes that the sizes of the name and info field are each set to 23 (+1 for NULL termination) characters and that the number of reserved entries is four.

- *Post-Defragmentation Header Table*— this table of file headers (plus defragmentation information) resides at the end of the TFS space. TFS creates one entry in this table for each active (non-deleted) file that exists at the time of a defragmentation cycle.

- *Defragmentation State Table*— two 32-bit CRCs for each sector. One CRC is computed on the sector before defragmentation and one CRC is computed after the sector has been processed by the defragmentation algorithm.

- *Spare Sector*— a flash sector that the defragmentation algorithm uses for scratch pad space. The spare sector must be at least as large as any other sector within TFS space.

- *Double Buffer*— when updating a file. In other words, if file A exists in TFS flash space, and, at some point file A is updated, the old file A is not deleted until the new file A is successfully created. The result is that the system must be prepared for the fact that, at one point in the file addition process, both the old and new file will exist.

Ignoring the double-buffer overhead, you use the following equation to compute the total overhead introduced by TFS:

```
overhead = ((FTOT * (HDRSIZE + DEFRAGHDRSIZE + 16)) + SPARESIZE +
    (SECTORCOUNT * 8))
```

Where:

- FTOT is the number of files to be stored.

- HDRSIZE is the size of a TFS file header (currently 92 bytes).
- DEFRAGHDRSIZE is the size of a TFS defragmentation header (currently 64 bytes)
- SPARESIZE is the size of the spare sector.
- SECTORCOUNT is the number of sectors allocated to TFS (not including spare).

Note that a file marked for deletion requires less overhead than an active file, because a deleted file does not require a defragmentation header. Thus deleting a file still frees up some memory space even though the file is not actually erased from the flash memory.

Defragmentation

The underlying flash technology does not allow a random range of memory within the device to be erased. Hence, when a file is deleted, it is simply marked as deleted in the header and left in the flash memory. To make the space occupied by deleted files available for reuse, the "empty" ranges are relocated into locations that can be erased. Figure 7.3 illustrates this defragmentation process. The heavily shaded areas represent the file headers; the lightly shaded areas represent the deleted files.

Figure 7.3   TFS Defragmentation Process.

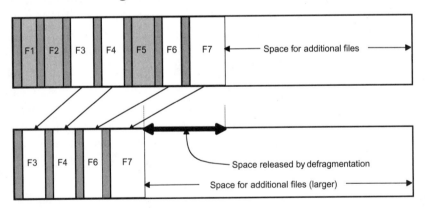

**TFS Flash Space Before and
After Defragmentation**

Several different methods exist for performing the cleanup or defragmentation process. Like most other embedded systems issues, the chosen technique depends largely on the characteristics of the application environment, the available hardware, and the tradeoff between complexity vs. capability. You can certainly find more complex ways of handling defragmentation than the method used with MicroMonitor, but usually, that added complexity makes the implementation of the entire file system much more complicated. The goal here is to keep the file storage simple and linear, guaranteeing that any one file can be assumed by the application to exist in contiguous space in the flash memory. The following discussion covers two different approaches. The first is quite simple but has its flaws (which, depending on the system, might be acceptable). The second is more robust and, with a few added options, can be quite flash-friendly.

Simple but Potentially Hazardous

The easiest solution for defragmentation is to concatenate each of the "non-deleted" files into RAM space, erase all the flash space allocated for TFS file storage, and then copy the entire concatenation back into the flash. On the positive side, this solution is simple and eliminates the need to pre-allocate one of the flash sectors as a spare. On the negative side, this solution assumes that a block of RAM that is statically allocated for this job is as big as the flash space allocated to TFS. Worse, if the system is reset or takes a power hit during defragmentation, the file system will probably be corrupted.

More Complicated, but Much More Robust

A more practical approach is to provide a means of defragmentation that is robust enough to allow the system to reset at any point in the defragmentation process. This approach does not use a large block of RAM, but it does require that one non-volatile block of memory (at least as large as the largest sector that TFS covers) be pre-allocated to the defragmentation process. In TFS, this block of memory is the "spare sector," the sector in the flash space immediately following the last sector used by TFS for file storage. Because this spare sector most likely is too small to hold a temporary copy of all active (non-deleted) files, the defragmentation process gets quite a bit more complicated. The copy must now be done in chunks instead of all at once.

While this approach is more complicated, it has the advantage of being immune to corruption as a result of a power hit or reset. This defragmentation process can be restarted at any point. The one disadvantage of this technique is that the spare sector is cycled frequently. It is the spare sector that is likely to reach the technological limit (number of erase cycles) and begin to fail. The point at which this limit is reached is very dependent on the device, the number of sectors dedicated to TFS, and the rate at which files are deleted and recreated. One major improvement to this scheme (to enhance the overall lifetime of the flash device) is to use battery-backed RAM in place of the spare sector, but, obviously, this luxury is unlikely to be approved for a budget-sensitive application.

Implementing a power-safe defragmentation is no cakewalk. This part was by far the toughest piece of code to implement for MicroMonitor. The defragmentation process uses three different pieces of flash space:

- The spare sector, which has already been pre-allocated.
- The defragmentation state table, which contains two 32-bit CRCs for each sector used by TFS for file storage. This information allows an interrupted defragmentation process to determine, after it has restarted, what sector it was processing when it was interrupted.
- The post-defragmentation header table, which is a table of the headers of all the files that are to survive the defragmentation (all the non-deleted files). The post-defragmentation header is a table of header structures similar to the header structure discussed above. These headers are used with the defragmentation state table to restart an interrupted defragmentation.

TFS Implementation

To cover all of the code in TFS would involve getting into details that are beyond the scope of this text. I will, however, use the remainder of this chapter to walk through the major blocks of TFS code. (The entire implementation is, of course, on the CD.) I will cover several key points in the design and implementation of TFS. The next few sections cover the process of flash defragmentation, file addition and deletion, the TFS file loader, file compression, and the ability to execute in place despite TFS's load model.

The Power-Safe Defragmentation Process

This defragmentation process conceptually shifts all of the active files in the TFS storage space toward the front of the flash address space and all of the space that was occupied by deleted files toward the end of the flash address space. After rearranging the files, the procedure erases all of the space following the last active file, making space that was occupied by inactive files available for new file storage. At first glance, this process doesn't sound too complicated, but there is one complicating "gotcha." At any point in the defragmentation process, the hardware can be reset or powered off, and the defragmentation algorithm needs to be able to recover without losing any of the files that existed in TFS prior to the start of the interrupted defragmentation.

We start with an example TFS space containing seven sectors for storage and a spare sector. For this discussion, I am assuming that all the sectors are of equal size but that is not a requirement. The example in Figure 7.4 shows TFS space with four files (F1, F2, F3, and F4), two areas of dead space (deleted files), a small amount of available space, and the space needed for defragmentation overhead (spare sector and state storage).

Note that the relative sizes are inaccurate (typically, a header is about 92 bytes, and a sector can range in size from 2K to 256K, depending on the device).

Figure 7.4   Example File Store Configuration.

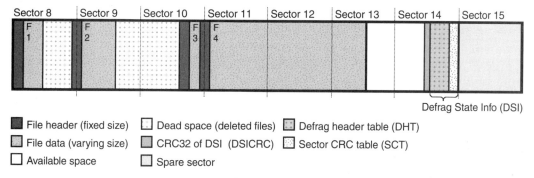

Sector 8 | Sector 9 | Sector 10 | Sector 11 | Sector 12 | Sector 13 | Sector 14 | Sector 15

Defrag State Info (DSI)

■ File header (fixed size)   ▫ Dead space (deleted files)   ▨ Defrag header table (DHT)

▨ File data (varying size)   ◼ CRC32 of DSI (DSICRC)   ▥ Sector CRC table (SCT)

▢ Available space   ▫ Spare sector

This figure shows how TFS space might be allocated after the system had been in use for a while. The segments labelled F1, F2, F3, and F4 are active files. Notice that there are also segments of dead space associated with deleted files.

Defragmentation becomes necessary when the file you want to add is larger than the available space but not larger than the total available space plus all of the dead space fragments. The goal is to push all of the files to the left (lower address) and all of the dead space to the right (higher address space). This process turns the dead space into available space, allowing TFS to append a new file to the linear list. The three high-level steps to this defragmentation algorithm are:

1. *DSI Creation* — Build the defragmentation state information (DSI) based on the current state of the sectors and active (non-deleted) files. The DSI consists of three parts: a sector CRC table (SCT), a post-defragmentation header table (DHT), and a CRC of the two tables (DSICRC).

2. *File Relocation* — Start with the first sector of TFS space and perform the following steps on each sector:

   • Determine if anything is to change within the sector. If not, increment to the next sector.

- Copy the sector to be modified (the "active" sector) to the spare sector.
- Erase the active sector.
- Using the information in the DHT, scan through each non-deleted file to see if any part of it (header or data) is to be relocated into the active sector. This process must take into account the fact that the file transfer can be from a later sector or from the spare sector (depending on from where the file is relocated).

3. *Cleanup* — Clean up all remaining space after the last relocated file (so that the space becomes part of the new block of available space), and erase the spare sector.

The SCT contains two 32-bit CRCs per sector. The SCT is a fixed size, based on the number of sectors in the TFS area covered by the table. The CRCs in this table are used to help a restarted defragmentation process figure out which sectors have already been defragmented, thus allowing the restart to continue from where it was interrupted. The DHT contains one header per non-deleted file. This header is not a file header; it is the data needed by the defragmentation process to relocate each file to its new space in flash memory. After both the SCT and DHT have been constructed in flash memory, a 32-bit CRC of those tables is placed at the base of the DSI space as a mechanism to verify that the DSI space is valid. The DSI area is considered under construction if any of the area is not erased but the CRC test fails.

The defragmentation initiation routine is coded as a nested loop. The outer loop steps through each sector dedicated to TFS for file storage. At any point in time, only one sector is considered to be the active sector. The first step in the outer loop is to determine if anything in the sector is going to change as a result of the defragmentation. If not, then the outer loop steps to the next sector. Prior to any work (flash writes) being done on the active sector, the active sector is copied to the spare and then erased. At this point, the inner loop begins. For each file in the DHT, the inner-loop determines if the space that the file will occupy after relocation overlaps the active sector in any way. If an overlap occurs, then that portion of the file is copied to the active sector. Note that the portion copied could be the entire file or any sub-section of the file — for example, the header and part of the data, part of the header, or part of the data. How much is copied depends on how the relocated version of the file overlaps the active sector.

Note that the source of the copy may be a later sector (some TFS sector after the currently active sector) or the spare sector. The source data will be in the spare if the relocated file is moved from some location that was previously in the now active sector. Figures 7.5–7.10 give a pictorial view of the relocation process for the example TFS configuration.

In Figure 7.5, the first sector (sector 8) is copied to the spare and erased. Then the data that is destined to reside in sector 8 after defragmentation is copied back into sector 8. Notice that some of the data comes from the spare sector and some from a later sector.

Figure 7.6 repeats this process with sector 9. The data in the active sector is copied to the spare sector, the active sector is erased, and the new data is copied into the active sector. Some data comes from the spare sector, and some from a later sector.

Figure 7.7 is almost the same. Notice that sector 10 is the active sector copied to the spare sector, but that nothing is copied back from that spare sector to the active sector. Since nothing from sector 10's original contents is retained, there is really no need to copy the active sector. I only show this step for clarity. The next two figures (Figure 7.8 and Figure 7.9) finish up the defragmentation on active sectors 11 and 12, applying the same process.

Figure 7.5   Defragmentation Active Sector = 8.

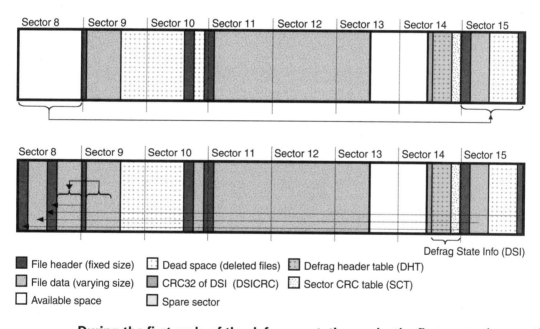

During the first cycle of the defragmentation cycle, the first sector (sector 8) is copied to the spare sector, and then it is refilled with a compacted image. Note that the compaction operation can bring material from anywhere in the file system.

Figure 7.6 Defragmentation Active Sector = 9.

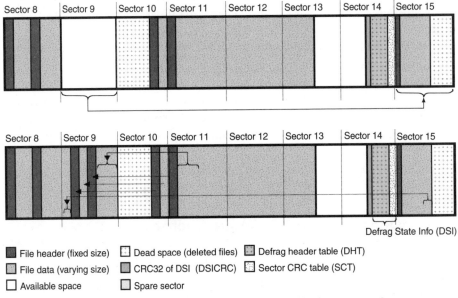

File header (fixed size)   Dead space (deleted files)   Defrag header table (DHT)

File data (varying size)   CRC32 of DSI (DSICRC)   Sector CRC table (SCT)

Available space   Spare sector

This figure details the defragmentation cycle for sector 9.

Figure 7.7 Defragmentation Active Sector = 10.

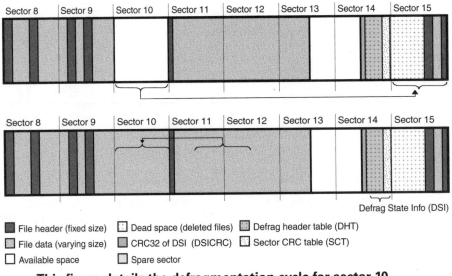

File header (fixed size)   Dead space (deleted files)   Defrag header table (DHT)

File data (varying size)   CRC32 of DSI (DSICRC)   Sector CRC table (SCT)

Available space   Spare sector

This figure details the defragmentation cycle for sector 10.

Figure 7.8   Defragmentation Active Sector = 11.

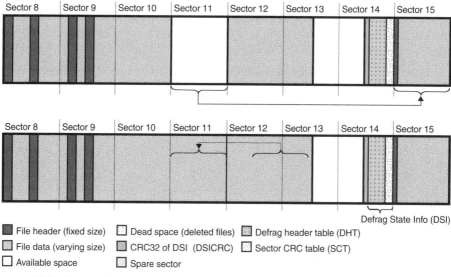

■ File header (fixed size)	□ Dead space (deleted files) ▦ Defrag header table (DHT)
▨ File data (varying size)	▩ CRC32 of DSI (DSICRC) ⊡ Sector CRC table (SCT)
□ Available space	▨ Spare sector

This figure details the defragmentation cycle for sector 11.

Figure 7.9   Defragmentation Active Sector = 12.

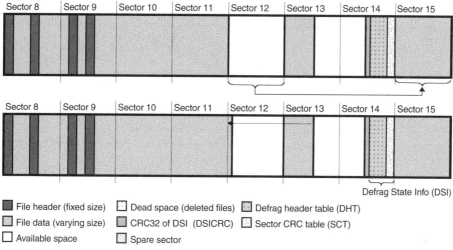

■ File header (fixed size)	□ Dead space (deleted files) ▦ Defrag header table (DHT)
▨ File data (varying size)	▩ CRC32 of DSI (DSICRC) ⊡ Sector CRC table (SCT)
□ Available space	▨ Spare sector

This figure details the defragmentation cycle for sector 12.

Figure 7.10 Defragmentation Clean Up and Completion.

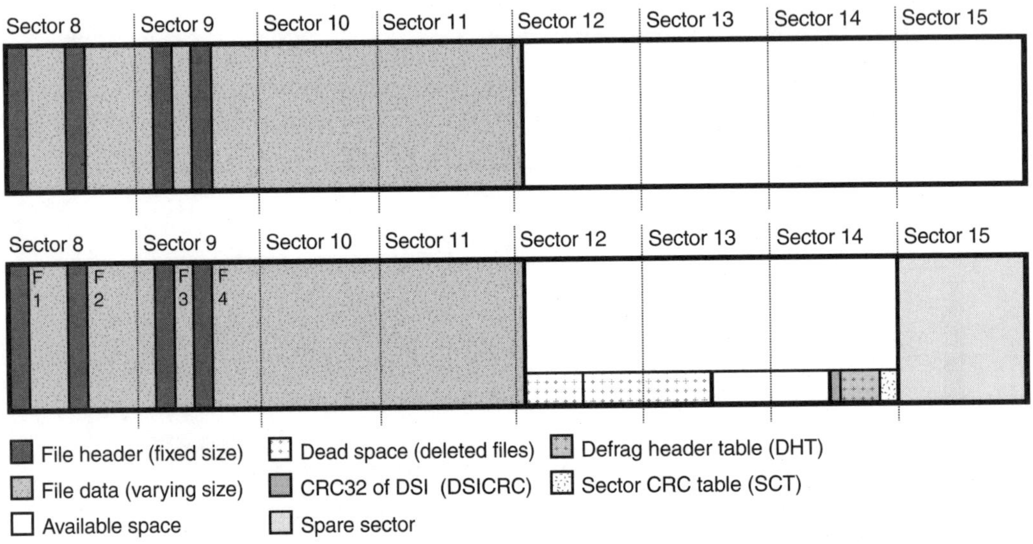

After sector 12 is processed, all that remains is to clean up and erase sectors 13, 14 and 15. Figure 7.10 shows the final result of the defragmentation, along with a shadow image of where the dead space has been shifted conceptually (the shortest segments after the last file). Notice that the size of the available space has significantly increased.

The Non-Power-Safe `tfsclean()` Function

Returning to the opposite end of the complexity spectrum, the non power-safe defragmentation algorithm mentioned on page 145 can be coded quite simply. The function that does the defragmentation is called `tfsclean()` (see Listing 7.3). This function takes a single parameter, a `TDEV` structure pointer. The `TDEV` structure tells `tfsclean()` which flash device to defragment (there may be multiple flash devices in TFS).

Listing 7.3   `tfsclean()`.

```
int
_tfsclean(TDEV *tdp)
{
    TFILE   *tfp;
    uchar   *tbuf;
```

```
ulong    appramstart;
int      dtot, nfadd, len, err;

if (TfsCleanEnable < 0)
    return(TFSERR_CLEANOFF);


appramstart = getAppRamStart();


/* Determine how many "dead" files exist. */
dtot = 0;
tfp = (TFILE *)tdp->start;
while(validtfshdr(tfp)) {
    if (!TFS_FILEEXISTS(tfp))
        dtot++;
    tfp = nextfp(tfp,tdp);
}


if (dtot == 0)
    return(TFS_OKAY);

printf("Reconstructing device %s with %d dead file%s removed...\n",
    tdp->prefix, dtot,dtot>1 ? "s":"");


tbuf = (char *)appramstart;
tfp = (TFILE *)(tdp->start);
nfadd = tdp->start;
while(validtfshdr(tfp)) {
    if (TFS_FILEEXISTS(tfp)) {
        len = TFS_SIZE(tfp) + sizeof(struct tfshdr);
        if (len % TFS_FSIZEMOD)
            len += TFS_FSIZEMOD - (len % TFS_FSIZEMOD);
        nfadd += len;
        err = tfsmemcpy(tbuf,(uchar *)tfp,len,0,0);
        if (err != TFS_OKAY)
            return(err);
        ((struct tfshdr *)tbuf)->next = (struct tfshdr *)nfadd;
        tbuf += len;
```

```
        }
        tfp = nextfp(tfp,tdp);
    }


    /* Erase the flash device: */
    err = _tfsinit(tdp);
    if (err != TFS_OKAY)
        return(err);


    /* Copy data placed in RAM back to flash: */
    err = AppFlashWrite((ulong *)(tdp->start),(ulong *)appramstart,
        (tbuf-(uchar*)appramstart));
    if (err < 0)
        return(TFSERR_FLASHFAILURE);


    return(TFS_OKAY);
}
```

This function first checks to see if defragmentation has been disabled for some reason (see Listing 7.3). If so, it returns TFSERROR_CLEANOFF. The copy must have RAM space into which to concatenate all the active files. I assume that it can use the RAM immediately above the end of the .bss space used by MicroMonitor. The function getAppRamStart() returns a pointer to the start of this RAM. The tfsclean() function blindly assumes there is enough RAM space here to cover the possibility that the entire TFS flash device might be copied. (The memory map of the application must take this possibility into account.) The code scans through the file list of the specified device looking for files that have been deleted. If no deleted files exist, there is no need to do any cleanup, allowing an early, successful return.

The second while() loop performs the actual copy and concatenation. Each active file is copied back-to-back into the RAM space, starting at appramstart. Notice that the next pointer in each TFS header is updated in the copied header so that the new header properly reflects the fact that the file is in different flash space. Upon completion of the concatenation, the flash space allocated to TFS file storage is erased with the call to tfsinit(), using the same TDEV structure pointer that was passed to tfsclean(). The final step, now that the flash memory has been erased, is to copy all of the concatenated files from RAM back to the base of the flash device.

Adding and Deleting Files

At first it might seem simple enough to just add another file header and file data block to the end of the current file list in flash. In the ideal situation, it would be. In reality, there are a lot of cases to consider. This section walks through the process of adding (with `tfsadd()`) and deleting (with `tfsunlink()`) files to/from TFS.

The `tfsadd()` Function

At a high level, TFS takes the following steps to add a file to the file system:

1. Does a file with the same name already exist in TFS?
   - If yes and if the existing file content is identical to the incoming content, then return success.
   - If yes but the new file content is different from the current file, the current file is marked *stale,* and the process of adding the new file continues.
   - If no, continue.
2. Run 32-bit CRC on the incoming data.
3. Is there enough room to store the file?
   - If yes, continue.
   - If no, defragment the TFS flash space. If after defragmentation there is enough space, then continue. If there is not enough space, return indicating that there is not enough flash space left.
4. Run a second 32-bit CRC on the incoming data. If first and second CRC values differ, then return an error (The reason for this two-pass CRC is described below.).
5. Transfer the data to flash memory, then build the new TFS file header, and copy that to flash.
6. If a file was previously marked *stale*, then mark it deleted. All done.

The next few listings (Listings 7.4 to 7.13) are chunks of the `tfsadd()` function. This function deals with all of the complexities of adding a new file to TFS. The parameters `name`, `info`, and `flags` are character strings (see Listing 7.4). The variable `name` is the string to be used as the filename; the string `info` is used optionally to describe the file. The `flags` parameter is a string of ASCII characters that describe the attributes to be applied to the file. Note that `info` and `flags` can be `NULL`, in which case `tfsadd()` supplies defaults. The remaining arguments are `src` and `size`. The `src` argument is a pointer to the actual data that is to become the data portion of the file in TFS storage space, and `size` is the number of bytes to be considered for storage.

Listing 7.4   tfsadd().

```c
int
tfsadd(char *name, char *info, char *flags, uchar *src, int size)
{
    TDEV    *tdp;
    TFILE   *fp, tf;
    ulong   endoftfsflash, nextfileaddr, state_table_overhead;
    ulong   crc_pass1, crc_pass2, bflags;
    int     ftot, cleanupcount, err, stale, ssize;

    if (!info) info = "";
    if (!flags) flags = "";
```

The user can trace several functions in TFS. Set the `tfsTrace` variable to enable tracing (see Listing 7.5). The result of enabling tracing is that the call to `tfsadd()` is printed to the console for observation by the user.

Listing 7.5   The Trace Feature.

```c
    if (tfsTrace > 0)
        printf("tfsadd(%s,%s,%s,0x%lx,%d)\n",
            name,info,flags,(ulong)src,size);
```

TFS includes a "perror-like" function that allows the user to convert a returned error code to some error message. Error checking can return specific codes that can later be passed back into another TFS API function for expansion to a more detailed description. The error checks done in Listing 7.6 demonstrate this feature.

The call to `tfsFileIsOpened()` near the end of Listing 7.6 is performed so that an executing script (scripts are executed directly out of flash) is not accidentally deleted by some unaware task.

Listing 7.6   Checking Operation Validity.

```
/* Check for valid size and name: */
if ((size <= 0) || (!name))
    return(TFSERR_BADARG);

/* If name or info field length is too long, abort now... */
if ((strlen(name) > TFSNAMESIZE) ||
    ((info) && (strlen(info) > TFSINFOSIZE)))
    return(TFSERR_NAMETOOBIG);

/* If the file is currently opened, then don't allow the add... */
if (tfsFileIsOpened(name))
    return(TFSERR_FILEINUSE);
```

Listing 7.7   Processing Attribute Flags.

```
/* If incoming flags are illegal, abort now... */
if (*flags == 0) {
    bflags = 0;
}
else {
    err = tfsflagsatob(flags,&bflags);
    if (err != TFS_OKAY)
        return(err);
}
```

The flags string passed in as an argument must be converted to a bit field (unsigned long for this implementation) with certain bit settings representing specific characters in the flags string. (Accepting the flags input in character form makes it easy to allow a user to specify a set of flags at the CLI.) The call to tfsflagsatob() constructs the bit field and returns an error if the conversion fails.

Listing 7.8   Computing the Initial Checksum.

```
/* Take snapshot of source crc. */
crc_pass1 = crc32(src, size);
```

Before beginning a copy to flash, the code computes a 32-bit CRC on the incoming data. Actually, this CRC is computed multiple times so that `tfsadd()` can detect changing source data. This step is useful for two reasons:

- if the incoming data is changing, it is likely that the source address is incorrect.
- the incoming pointer should not be pointing to raw data in TFS space. If the incoming pointer is pointing to raw data and a defragmentation occurs, data in TFS is shifted.

Just before beginning the meat of the copy, the incoming name is checked against the possible list of multiple flash devices under TFS (see Listing 7.9). If the prefix of the incoming name matches the name of one of the devices, TFS assumes that the file is to be added to the associated flash device.

Listing 7.9   Identifying Flash Device.

```
/* Establish the device that is to be used for the incoming file
 * addition request... The device used depends on the prefix of
 * the incoming file name. If the incoming prefix doesn't match
 * any of the devices in the table, then place the file in the
 * first device in the table (assumed to be the default).
 */
for(tdp=tfsDeviceTbl;tdp->start != TFSEOT;tdp++) {
    if (!strncmp(name,tdp->prefix,strlen(tdp->prefix)))
        break;
}
if (tdp->start == TFSEOT)
    tdp = tfsDeviceTbl;
```

Listing 7.10   Finding the Last Header.

```
tryagain:
    fp = (TFILE *)tdp->start;

    /* Find end of current storage: */
    ftot = 0;
    while (fp) {
        if (fp->hdrsize == ERASED16)
            break;
```

```
        if (TFS_FILEEXISTS(fp)) {
            ftot++;
            if (fp->flags & TFS_NSTALE) {
                if (!strcmp(TFS_NAME(fp),name)) {
                /* If file of the same name exists AND it is identical to
                 * the new file to be added, then return TFS_OKAY and be
                 * done; otherwise, remove the old one and continue.
                 * Don't do the comparison if src file is in-place-modify
                 * because the source data is undefined.
                 */
                    if ((!(bflags & TFS_IPMOD)) &&
                        (!tfscompare(fp,name,info,flags,src,size)))
                        return(TFS_OKAY);

                /* If a file of the same name exists but is different than
                 * the new file, make the current file stale, then after
                 * the new file is added we will delete the stale one.
                 */
                    stale = 1;
                    err = tfsmakeStale(fp);
                    if (err == TFS_OKAY)
                        goto tryagain;
                    else
                        return(err);
                }
            }
        }
        fp = nextfp(fp,tdp);
    }
    if (!fp)    /* If fp is 0, then nextfp() (above) detected corruption. */
        return(TFSERR_CORRUPT);
```

TFS searches the appropriate flash device looking for the last file stored on the device (so that it can append the new file to the end of the current list). This search consists of stepping through the linked list. During this search, TFS also verifies the sanity of each of the file headers. The call to nextfp() does some basic checks. At some point TFS finds the last header or returns TFS_CORRUPT, indicating that headers are incorrect. If the situation where the file to be added already exists (same name) in TFS, additional steps might be necessary.

- If the file exists and is identical in data, flags, and information field to the incoming file, the code immediately returns. Because the two file images are identical, there is no harm in skipping the copy to flash. In fact, doing so extends the component life by avoiding a flash erase/program cycle.

- If the file exists and is different, then the existing file is marked STALE. This file will eventually be replaced with the new file, but the code delays until the new file is successfully copied before actually deleting the current version.

- If the file does not already exist, the new file is added with none of the preceding complications.

When TFS finds the end of the current list of files, it must determine whether there is enough space to add the incoming file (see Listing 7.11). If enough space is available, the file is appended to the list. If there isn't enough space, the add routine initiates a defragmentation cycle.

When computing available file space, one must consider the overhead required for defragmentation. This overhead includes the spare sector, as well as the space needed for the defragmentation header and sector CRC table, both of which are built downward from the end of TFS space during defragmentation. After defragmentation is completed, TFS scans through the list a second time, finds the end point, and determines if there is now enough space. If yes, the add operation can continue; if not, the routine returns TFSERR_FLASHFULL.

Listing 7.11   **Checking for Free Space.**

```
/* Calculate location of next file (on mod16 address). This will be
 * initially used to see if we have enough space left in flash to store
 * the current request; then, if yes, it will become part of the new
 * file's header.
 */
nextfileaddr = ((ulong)(fp+1)) + size;
if (nextfileaddr & 0xf)
    nextfileaddr = (nextfileaddr | 0xf) + 1;


/* Make sure that the space is available for writing to flash...
 * Remember that the end of useable flash space must take into
 * account the fact that some space must be left over for the
 * defragmentation state tables. Also, the total space needed for
 * state tables cannot exceed the size of the sector that will contain
 * those tables.
```

```
    */
    state_table_overhead = ((ftot+1) * DEFRAGHDRSIZ) +
        (tdp->sectorcount * sizeof(long));

    if (addrtosector((uchar *)(tdp->end),0,&ssize,0) < 0)
        return(TFSERR_MEMFAIL);

    if (state_table_overhead >= (ulong)ssize)
        return(TFSERR_FLASHFULL);

    endoftfsflash = (tdp->end + 1) - state_table_overhead;

    if ((nextfileaddr >= endoftfsflash) ||
        (!tfsSpaceErased((uchar *)fp,size+TFSHDRSIZ))) {
        if (!cleanupcount) {
            err = tfsautoclean(0,0,0,0,tdp,0,0);
            if (err != TFS_OKAY) {
                printf("tfsadd autoclean failed: %s\n",
                    (char *)tfsctrl(TFS_ERRMSG,err,0));
                return(err);
            }
            cleanupcount++;
            goto tryagain;
        }
        else
            return(TFSERR_FLASHFULL);
    }
```

Listing 7.12   Testing for Stable Data.

```
/* Do another crc on the source data. If crc_pass1 != crc_pass2 then
 * somehow the source is changing. This is typically caused by the fact
 * that the source address is within TFS space that was automatically
 * defragmented above. Since we are aborting the creation of the file,
 * we must undo any stale file that may have been created above.
 * No need to check source data if the source is in-place-modifiable.
 */
```

```
if (!(bflags & TFS_IPMOD)) {
    crc_pass2 = crc32(src,size);
    if (crc_pass1 != crc_pass2) {
        if (stale)
            tfsstalecheck(0);
        return(TFSERR_FLAKEYSOURCE);
    }
}
else
    crc_pass2 = ERASED32;
```

It is almost time to do the flash write operations. The next step is to perform a second CRC on the incoming data (see Listing 7.12). If the CRCs do not match, the routine returns an error indicating that the incoming data is not stable.

In preparation for the actual write, `tfsadd()` creates a new file header in the local structure `tf` (on the stack)(see Listing 7.13). After the new file header is created, the data portion of the incoming file is copied to flash and, finally, the file header is copied to flash. The file data is copied prior to the header so that the header is the very last flash write, making it easier to detect an interrupted write. After the new file is successfully copied, `tfsadd()` performs one more CRC to verify that the flash copy was successful. TFS can then delete any stale file that was left. The last step is a call to `tfslog()`, which, if enabled, keeps a log of the file operations that actually modify the flash memory.

Listing 7.13   Creating the Header.

```
memset((char *)&tf,0,TFSHDRSIZ);

/* Copy name and info data to header. */
strcpy(tf.name, name);
strcpy(tf.info, info);
tf.hdrsize = TFSHDRSIZ;
tf.hdrvrsn = TFSHDRVERSION;
tf.filsize = size;
tf.flags = bflags;
tf.flags |= (TFS_ACTIVE | TFS_NSTALE);
tf.filcrc = crc_pass2;
tf.modtime = tfsGetLtime();
```

```
    tf.next = 0;
    tf.hdrcrc = 0;
    tf.hdrcrc = crc32((uchar *)&tf,TFSHDRSIZ);
    tf.next = (TFILE *)nextfileaddr;

    /* Now copy the file and header to flash.
     * Note1: the header is copied AFTER the file has been
     * successfully copied. If the header was written successfully,
     * then the data write failed, the header would be incorrectly
     * pointing to an invalid file. To avoid this, simply write the
     * data first.
     * Note2: if the file is in-place-modifiable, then there is no
     * file data to be written to the flash. It will be left as all FFs
     * so that the flash can be modified by tfsipmod() later.
     */

    /* Write the file to flash if not TFS_IPMOD: */
    if (!(tf.flags & TFS_IPMOD)) {
        if (tfsflashwrite((ulong *)(fp+1),(ulong *)src,size) == -1)
            return(TFSERR_FLASHFAILURE);
    }

    /* Write the file header to flash: */
    if (tfsflashwrite((ulong *)fp,(ulong *)(&tf),TFSHDRSIZ) == -1)
        return(TFSERR_FLASHFAILURE);

    /* Double check the CRC now that it is in flash. */
    if (!(tf.flags & TFS_IPMOD)) {
        if (crc32((uchar *)(fp+1), size) != tf.filcrc)
            return(TFSERR_BADCRC);
    }

    /* If the add was a file that previously existed, then the stale flag
     * will be set and the old file needs to be deleted...
     */
    if (stale) {
        err = _tfsunlink(name);
```

```
        if (err != TFS_OKAY)
            printf("%s: %s\n",name,tfserrmsg(err));
    }

    tfslog(TFSLOG_ADD,name);
    return(TFS_OKAY);
}
```

The `tfsunlink()` Function

The file delete function, `tfsunlink()` (see Listing 7.14) does not require as much error checking as `tfsadd()` because the only incoming argument is the name of the file to be deleted. As did `tfsadd()`, the unlink function implements the trace mechanism and checks to see if the file is currently open. The delete code then retrieves a pointer to the files by calling `tfsstat()`. If `tfsstat()` returns NULL, `tfsunlink()` assumes there is no file in TFS with the incoming name and returns the appropriate error code. If `tfsstat()` returns a pointer, then that file header's TFS_ACTIVE bit is cleared to indicate that the file has been deleted. The final step is to call `tfslog()` to record the flash transaction.

Listing 7.14   `tfsunlink()`.

```
int
tfsunlink(char *name)
{
    TFILE *fp;
    ulong flags_marked_deleted;

    if (tfsTrace > 0)
        printf("_tfsunlink(%s)\n",name);

    /* If the file is currently opened, then don't allow the deletion... */
    if (tfsFileIsOpened(name))
        return(TFSERR_FILEINUSE);

    fp = tfsstat(name);
    if (!fp)
        return(TFSERR_NOFILE);
```

```
    if (TFS_USRLVL(fp) > getUsrLvl())
        return(TFSERR_USERDENIED);

    flags_marked_deleted = fp->flags & ~TFS_ACTIVE;
    if (tfsflashwrite((ulong *)&fp->flags,
        &flags_marked_deleted,sizeof(long)) < 0) {
        return(TFSERR_FLASHFAILURE);
    }

    tfslog(TFSLOG_DEL,name);
    return (TFS_OKAY);
}
```

To Load or Not to Load

TFS supports two major types of executable files: binary and script. Scripts are simple ASCII files containing CLI commands that are executed one line at a time. Scripts are executed directly from the flash memory in which they are stored. As of this writing, the binary executables can be in ELF, COFF, or AOUT format. These three formats are very similar; each consists of a file header, section headers, and a bunch of sections. Unlike the script executable, a binary file is executed after copying sections of the formatted file from TFS storage to space in RAM. The program then executes out of RAM. This process is commonly called loading a file. Loading is a very common practice on workstation/server-type operating systems because, in those environments, it isn't physically possible for the CPU to fetch from disk. In an embedded systems application, there is no disk. Instead the applications reside in flash memory which appears as local memory to the CPU. This issue means that the embedded systems processor can fetch applications directly out of flash memory. (As a matter of fact, MicroMonitor does execute directly out of flash.) Thus, whether an embedded system monitor loads an application or executes it directly from the file system is a design choice. There are tradeoffs on both sides of the decision.

The advantages of loading include:

- No need to re-invent a file format;
- You can run multiple applications on the same target by building them with non-overlapping absolute address maps;
- RAM space on the target is likely to be wider and therefore more efficient for instruction fetching;

- With the instructions in writable memory space, you can easily insert traps (or breakpoints) into the instruction stream;

- The executable program can be compressed and therefore can require less flash space.

On the other hand, loading has a significant disadvantage: the transfer of text and initialized data sections from flash memory to RAM consumes time and memory.

The optimum approach depends on the nature of your application and how much memory you have. Since I am presenting a platform that provides a buffer between the application and the flash memory (allowing the application to treat flash memory as namespace instead of address space), I have already accepted the fact that I am adding overhead in order to provide a platform that is easier to maintain. I have therefore designed TFS to support loading.

In general, I consider it reasonable to sacrifice efficiency for the sake of maintainability. Throughout the design of TFS, when faced with this trade-off, I've opted for maintainability.

Loader Implementation

Listing 7.15 shows a snippet of the loader for the ELF file format. The parameters shown in Listing 7.15 include the following:

- `fp` is a pointer to the TFS file header structure associated with this ELF file;

- `verbose` enables extra reporting;

- `entrypoint` is a pointer to a `long` that, if non-zero, is loaded with the address of the entry point for this ELF file;

- `verifyonly` is a flag that tells this function it should only compare what is already loaded to what would be loaded.

Note that Listing 7.15 requires multiple levels of headers. The TFS header has nothing to do with ELF itself. The TFS header is simply the header used for managing the storage of the files in the flash memory. Each file in TFS has two parts: the header and the data. In this case, the data is an ELF file, and the ELF file has another set of headers. This function has to deal with both header types, which can sometimes contribute to a certain amount of confusion.

Listing 7.15   **ELF File Format Loader.**

```
/* tfsloadelf():
 *  The file pointed to by fp has been determined to be an ELF file.
 *  This function loads the sections of that file into the designated
 *  locations.
 *  Caches are flushed after loading each loadable section.
 */
int
tfsloadebin(TFILE *fp,int verbose,long *entrypoint,int verifyonly)
{
    Elf32_Word  size, notproctot;
    int     i, err;
    char        *shname_strings;
    ELFFHDR *ehdr;
    ELFSHDR *shdr;

    /* Establish file header pointers... */
    ehdr = (ELFFHDR *)(TFS_BASE(fp));
    shdr = (ELFSHDR *)((int)ehdr + ehdr->e_shoff);
    err = 0;

    /* Verify basic file sanity... */
    if ((ehdr->e_ident[0] != 0x7f) || (ehdr->e_ident[1] != 'E') ||
        (ehdr->e_ident[2] != 'L') || (ehdr->e_ident[3] != 'F'))
        return(TFSERR_BADHDR);

    /* Store the section name string table base: */
    shname_strings = (char *)ehdr + shdr[ehdr->e_shstrndx].sh_offset;

    notproctot = 0;

    /* For each section header, relocate or clear if necessary... */
    for (i=0;!err && i<ehdr->e_shnum;i++,shdr++) {
        if ((size = shdr->sh_size) == 0)
            continue;
```

```
        if ((verbose) && (ehdr->e_shstrndx != SHN_UNDEF))
            printf("%-10s: ", shname_strings + shdr->sh_name);

    if (!(shdr->sh_flags & SHF_ALLOC)) {
        notproctot += size;
        if (verbose)
            printf("     %7ld bytes not processed (tot=%ld)\n",
                size,notproctot);
        continue;
    }
    if (shdr->sh_type == SHT_NOBITS) {
        if (tfsmemset((char *)(shdr->sh_addr),0,size,
            verbose,verifyonly) != 0)
            err++;
    }
    else {
        if (TFS_ISCPRS(fp)) {
            int     outsize;

            outsize = decompress((char *)(ehdr)+shdr->sh_offset,
                    size,(char *)shdr->sh_addr);
            if (outsize == -1) {
                err++;
                continue;
            }
            if (verbose)
                printf("dcmp %7d bytes from 0x%08lx to 0x%08lx\n",
                    outsize,(ulong)(ehdr)+shdr->sh_offset,
                    shdr->sh_addr);
        }
        else {
            if (tfsmemcpy((char *)(shdr->sh_addr),
                (char *)((int)ehdr+shdr->sh_offset),
                size,verbose,verifyonly) != 0)
                err++;
        }
```

```
            /* Flush caches for each loadable section... */
            flushDcache((char *)shdr->sh_addr,size);
            invalidateIcache((char *)shdr->sh_addr,size);
        }
    }

    if (err)
        return(TFSERR_MEMFAIL);

    if (verbose & !verifyonly)
        printf("entrypoint: 0x%lx\n",ehdr->e_entry);

    /* Store entry point: */
    if (entrypoint)
        *entrypoint = (long)(ehdr->e_entry);

    return(TFS_OKAY);
}
```

Listing 7.15 begins by setting up structure overlays for the ELF file header structure (ehdr). The section header pointer (shdr) is established based on an offset (e_shoff) from the location of the file header.

The test following these pointer initializations performs some basic format validation by confirming that the header contains the required ELF signatures. (Without getting into a lot of detail on ELF itself, shname_strings is another offset further into the file that points to a table of strings. For my purposes, this pointer helps display different section names in more detail as I parse through the various section headers.)

The following loop drives the processing of the ELF file sections. Immediately, the section name is printed, and the SHF_ALLOC flag is tested. This flag indicates whether or not the section has space directly associated with the executable image. For example, a .text section would have this flag set because .text contains instructions for the CPU. A symbol table section would not have this flag set because it doesn't have anything to do with the actual process image. Following additional checks, the section is either copied to RAM, or, if sh-type is set to SHF_NOBITS, the memory space is cleared.

Notice the TFS_ISCPRS(fp) macro. TFS_ISCPRS(fp) is an extension to the ELF file format that is unique to TFS. MicroMonitor allows each section within the ELF file to be compressed. Hence, when this macro returns true, the loader decompresses out of flash memory and into the destination memory space. (The next section covers this feature in greater detail.)

Each time a copy operation completes, the loader forces D-cache to be flushed and the I-cache to be invalidated. These cache operations are necessary because when the loader is copying .text sections from one point in memory to another, it is essentially copying instructions from one point in memory to another. During the copy, the instructions just look like data to the CPU, so if the CPU has a data and instruction cache, there is the possibility that the instructions are in the data cache. If the caches are not flushed/invalidated prior to the CPU attempting to execute the code that was just copied, it is possible that a drastic error can occur because the instructions are in the data cache and not in physical memory.

Once the copy loop completes, the loader stores the entry point and returns.

File Decompression

As I discussed earlier, a typical application executable might be COFF, ELF, or AOUT. Each of these file formats has multiple sections of text and data that must be transferred from the flash space to some RAM/DRAM space from where applications execute. TFS extends the normal format of these files by allowing the individual sections within the file to be compressed. By default, the executable is uncompressed, and the data is transferred from flash memory to RAM.

TFS supports section-by-section compression to allow the section headers to remain uncompressed even though the balance of the file is compressed. If compression were implemented as an all-or-nothing file-level option, the entire file would need to be decompressed into RAM to extract the section information — only to be recopied to its load position once that information could be extracted from the section information.

The alternative is to compress only the individual sections within the file. This section-at-a-time decompression leaves all of the relocation information of the formatted executable readily available yet still provides the advantages of compression — avoiding the double-memory copy that would be needed if the entire file were compressed.

Figure 7.11   TFS File Decompression Strategy.

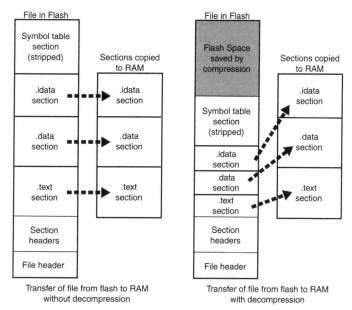

All sections of the file are compressed within the format of the file. This allows the ELF format to stay intact, but still supports a compressed image.

Execute In Place

The previous two sections talk about how TFS transfers sections of a formatted file (i.e., an ELF format file) from the flash space in which it resides to the DRAM space from which it was configured to run. No code actually executes out of the flash space allocated to TFS. A memory copy (and possibly a decompression) is always involved. The previously mentioned disadvantage of this approach is that the .text space used by the application is copied to RAM when it really doesn't need to be (since .text space is not considered writable). An alternative to this loading process is execute-in-place (XIP), meaning that the .text section of the program resides in flash and the CPU executes it out of flash directly, with no memory copy required.

The attractiveness of namespace (rather than address space) is the very reason why TFS does not support XIP. XIP (without address translation) requires that the program reside at a fixed location in memory, and TFS cannot guarantee that any file in the file system will be at a fixed location. TFS does, however, allow you to leave the program in flash memory and execute directly out of flash memory. Actually, TFS isn't even aware of the program, but, because of TFS's ability to reside in some portion of a flash device, MicroMonitor can still execute a program in XIP mode.

The standard way to design the monitor/application flash memory map is shown in the "No XIP Support" map (see Figure 7.12). The monitor is at the base of the flash space with all remaining space dedicated to TFS. If a program is to run in XIP mode, the base of TFS can be shifted up (as in the "XIP Support" side of Figure 7.12), and some fixed number of sectors can be dedicated to the XIP program. Note that MicroMonitor and the program still has access to TFS for data storage, but the program itself is not in TFS.

Figure 7.12   XIP vs. Non-XIP Flash Support.

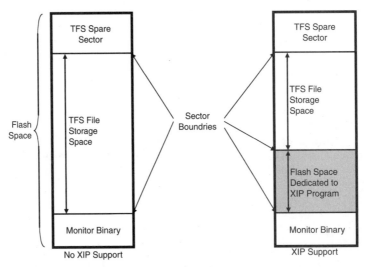

The monitor supports XIP simply because the starting point of TFS can be adjusted so that a fixed number of flash sectors are dedicated to the storage of the XIP program.

Summary

Needless to say, TFS requires much more code than you've seen in this chapter. TFS includes a full set of API functions to support read, write, seek, open, close, and other file operations. The complete package also includes MicroMonitor commands that expose these functions as part of the CLI. Going into detail on every function within TFS would take up too much space. Besides, once you understand some of the basics, the remaining code is easy to follow. I hope this chapter has succeeded in introducing you to the basic features of a flash file system. Please refer to the CD for the complete code listings.

8

Chapter 8

Executing Scripts

Now that the monitor design includes a flash file system and a command line interface, I will extend the system so that a file can execute as a script. Actually, the scripting feature turns out to be a pretty simple addition — one that adds a lot of flexibility to MicroMonitor. A single script-running function, with the help of a few script-running-specific commands in MicroMonitor's command set, provides a versatile environment for simple script execution.

The Script Runner

The script runner function (`tfsscript()`) (see Listing 8.1) treats a file as a list of commands. The function reads each line of the file and executes the line as a command. Some commands affect the script runner directly, for example `goto`, `gosub`, `return`, and `exit`. I will discuss these commands in detail later.

Listing 8.1   tfsscript().

```
int
tfsscript(TFILE *fp, int verbose)
{
    char    lcpy[CMDLINESIZE];
    int     tfd, lnsize;

    /* TFS does not support calling a script from within a subroutine. */
    if (ReturnToDepth != 0)
        return(TFSERR_SCRIPTINSUB);

    tfd = tfsopen(fp->name,TFS_RDONLY,0);
    if (tfd < 0)
        return(tfd);

    ReturnToTfd = tfd;

    while(1) {
        lnsize = tfsgetline(tfd,lcpy,CMDLINESIZE);
        if (lnsize == 0)     /* end of file? */
            break;
        if (lnsize < 0) {
            printf("tfsscript(): %s\n",tfserrmsg(lnsize));
            break;
        }
        if ((lcpy[0] == '\r') || (lcpy[0] == '\n')) /* empty line? */
            continue;

        lcpy[lnsize-1] = 0;              /* Remove the newline */

        /* Just in case the goto tag was set outside a script, */
        /* clear it now. */
        if (ScriptGotoTag) {
            free(ScriptGotoTag);
            ScriptGotoTag = (char *)0;
        }
```

```
        ScriptExitFlag = 0;

        /* Execute the command line: */
        tfsDocommand(lcpy,verbose);

        /* Check for exit flag.  If set, then in addition to terminating the
         * script, clear the return depth here so that the "missing return"
         * warning  is not printed.  This is done because there is likely
         * to be a subroutine with an exit in it and this should not
         * cause a warning.
         */
        if (ScriptExitFlag) {
            ReturnToDepth = 0;
            break;
        }


        /* If ScriptGotoTag is set, then attempt to reposition the line
         * pointer to the line that contains the tag.
         */
        if (ScriptGotoTag) {
            int     tlen;

            tlen = strlen(ScriptGotoTag);
            tfsseek(tfd,0,TFS_BEGIN);
            while(1) {
                lnsize = tfsgetline(tfd,lcpy,CMDLINESIZE);
                if (lnsize == 0) {
                    printf("Tag '%s' not found\n", ScriptGotoTag+2);
                    free(ScriptGotoTag);
                    ReturnToDepth = 0;
                    ScriptGotoTag = (char *)0;
                    tfsclose(tfd,0);
                    return(TFS_OKAY);
                }
                if (!strncmp(lcpy,ScriptGotoTag,tlen)) {
                    free(ScriptGotoTag);
                    ScriptGotoTag = (char *)0;
```

```
                    break;
                }
            }
        }
    }
    tfsclose(tfd,0);
    if (ScriptExitFlag & REMOVE_SCRIPT)
        tfsunlink(fp->name);
    if (ReturnToDepth != 0) {
        printf("Warning: '%s' missing return.\n",fp->name);
        ReturnToDepth = 0;
    }
    return(TFS_OKAY);
}
```

Initially ignoring a few of the global variables used in Listing 8.1, let's begin with the basics. The `tfsscript()` function starts by opening a TFS file by calling `tfsopen()`[1]. Assuming the file exists, the script runner then enters a loop that repeats for each line in the file. At the top, the loop calls `tfsgetline()` to retrieve the next line in the file. If the line is empty, the loop immediately skips to the next line; otherwise, the line is passed to the function pointed to by `tfsDocommand`. The `tfsDocommand` variable is a function pointer that is loaded with a pointer to the `docommand()` function by default. (I will explain why this is a loaded function pointer instead of just a normal function call in a later chapter.) Ignoring the `ScriptGotoTag` branch for a moment, it becomes clear that the script runner is not terribly complex. The function steps through each line of the script file and passes that line to the command handler. When the function reaches the end of the file, the function closes and returns.

Exit

The global variables in `tfsscript()` provide the script runner with the ability to jump to tags (`goto` command) and branch to (`gosub` command) or return from (`return` command) subroutines. At any point in the script, the `exit` command can cause the whole thing to terminate. Each of these commands (`goto`, `gosub`, `return`, and `exit`) execute through `docommand()`. Listing 8.2 shows the `exit` command.

---

1. Notice that we are discussing the monitor code. The monitor not only provides the application with the ability to use TFS, but the monitor itself uses the TFS API.

Listing 8.2   The exit **Command.**

```
int ScriptExitFlag;

char *ExitHelp[] = {
    "Exit a script",
    "-[r]",
    "Options:",
    " -r   remove script after exit",
    0,
};

int
Exit(int argc, char *argv[])
{
    ScriptExitFlag = EXIT_SCRIPT;
    if ((argc == 2) && (!strcmp(argv[1],"-r")))
        ScriptExitFlag |= REMOVE_SCRIPT;
    return(CMD_SUCCESS);
}
```

If a line in the script contains the command line exit, the above code executes out of tfsscript(), and, as a result, the global variable ScriptExitFlag is set to EXIT_SCRIPT. If the -r option is present, the REMOVE_SCRIPT bit would also be set in the global variable ScriptExitFlag. Referring to the tfsscript() function of Listing 8.1, notice that after tfsDocommand() returns, the code looks to see if the ScriptExitFlag variable has been modified. If ScriptExitFlag is non-zero, the loop is terminated, and the file is closed. If the REMOVE_SCRIPT bit is set in ScriptExitFlag, then the script is automatically removed.

Goto

The tfsscript() function also provides one global ScriptGotoTag variable. The syntax of the goto command is goto {tagname}, so the goto command sets up the ScriptGotoTag (a char pointer — see Listing 8.3) to point to the tag that was passed from the command line as the parameter of a goto. Referring to the tfsscript() function (see Listing 8.1), if the ScriptGotoTag variable is set after the return from tfsDocommand(), the currently opened script is searched for the line that starts with a pound sign, a space, and the tag. For example, the line goto TOPOFLOOP causes tfsscript() to search through the currently running script for the line # TOPOFLOOP. The file pointer is then set to this new location in the script, and execution continues.

Listing 8.3   The goto **Command.**

```
char    *ScriptGotoTag;

/* gototag():
 *  Used with tfsscript to allow a command to adjust the pointer into the
 *  script that is currently being executed.  It simply populates the
 *  "ScriptGotoTag" pointer with the tag that should be branched to next.
 */
void
gototag(char *tag)
{
    if (ScriptGotoTag)
        free(ScriptGotoTag);
    ScriptGotoTag = malloc(strlen(tag)+8);
    sprintf(ScriptGotoTag,"# %s",tag);
}

char *GotoHelp[] = {
    "Branch to file tag",
    "{tagname}",
    0,
};

int
Goto(int argc, char *argv[])
{
    if (argc != 2)
        return(-1);
    gototag(argv[1]);
    return(CMD_SUCCESS);
}
```

gosub **and** return

To wrap up the details of tfsscript(), I describe the script runner's ability to branch to and return from subroutines: gosub and return.

Listing 8.4   **The** gosub **and** return **Commands.**

```
char *GosubHelp[] = {
    "Call a subroutine",
    "{tagname}",
    0,
};


int
Gosub(int argc, char *argv[])
{
    if (argc != 2)
        return(-1);
    gosubtag(argv[1]);
    return(CMD_SUCCESS);
}

char *ReturnHelp[] = {
    "Return from subroutine",
    "",
    0,
};


int
Return(int argc, char *argv[])
{
    if (argc != 1)
        return(-1);
    gosubret(0);
    return(CMD_SUCCESS);
}
```

The front ends to each of these commands (Listing 8.4) are essentially identical except that one calls `gosubtag()` and one calls `gosubret()` (Listing 8.5).

Listing 8.5 `gosub` **and** `return` **Under the Hood.**

```
#define MAXGOSUBDEPTH   15

static long ReturnToTbl[MAXGOSUBDEPTH+1];
static int  ReturnToDepth, ReturnToTfd;

void
gosubtag(char *tag)
{
    if (ReturnToDepth >= MAXGOSUBDEPTH) {
        printf("Max return-to depth reached\n");
        return;
    }
    ReturnToTbl[ReturnToDepth] = tfstell(ReturnToTfd);
    ReturnToDepth++;
    gototag(tag);
}


void
gosubret(char *ignored)
{
    if (ReturnToDepth <= 0)
        printf("Nothing to return to\n");
    else {
        ReturnToDepth--;
        tfsseek(ReturnToTfd, ReturnToTbl[ReturnToDepth], TFS_BEGIN);
    }
}
```

The `gosub` command calls `gosubtag()`, which records the location in the file to which the subroutine must return. The next element in the `ReturnToTbl[]` array is populated with the value returned by `tfstell()`. The `ReturnToTbl[]` array is essentially a stack of return locations (in the form of file offsets). Function `gosubtag()` then calls `gototag()`, which I discussed earlier. The `return` command unwinds the calling linkage by calling gosubret(). Function gosubret() pops the return location from the ReturnToTbl[] table and returns to the appropriate point in the file (using tfsseek()). The return stack depth is decreased by one, and a seek to that return point in the file is performed. The maximum call nesting is limited by the size of the ReturnToTbl[] table. The gosubtag() function tests for calls that exceed this limit.

Conditional Branching

Several other commands provide additional capabilities for enhancing the script execution environment, although none of these additional commands interacts directly with the tfsscript() function as do exit, goto, gosub, and return. The one remaining command implementation that is worth detailing is the if command. The if command provides MicroMonitor with the conditional branching capabilities needed for any programming environment. The implementation of if uses the facilities I've already introduced with gosub, goto, exit, and return.

Listing 8.6   Conditional Branch Support: The if Command.

```
char *IfHelp[] = {
    "Conditional branching",
    "-[t:] [{arg1} {compar} {arg2}] {action} [else action]",
    " Numeric/logic compare:",
    "  gt lt le ge eq ne and or",
    " String compare:",
    "  seq sne",
    " Other tests (-t args):",
    "  gc, ngc, iscmp {filename}",
    " Action:",
    " goto tag | gosub tag | exit | return",
    0,
};


int
If(int argc, char *argv[])
{
    int opt, arg, true, if_else, offset;
    void    (*iffunc)(), (*elsefunc)();
```

```
long    var1, var2;
char    *testtype, *arg1, *arg2, *iftag, *elsetag;



testtype = 0;
while((opt=getopt(argc,argv,"t:")) != -1) {
    switch(opt) {
    case 't':
        testtype = optarg;
        break;
    default:
        return(CMD_PARAM_ERROR);
    }
}

elsetag = 0;
elsefunc = 0;
offset = true = if_else = 0;
```

The goal of the if command is to make some type of test or comparison and, based on the result of that test, to take some kind of action. The comparison is generally based on comparing the content of a shell variable to some constant or to another shell variable. The variables can be string or numerically based. The -t option allows the user to check for the presence of a character on the console port or to determine if a file is compressed or not.

The basic syntax of the if command is

```
if {comparison between A & B is true}{perform actionX}
    [else {perform actionY}]
```

or

```
if {-t testtype}{perform actionX}[else {perform actionY}]
```

where the test performed by testtype can be true or false.

The if command offers two potential outcomes, so there must be two different. function pointers to load with the appropriate function that performs the requested action (iffunc and elsefunc). Referring to Listing 8.6, the command line is first tested for the -t option. If present, then the appropriate flag is set.

Listing 8.7   Parsing Else Clauses.

```
/* First see if there is an 'else' present... */
    for (arg=optind;arg<argc;arg++) {
        if (!strcmp(argv[arg],"else")) {
            if_else = 1;
            break;
        }
    }


    if (if_else) {
        elsetag = argv[argc-1];
        if (!strcmp(argv[argc-1],"exit")) {
            offset = 2;
            elsefunc = exitscript;
        }
        else if (!strcmp(argv[argc-1],"return")) {
            offset = 2;
            elsefunc = gosubret;
        }
        else if (!strcmp(argv[argc-2],"goto")) {
            offset = 3;
            elsefunc = gototag;
        }
        else if (!strcmp(argv[argc-2],"gosub")) {
            offset = 3;
            elsefunc = gosubtag;
        }
        else
            return(CMD_PARAM_ERROR);
    }

    iftag = argv[argc-offset-1];
    if (!strcmp(argv[argc-offset-1],"exit"))
        iffunc = exitscript;
    else if (!strcmp(argv[argc-offset-1],"return"))
        iffunc = gosubret;
```

```
    else if (!strcmp(argv[argc-offset-2],"goto"))
        iffunc = gototag;
    else if (!strcmp(argv[argc-offset-2],"gosub"))
        iffunc = gosubtag;
    else
        return(CMD_PARAM_ERROR);
```

Further parsing (Listing 8.7) determines if the else keyword is present on the command line. If so, the branching code loads the elsefunc function pointer with the else action. This action can be a goto, gosub, exit, or return. Next, the following four-way branch loads the iffunc function pointer with a corresponding action.

Listing 8.8   Performing the Test or Comparison.

```
if (testtype) {
    if (!strcmp(testtype,"gc")) {
        if (gotachar())
            true=1;
    }
    else if (!strcmp(testtype,"ngc")) {
        if (!gotachar())
            true=1;
    }
    else if (!strcmp(testtype,"iscmp")) {
        TFILE *tfp;

        tfp = tfsstat(argv[optind]);
        if (tfp) {
            if (TFS_ISCPRS(tfp))
                true=1;
        }
        else
            printf("'%s' not found\n",argv[optind]);
    }
    else
        return(CMD_PARAM_ERROR);
}
else {
```

```
        arg1 = argv[optind];
        testtype = argv[optind+1];
        arg2 = argv[optind+2];

        var1 = strtoul(arg1,(char **)0,0);
        var2 = strtoul(arg2,(char **)0,0);

        if (!strcmp(testtype,"gt")) {
            if (var1 > var2)
                true = 1;
        }
        else if (!strcmp(testtype,"lt")) {
            if (var1 < var2)
                true = 1;
        }
        else if (!strcmp(testtype,"le")) {
            if (var1 <= var2)
                true = 1;
        }
        else if (!strcmp(testtype,"ge")) {
            if (var1 >= var2)
                true = 1;
        }
        else if (!strcmp(testtype,"eq")) {
            if (var1 == var2)
                true = 1;
        }
        else if (!strcmp(testtype,"ne")) {
            if (var1 != var2)
                true = 1;
        }
        else if (!strcmp(testtype,"and")) {
            if (var1 & var2)
                true = 1;
        }
        else if (!strcmp(testtype,"or")) {
```

```
        if (var1 | var2)
            true = 1;
    }
    else if (!strcmp(testtype,"seq")) {
        if (!strcmp(arg1,arg2))
            true = 1;
    }
    else if (!strcmp(testtype,"sne")) {
        if (strcmp(arg1,arg2))
            true = 1;
    }
    else
        return(CMD_PARAM_ERROR);
}
```

Next, referring to Listing 8.8, the test or comparison is executed, and the `true` flag is set based on the result.

Listing 8.9   Execute the Appropriate Action.

```
/* If the true flag is set, call the 'if' function.
 * If the true flag is clear, and "else" was found on the command
 * line, then call the 'else' function...
 */
if (true)
    iffunc(iftag);
else if (if_else)
    elsefunc(elsetag);

return(CMD_SUCCESS);
}
```

Finally, based on the setting of the `true` flag and the content of the `iffunc` and `elsefunc` pointers, the conditional action is performed (Listing 8.9). All in all, you get an amazing amount of script functionality from a surprisingly small, simple piece of code. Refer to the CD for command functions for `read`, `item`, `sleep`, `echo`, and other script-related commands.

A Few Examples

I've described some of the implementation behind scripts. Now, I'll present a few examples that illustrate how scripts can be used. Some of the command details in the examples are not documented in this text; refer to the CD for complete details.

Example #1: `ping`

Instead of providing gobs of commands in the command table, MicroMonitor's command set philosophy is to provide low-level capabilities that can be combined through scripting to form a variety of higher-level capabilities. This script is an example of that philosophy. It builds on the capabilities of the `icmp` command to create a `ping` command. The `icmp` command supports some ICMP features at the MicroMonitor command line. The `echo` argument to the `icmp` command is basically a ping; however, the command `ping` is not in MicroMonitor's command set because it can be built with a script (see Listing 8.10).

Listing 8.10   Building `ping`.

```
#
# PING:
# Script using "icmp echo" and "argv" commands:
# Syntax: ping IP_ADDRESS [optional ping count]
#
argv -v
if $ARGC eq 2 goto PING_1
if $ARGC eq 3 goto PING_N
echo $ARG0: requires IP address
exit

# PING_1:
icmp echo $ARG1
exit

# PING_N:
icmp -c $ARG2 echo $ARG1
exit
```

The `argv -v` command retrieves command line arguments passed to `ping` and populates shell variables appropriately. For this example, if the script was invoked as

```
ping 135.3.94.1 6
```

`$ARG0` would contain `ping`, `$ARG1` would contain `135.3.94.1`, `$ARG2` would contain 6, and `$ARGC` would contain 3. Notice the use of comments, conditional branching, and `goto` tags. The `PING_1` and `PING_N` tags mark the start of the two different logical paths taken depending on the command line argument count. The rest is pretty easy to understand.

Example #2: Shell Arrays

Listing 8.11 uses the nested shell variable capability in MicroMonitor's command interpreter to implement simple arrays. All syntax is similar to that of Listing 8.10, but this example demonstrates the use of MicroMonitor's nested shell variable capability.

Listing 8.11   Implementing Simple Arrays.

```
#
# Build a list (or array) of vegetables:
#
set VEG_1 Lettuce
set VEG_2 Broccoli
set VEG_3 Carrot
set VEG_4 Corn

set idx 1
set max 4

#
# Now print the list of vegetables using the 'idx' shell variable
# as an index:
#
# TOP:
if $idx gt $max exit       # Exit loop when idx is greater than max.
echo ${VEG_${idx}}         # Use nested shell var to print $VEG_N.
set -i idx                 # Increment content of idx.
goto TOP                   # Do it again.
```

The output of the script of Listing 8.11 would be

```
Lettuce
Brocoli
Carrot
Corn
```

The `set` command assigns a value to a shell variable. When the CLI processor parses the line

```
echo ${VEG_${idx}}
```

it makes two passes through the shell variable processing stage. The first pass converts `${idx}` to its value, and the second pass converts `${VEG_N}` (where N is the value of `$idx`) to its value. Note that the `idx` shell variable is used like an index into an array of names, where the array is called VEG_.

Example #3: Subroutines, Conditional Branching, and TFS, etc.

The script in Listing 8.12 further demonstrates the use of conditional branching and subroutines. Listing 8.12 uses some of the features of the `tfs` command as part of the demonstration. The script loads an executable file from TFS flash memory to DRAM. The script informs the user if the file is compressed.

Listing 8.12   Using a Script to Load an Executable.

```
#
# Load file:
# Script syntax: fload {filename}
#
argv -v
if $ARGC ne 2 goto USAGE

# See if file exists...
tfs size $ARG1 FSIZE
if $FSIZE seq \$FSIZE goto NOFILE

# See if file is compressed...
if -t iscmp $ARG1 gosub COMPRESSED else gosub NCOMPRESSED
```

```
# Verbosely load the file to dram...
tfs -v ld $ARG1
exit

#
# COMPRESSED:
#
echo File $ARG1 is compressed.
echo
return

#
# NCOMPRESSED:
#
echo File $ARG1 is not compressed.
echo
return

#
# NOFILE:
#
echo File $ARG1 not found.
exit

#
# USAGE:
#
echo Usage: $ARG0 {filename}
exit
```

After basic argument testing, the script uses the tfs size command to populate the shell variable FSIZE with the size of the file. If the file is present, FSIZE will be set accordingly; otherwise FSIZE will be cleared. If the FSIZE variable is cleared, the CLI processor leaves the $FSIZE string untouched, so $FSIZE and \$FSIZE would then appear as identical strings because the backslash in the second string would be removed by the CLI parsing. The second if statement (if $FSIZE seq ...) deals with this comparison. The third if demonstrates the additional testing capability of if using the -t option. In this test, the if is testing the file to determine whether or not it is compressed. The COMPRESSED tag points to a subroutine, and NOFILE and USAGE are simple branch destinations, each of which prints out some user message. Finally, the file is loaded. The output of the script when passed the name of a non-compressed file (in this case, file abc) is shown in Listing 8.13.

Listing 8.13   The Load Statistics.

```
File abc is not compressed.

.text     : copy  852808 bytes from 0xf0142fdc to 0x00080000
.rodata   : copy   68964 bytes from 0xf0213324 to 0x00150348
.data     : copy   61984 bytes from 0xf022408c to 0x001610b0
.ctors    : copy      12 bytes from 0xf02332ac to 0x001702d0
.dtors    : copy      12 bytes from 0xf02332b8 to 0x001702dc
.got      : copy      16 bytes from 0xf02332c4 to 0x001702e8
.sbss     : set      916 bytes  at   0x001702f8 to 0x00
.bss      : set    91252 bytes  at   0x00170690 to 0x00
.comment  :        17160 bytes not processed (tot=17160)
.shstrtab :          101 bytes not processed (tot=17261)
entrypoint: 0x80000
```

The preceding scripts demonstrate the scripting capability of the script runner. The scripts also show the versatility of some of the commands built into MicroMonitor's CLI table. For full documentation of the command set, refer to the CD.

Summary

If the phrase "embedded systems" conjures images of frustrated engineers struggling to squeeze another 15 bytes out of their code so that it fits in the 1K on-chip memory, then scripting capabilities might seem like an unaffordable luxury. It really isn't. First, modern silicon economies are such that most applications can easily afford the necessary code space — especially during development. Later, if needed, the monitor can be reconfigured to minimize its footprint.

Second, as the preceding examples illustrated, scripting can be a very powerful tool for creating system-level capabilities and development tools.

Finally, a scripting capability encourages you to strive for modularity in your code. Including a script runner allows you to write the bulk of the monitor and your application as relatively independent, primitive functions that are aggregated into meaningful capabilities by various scripts. You can do the same thing in programming code, but the script is easier to write, modify, and maintain. Because the script depends on the monitor for its execution context, in many cases, scripts are significantly smaller than equivalent programs.

9

Chapter 9

Network Connectivity

The Ethernet is now so pervasive that even embedded systems can no longer ignore it. Ethernet is a bit more complicated than simple RS-232 as a communication interface, but it is also priceless once you get it up and running.

The TCP/IP protocol stack is encapsulated into protocol layers. Each layer of the protocol considers the layer above it to be just a block of data (or payload). That's all the layer knows. The payload for Ethernet is IP or ARP, the payload for IP is ICMP, UDP or TCP (and others), and then UDP and TCP carry others (like TFTP, HTTP, and FTP). FTP rides on TCP, TCP rides on IP, and IP rides on Ethernet. You can think of the TCP/IP protocol stack as a line of dump trucks. Each truck is small enough to fit inside the one in front of it. The front dump truck doesn't care what is inside its cargo area, so the fact that it is another smaller dump truck makes no difference. Each truck transfers its payload from source to destination. What happens to the payload after the transfer is of no concern to the dump truck that just dumped it.

NOTE

If you really want to learn about networking, buy a book on networking. I can't cover the whole subject in this chapter. The goal of this chapter is to discuss briefly some of the basic protocols and step through what is needed to connect an embedded system to an IP network.

To connect an embedded system to an IP network, you must interface with some Ethernet device and write a packet processor.

Ethernet

Everything starts with the biggest dump truck: the Ethernet frame. The packet format for Ethernet is

Destination Host Address	6 bytes
Source Host Address	6 bytes
Frame Type	2 bytes
Payload	1500 bytes

The destination address, as you will see momentarily, can be a specific MAC address or a broadcast address. MAC addresses are usually formatted as six colon-delimited bytes. Each byte spans the full 8-bit range of 0–255, and the values are typically represented with ASCII-coded hexadecimal. For example, a valid Ethernet MAC address is 00:60:1D:02:08:B5. Notice that each packet received contains the MAC address of the sender (source).

ARP

Every device on an Ethernet/IP network has two addresses — the MAC address at the Ethernet layer and the IP address at the network layer. To communicate with a device over Ethernet, you need to know the device's MAC address. However, because you are running IP on top of the Ethernet layer, you need to be able to address other devices using their IP address, not their MAC address. The Address Resolution Protocol (ARP) allows us to do this. Besides IP, ARP is the only Ethernet payload I discuss in this chapter. (There are others, but they are beyond the scope of this discussion.) The ARP packet format looks like this

Hardware	2 bytes
Protocol	2 bytes
Hlen	1 byte
Plen	1 byte
Operation	2 bytes
Sender Hardware Address	6 bytes
Sender IP Address	4 bytes
Target Hardware Address	6 bytes
Target IP Address	4 bytes

Notice that ARP does not have a payload, so there is no further encapsulation. The only purpose of ARP is to resolve the MAC/IP address combination. Every device on a network must support the ability to receive an incoming ARP request and respond to that request if appropriate.

ARP resolves what would appear to be a catch-22. The device that wants to communicate with the target must ask the target what its MAC address is, but, to do so, it must already know the address of the target! This dilemma is resolved by broadcasting the ARP request to all devices on the subnet using a special broadcast Ethernet address (FF:FF:FF:FF:FF:FF).

All devices on a network must be able to receive an Ethernet broadcast. Part of the message broadcast is the fact that the message is of type ARP. The incoming ARP request contains the IP address of the device for which the requester is trying to get the MAC address (the target IP address). The ARP packet handler for each device that receives the broadcasted request must compare this IP address to its own IP address. If there is a match, the device sends an ARP response to the requester using the hardware (MAC) and IP addresses taken from the incoming packet.

Once this information is retrieved by the requester, it is saved in the requester's local memory for some period of time. (This local storage is called an *ARP cache*.) Storing the MAC address allows the device to retrieve the MAC address for the given IP address later without having to issue another ARP request. The low-level drivers of a network stack protocol are constantly peeking at the incoming packets and storing away fresh MAC/IP combinations in the ARP cache. If the entry in the cache is not used for some period (could be anywhere from 2 to 20 minutes), the entry is removed (or flushed) from the cache.

IP

Internet Protocol (IP) is the workhorse of all TCP/IP networks. The packet header looks like this

Version and Header Length	1 byte
Type of Service	1 byte
Length of Packet	2 bytes
Identification	2 bytes
Fragment Offset Field	2 bytes
Time to Live	1 byte
Protocol	1 byte
Checksum	2 bytes
Source IP Address	4 bytes
Destination IP Address	4 bytes
Payload	Max of 64K

Unlike ARP, IP always has a payload. The purpose of IP is to carry data from place to place (a perfect dump truck). The payload is accompanied by information regarding the size and number of devices that have handled the packet as it made its way to the target. Different types of network devices use portions of this packet header for different things. In this case, I am primarily interested in the protocol, length of packet, checksum, source address, and destination address fields. The protocol field is what tells us what is in the payload. For our discussion, the payload is ICMP, UDP, TCP, or unknown. The checksum is a basic sanity check for the packet. The source and destination addresses are the IP address of the device that sent the packet and of the device that is supposed to receive the packet. Our packet processor must look at all of these fields to accept or reject the packet, as well as to determine where the packet needs to go in the next phase of processing.

ICMP

Something in the protocol must make sure that the dump trucks are running properly and that they follow the right route to their destination. This task is partially the responsibility of the Internet Control Message Protocol (ICMP). MicroMonitor only implements a small portion of ICMP. For my purposes, the most important part of ICMP is the *echo* capability. ICMP echo is commonly referred to as ping. The purpose of ping is to allow one network device to find out if another device is on the network and healthy. A device that sends an ICMP echo request is attempting to determine if another device is healthy. A device that receives an ICMP echo request responds to confirm that it is alive. ICMP support is important if you want other devices to be able to determine whether the target system is present on the network. One other important use of ICMP (in this case) is that I need to be able to tell a sender if a packet is undeliverable. For example, MicroMonitor does not support Network File System (NFS), so if the system receives an NFS request, it should respond to the sender with an ICMP Unreachable Protocol message to let the sender know that the request is undeliverable.

NOTE

There is one other handy use of ICMP echo in embedded systems. Earlier in this chapter, I mentioned the ARP cache. The ARP cache is very useful on a stable network. When a device is attached to the network, its MAC and IP addresses are fairly constant (assuming no DHCP licensing for now). In a development environment, however, where network-attached devices are being built and debugged, the network configuration is somewhat less stable. In this environment, the ARP cache mechanism can get in the way, particularly if you need to recycle a particular IP address.

For example, assume that you are working on several network-enabled projects and that the network administrator has assigned you a single IP address for hardware testing. At first glance, this arrangement seems reasonable; though you are working with several different embedded systems targets, you will have only one turned on at a time. So you set up each device with the same IP address. When you connect to the first device using IP/UDP, everything works fine. Your host identifies the device as IP address 135.3.94.138 and MAC address 00:60:1d:02:0b:fe. Your host silently adds this relationship to its ARP cache.

Now you shut down device_1 and turn on device_2. It is also configured at IP 135.3.94.138 but has a MAC address of 00:60:1d:02:0b:f0. When you try to talk to this device, your host says it can't find the device.

If at this point you issue the command arp -a (or some equivalent) to dump the content of the host's ARP cache, you will see that your host still thinks that 135.3.94.138 has a MAC address of 00:60:1d:02:0b:fe (because the host put that IP/MAC combination into its ARP cache during the earlier interaction with device_1). If you don't have the ability to flush your host's ARP cache manually, you have two choices. You can wait until your machine automatically flushes the cache, which could be several minutes. Alternatively, you can issue an ICMP echo from your target to any other device on the subnet. The host's network interface would see this broadcast and update its ARP cache immediately. Now communication between your host and device_2 works properly.

UDP and TCP

The contents of an IP payload can vary, but most IP packets contain User Datagram Protocol (UDP) or Transmission Control Protocol (TCP). At the IP level, you cannot determine much about the packet other than its size and sender. If the incoming IP payload is UDP, you can find information about who is talking to whom in the UDP header. For example, assume that you have a file server that can serve files to multiple machines. One user on machine_1 requests fileX, another user on machine_1 requests fileZ, while a user on machine_2 requests fileY, all at roughly the same time. First of all, how does the low-level protocol know that the incoming file request is for the file server application running on the machine? It is very likely that multiple servers are running on any one machine (for example TFTP, FTP, HTTP, or TELNET). When the file server application receives the request, how does it know to which client to respond? When the file server receives two requests from two different users on the same machine, how does it respond to the correct user? There's more involved than just IP addresses now. Things start to get more complicated because we are on machines with a single IP address but multiple users or applications trying to communicate with each other over the network.

The packet header for UDP is as follows. It is made up of a header and a pseudoheader. The pseudoheader is shown in italics and is built from information taken from the IP layer.

Source Port	2 bytes
Destination Port	2 bytes
Length of Packet	2 bytes
Checksum	2 bytes
Source Address	4 bytes
Destination Address	4 bytes
Zero	1 byte
Protocol	1 byte
Length of Packet	2 bytes

The pseudoheader is not part of the IP packet specification (hence the term "pseudo" header). The pseudoheader is constructed from the IP header below it and concatenated onto the UDP packet. The combination of source port, destination port, source IP address, and destination IP address allows the sender and receiver of these packets to keep track of not only the device (or machine) but also the application within the device (or machine) which is responsible for the packet.

TCP makes UDP look like a cakewalk. TCP is a very complicated and robust protocol that certainly requires more than just a few paragraphs. The most important distinction between UDP and TCP is that UDP does not guarantee that the packet will be received. UDP simply sends a packet to a destination; if the packet is not received, the application code must recover. TCP, on the other hand, does guarantee (within reason) that the packet will be received. With that guarantee comes a great deal of added code complexity and real-time overhead. TCP provides addressing similar to that offered by UDP but employs a very elaborate state-based handshake between sender and receiver to assure that a packet reaches its destination intact. MicroMonitor avoids this complexity by responding to all TCP connection requests with a connection reset.

DHCP/BOOTP

Bootstrap Protocol (BOOTP) and Dynamic Host Configuration Protocol (DHCP) are IP protocols that run when a network starts. DHCP is a modernization of BOOTP. These protocols allow a target to start up somewhat unaware of itself. The idea is that after the target has booted itself, it will talk to a BOOTP or DHCP server to retrieve configuration information about itself. Following is the format for a BOOTP header; DHCP is similar.

Op	1 byte
Htype	1 byte
Hlen	1 byte
Hops	1 byte
Transaction ID	4 bytes
Seconds	2 bytes
Unused	2 bytes
Client IP	4 bytes
Your IP	4 bytes
Server IP	4 bytes
Router IP	4 bytes
Client MAC Address	16 bytes
Server Host Name	64 bytes
Boot File Name	128 bytes
Vendor Specific Area	64 bytes

To retrieve its configuration data, the target device must issue a BOOTP broadcast request. Like Ethernet, IP also has an address that is dedicated to broadcast: 255.255.255.255. If there is a BOOTP server on the network, the BOOTP server might respond. The response includes information such as the server's IP address, the IP address that the target is to use, the IP address of the gateway on this subnet, the subnet mask, a boot file name, and an IP address from which to get this boot file. DHCP expands this capability to allow the target and server to establish a dynamic IP address. When the target boots up, it talks to a DHCP server to retrieve information similar to the BOOTP information but with the option that the IP address assigned to the device can be temporary, which is called *DHCP IP address leasing*. Typically, the server and client establish some time-out period after which the client must request an extension on the lease of the IP address. The client may or may not be granted the extension, depending on how the DHCP server is configured.

Applied to Embedded Systems

You may be wondering how all this information on network protocols relates to embedded systems firmware. The answer is that, because I am building the entire interface, I must deal with incoming packets at the Ethernet level. The Ethernet device itself guarantees that only packets destined for its own MAC address are accepted. The driver firmware is then usually responsible for dropping all packets, excluding broadcasts, that are not addressed to the local IP address.

To write the driver code, you need to understand how to detect when an incoming packet has arrived and how to retrieve the packet from the Ethernet controller. Both operations are very specific to the device itself, so you need to refer to the device documentation. Generally, an Ethernet device looks like a FIFO or uses buffer descriptors where each descriptor set describes an incoming or outgoing buffer (or packet).

The buffer descriptor model is pretty common and quite easy to work with once you get the hang of it. Each device imposes its own definition of what a buffer descriptor looks like. The buffer descriptor typically contains a command/status field, a length field, a field containing a pointer to the actual buffer, and a field pointing to the next buffer descriptor. This definition implies a linked list of structures where each structure points to a buffer.

Figure 9.1   Ethernet Driver Buffer Descriptors.

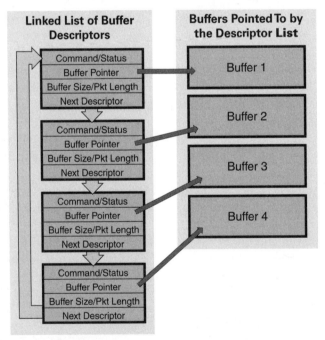

It is common for Ethernet controllers to communicate with applications about the location of data using a linked chain of buffer descriptors. Notice that the descriptors form a circularly linked list.

Figure 9.1 shows a typical buffer descriptor and buffer configuration. The number of descriptors and buffers depends entirely on the application and the amount of memory space available in the target system. The Ethernet device is usually given a pointer to the first buffer descriptor in the list, and, when data transfer begins, the device assumes that the buffer descriptors have been properly initialized.

Using 'C' Structures to Access Peripherals

It is very common in C to interface to a peripheral device by creating a structure that looks like the device and then overlaying that structure onto the address space that is occupied by the device. When doing this, you must be aware of some code generation issues that can otherwise be taken for granted. When using structures in normal programs, the compiler/CPU combination determines precisely how the structure is mapped on to memory. When you write a function to access a member in this structure, you can be assured that the underlying code will access the proper member at the appropriate offset from the base of the structure. You don't really need to know exactly how each member in the structure is mapped onto memory.

When using a C structure as a clean way to interface to a peripheral, you can't take anything for granted. The peripheral has a fixed format onto which you are building a structure that must match the peripheral's hardware. Suddenly, you must know exactly how the structure is formatted; otherwise, it will not properly align with the peripheral's hardware.

Without going into the various reasons why, the compiler may add "padding" between members of the structure. This "hidden" padding of the structure can confuse access to the device because although the hardware and software structures appear to match, the unseen padding causes a mismatch. In most cases, the solution to this problem is simple awareness. You need to tell the compiler that you don't want it to insert any padding in the structure definition. You essentially force the compiler to not do something that it would otherwise consider natural. If you investigate the cross-compiler documentation, you are likely to find some some special syntax (often called `pragmas`) that will direct the compiler to not insert any invisible padding into the relevant structure.

Listing 9.1   Initializing a Block of Buffer Descriptors.

```
struct rdesc {
    ulong   cmdstat;       /* Command/Status            */
    uchar   *bp;           /* Pointer to buffer         */
    ushort  bsize;         /* Size of buffer            */
    ushort  psize;         /* Size of received packet   */
    struct  rdesc  *ndp;   /* Pointer to next descriptor */
};


unsigned char RbufBase[BUF_SIZE * RX_DESCRIPTOR_COUNT];
struct  rdesc RdescBase[RX_DESCRIPTOR_COUNT];


for(i=0;i<RX_DESCRIPTOR_CNT;i++) {
    RdescBase[i].cmdstat = DEVICE_IS_IDLE;
    RdescBase[i].bsize = BUF_SIZE;
    RdescBase[i].psize = 0;
    RdescBase[i].bp = (uchar *)&RbufBase[i * BUF_SIZE];
    if (i == RX_DESCRIPTOR_CNT-1) {
        RdescBase[i].ndp = RdescBase;
    }
    else {
        RdescBase[i].ndp = &RdescBase[i+1];
    }
}
```

The example code in Listing 9.1 shows how one might initialize a block of buffer descriptors. The structure rdesc is used as the buffer descriptor and is declared to match the format of the descriptor as it would be defined by the device. One block of memory (RbufBase) is used for buffer allocation, and one block of memory (RdescBase) is used for buffer descriptor allocation. The for loop initializes the linked list. Note that this list is circular; the last item in the list points to the first.

The processPACKET() Function

In the case of packet reception, the firmware must retrieve the Ethernet payload and extract the packet type to determine if the packet is ARP or IP. If the packet is neither ARP nor IP, it is thrown away. That's about all the Ethernet code does. Next, the packet is passed to either the IP or ARP packet-processing function. If the packet is

ARP, the appropriate response is sent, and handling of the packet is complete. If the packet is IP, the software must further parse the header to determine which packet-processing subsection should process it. The interface handles UDP, DHCP/BOOTP, ICMP, and bits of TCP. So, based on the contents of the incoming packet, one of several different higher layer packet processors is called.

Listing 9.2   processPACKET().

```
/* processPACKET():
 *  This is the top level of the message processing after a complete
 *  packet has been received over ethernet.  It's all just a lot of
 *  parsing to determine whether the message is for this board's IP
 *  address (broadcast reception may be enabled), and the type of
 *  incoming protocol.  Once that is determined, the packet is either
 *  processed (TFTP, DHCP, ARP, ICMP-ECHO, etc...) or discarded.
 */
void
processPACKET(struct ether_header *ehdr, ushort size)
{
    int i;
    ushort  *datap, udpport;
    ulong   csum;
    struct ip *ihdr;
    struct Udphdr *uhdr;

    if (ehdr->ether_type == htons(ETHERTYPE_ARP)) {
        processARP(ehdr,size);
        return;
    }
    else if (ehdr->ether_type != htons(ETHERTYPE_IP)) {
        printPkt(ehdr,size,ETHER_INCOMING);
        return;
    }

    /* If we are NOT in the middle of a DHCP or BOOTP transaction, then
     * if destination MAC address is broadcast, return now.
     */
```

```
    if ((DHCPState == DHCPSTATE_NOTUSED) &&
        (!memcmp((char *)&(ehdr->ether_dhost),BroadcastAddr,6))) {
        return;
    }


    /* If source MAC address is this board, then assume we received our
     * own outgoing broadcast message...
     */
    if (!memcmp((char *)&(ehdr->ether_shost),BinEnetAddr,6)) {
        return;
    }
```

The processPACKET() function starts with Listing 9.2. The incoming parameters are the raw packet from the Ethernet driver and the size of the packet. The Ethernet header is tested immediately to see if the packet is ARP or IP. If the packet is ARP, execution branches to the ARP processing code. If the packet is some unrecognized protocol, it is printed to the console (as a diagnostic aid) before discarding it. The remaining code in this function assumes that the packet is IP. Any incoming broadcasts not associated with DHCP/BOOTP are dropped. Also, because the incoming packet might be the outgoing packet just sent by this target (depends on how the Ethernet interface device is configured), if the Ethernet source address of the incoming packet is the same as this target's address, the packet is dropped.

Listing 9.3   Verifying the Packet Integrity.

```
    ihdr = (struct ip *) (ehdr + 1);


    /* If not version # 4, return now... */
    if (getIP_V(ihdr->ip_vhl) != 4)
        return;


    /* IP address filtering:
     * At this point, the only packets accepted are those destined for this
     * board's IP address, plus, DHCP, if active.
     */
    if (memcmp((char *)&(ihdr->ip_dst),BinIpAddr,4)) {
        if (DHCPState == DHCPSTATE_NOTUSED)
            return;
```

```
        if (ihdr->ip_p != IP_UDP)
            return;
        uhdr = (struct Udphdr *)(ihdr+1);
        if (uhdr->uh_dport != htons(DhcpClientPort)) {
            return;
        }
    }


    /* Verify incoming IP header checksum...
     */
    csum = 0;
    datap = (ushort *) ihdr;
    for (i=0;i<(sizeof(struct ip)/sizeof(ushort));i++,datap++)
        csum += *datap;
    csum = (csum & 0xffff) + (csum >> 16);
    if (csum != 0xffff) {
        EtherIPERRCnt++;
        return;
    }


    printPkt(ehdr,size,ETHER_INCOMING);
```

The next phase is to overlay the IP structure (see Listing 9.3) onto the incoming packet and perform some validation. First, the code verifies that the packet conforms to IP, then that the incoming packet is addressed to the local IP address, and, finally, that the checksum matches the packet. If the packet passes all of this validation, I call `printPkt()` to display the packet (`printPkt()` only prints if verbosity has been enabled).

Listing 9.4   Dispatching for Protocol-Specific Processing.

```
    if (ihdr->ip_p == IP_ICMP) {
        processICMP(ehdr,size);
        return;
    }
    else if (ihdr->ip_p == IP_TCP) {
        processTCP(ehdr,size);
        return;
```

```
    }
    else if (ihdr->ip_p != IP_UDP) {
        int j;

        SendICMPUnreachable(ehdr,ICMP_UNREACHABLE_PROTOCOL);
        if (!(EtherVerbose & SHOW_INCOMING))
            return;
        for(j=0;protocols[j].pname;j++) {
            if (ihdr->ip_p == protocols[j].pnum) {
                printf("%s not supported\n",
                    protocols[j].pname);
                return;
            }
        }
        printf("<%02x> protocol unrecognized\n", ihdr->ip_p);
        return;
    }
```

The code in Listing 9.4 checks the IP packet type to determine how (if at all) to process the incoming IP packet. These checks are similar to the checks in Listing 9.2 for the incoming Ethernet frames. MicroMonitor supports some UDP, ICMP, and minimal TCP, so the logic calls processICMP() for incoming ICMP and processTCP() for incoming TCP. MicroMonitor then sends an ICMP Unreachable error response if the incoming packet is not UDP.

Listing 9.5   Processing UDP Packets.

```
    uhdr = (struct Udphdr *)(ihdr+1);

    /* If non-zero, verify incoming UDP packet checksum...
     */
    if (uhdr->uh_sum) {
        int     len;
        struct  UdpPseudohdr    pseudohdr;

        memcpy((char *)&pseudohdr.ip_src.s_addr,
            (char *)&ihdr->ip_src.s_addr,4);
        memcpy((char *)&pseudohdr.ip_dst.s_addr,
```

```
            (char *)&ihdr->ip_dst.s_addr,4);
        pseudohdr.zero = 0;
        pseudohdr.proto = ihdr->ip_p;
        pseudohdr.ulen = uhdr->uh_ulen;

        csum = 0;
        datap = (ushort *) &pseudohdr;
        for (i=0;i<(sizeof(struct UdpPseudohdr)/sizeof(ushort));i++)
            csum += *datap++;

        /* If length is odd, pad and add one. */
        len = ntohs(uhdr->uh_ulen);
        if (len & 1) {
            uchar   *ucp;
            ucp = (uchar *)uhdr;
            ucp[len] = 0;
            len++;
        }
        len >>= 1;

        datap = (ushort *) uhdr;
        for (i=0;i<len;i++)
            csum += *datap++;
        csum = (csum & 0xffff) + (csum >> 16);
        if (csum != 0xffff) {
            EtherUDPERRCnt++;
            return;
        }
    }
udpport = ntohs(uhdr->uh_dport);

if (udpport == MoncmdPort)
    processMONCMD(ehdr,size);
else if (udpport == DhcpClientPort)
    processDHCP(ehdr,size);
else if ((udpport == TftpPort) || (udpport == TftpSrcPort))
    processTFTP(ehdr,size);
```

```
      else {
         if (EtherVerbose & SHOW_INCOMING) {
            uchar *cp;
            cp = (uchar *)&(ihdr->ip_src);
            printf("  Unexpected IP pkt from %d.%d.%d.%d ",
               cp[0],cp[1],cp[2],cp[3]);
            printf("(sport=0x%x,dport=0x%x)\n",
               ntohs(uhdr->uh_sport),ntohs(uhdr->uh_dport));
         }
         SendICMPUnreachable(ehdr,ICMP_UNREACHABLE_PORT);
      }
   }
```

The processing in Listing 9.5 is similar to that in Listing 9.3 but one level up in the protocol. This code overlays the UDP structure onto the IP payload and runs a checksum verification of the UDP header and pseudoheader. This checksum might not be necessary if the incoming packet has the checksum value set to zero. Finally, the handler processes the incoming UDP port number and branches to the appropriate code deeper in the MicroMonitor software (TFTP, DHCP, or MONCMD). If the port is not one that MicroMonitor supports, the handler returns an ICMP error response.

NOTE

MONCMD is port 777 in the monitor. This port supports the ability to execute CLI commands over UDP.

In General

The implementation of the driver code is in C, and structures are overlaid onto the incoming packet to simplify the packet parsing. For example, the structure shown in Listing 9.6 could be used for the IP packet processing.

Listing 9.6 contains a few details of which you should be aware. First, depending on where the packet ends up in the memory space of the target, you need to consider different CPU alignment requirements. For example, some CPUs do not like to look at a two- or four-byte integer (short or long, respectively) unless the integer is aligned on an even address. If the data is on an odd address and C code attempts to access it, the processor can throw an *alignment exception*. Be aware of this issue, and make adjustments where necessary. If you can't predict the alignment of your memory buffer, you have no choice but to copy the two- or four-byte datum to an aligned space before accessing it.

Listing 9.6   A Structure Declaration for the IP Header.

```
struct ip_header {
    uchar  ip_vhl;      /* version and header length */
    uchar  ip_tos;      /* type of service           */
    ushort ip_len;      /* length of packet          */
    ushort ip_id;       /* identification            */
    ushort ip_offset;   /* fragment offset field     */
    uchar  ip_ttl;      /* time to live              */
    uchar  ip_proto;    /* protocol                  */
    ushort ip_csum;     /* checksum                  */
    ulong  ip_source;   /* source IP address         */
    ulong  ip_dest;     /* destination IP address    */
}
```

An added complication is the fact that the CPU of the target might be big or little endian. All data on a network is transferred in network-byte order, which is big endian. If you are lucky enough to be running with a big-endian CPU, big-endian data is no issue; if the CPU is little endian, things like packet length, checksum, and other multi-byte quantities in the headers must be endian-reversed. The network-to-host long (ntohl) host-to-network long (htonl), network-to-host short (ntohs) and host-to-network short (htons) conversion macros perform this endian reversal. On a big-endian machine, these macros do nothing; on a little-endian machine, they perform the conversion.

Summary

The goal of this chapter is not to create a complete network stack but rather to implement just enough of the Internet protocols so that the embedded system can talk to the rest of the network. The Ethernet driver (similar to our serial port driver) is written in polled mode, and only one packet is processed at a time. Because this system does not even enable interrupts, I do not have to worry about queuing up multiple packets. When polling determines that a packet has been received, the software processes the packet, sends a response if appropriate, then waits for another packet. This approach keeps things simple. In keeping with the "baby steps" philosophy, this approach provides a working first step for the driver. What you learn with this pass can be used on the next pass (if needed) that becomes interrupt driven. No time is lost, even if interrupts are eventually needed. This philosophy is applicable to any driver being written.

Chapter 10

File/Data Transfer

The monitor now includes a flash file system, serial port communications, and Ethernet connectivity. The next natural step is to provide a mechanism that allows file transfer to and from the target. The file transfer protocols presented in this chapter are not new but remain popular because of their simplicity. The monitor uses Xmodem and TFTP for RS-232 and Ethernet implementations respectively. Data can be transferred as raw memory or as a file for both protocols. The MicroMonitor package includes code for a PC-based TFTP client/server and PC-based Xmodem transfer. I will limit this discussion to the target side. Complete implementation details are beyond the scope of this discussion. (Refer to the CD for a full source listing.)

Both Xmodem and TFTP are "lock step" protocols, meaning that when one end sends some data, it doesn't send any new data until it receives acknowledgment from the other end indicating that the data was received. Although this design slows things down a bit, especially with respect to TFTP, the lock step approach offers the benefit of simplicity.

Xmodem

I think Xmodem has been around since dirt. Xmodem is one of those things that just won't go away, which is good because Xmodem can be found just about anywhere and it's not too difficult to implement. Xmodem has spawned many variants, including derivatives that support CRC versus checksum, 128- versus 1024-byte packets, and multiple files per transfer. I won't discuss these variants here, because my focus is MicroMonitor's Xmodem support — not the larger protocol. Keep in mind that MicroMonitor assumes that the target is communicating with the host via an error-free connection, so consequently the Xmodem implementation doesn't need to be very robust. The point of the discussion is to give you a feel for the Xmodem protocol as it is used in MicroMonitor and to let you experience a basic Xmodem implementation for a very "blue sky" environment.

This implementation of Xmodem is primarily based on two important functions: Xup() and Xdown(). These functions provide upload and download capability, respectively. Both functions use the same data structures to describe and track a transfer. Listing 10.1 shows the declaration for this structure.

Listing 10.1   The Xmodem Control Structure.

```
struct xinfo {
    uchar   sno;            /* Sequence number.                          */
    uchar   pad;            /* Unused, padding.                          */
    int     xfertot;        /* Running total of transfer.                */
    int     pktlen;         /* Length of packet (128 or 1024).           */
    int     pktcnt;         /* Running tally of number of packets processed. */
    int     filcnt;         /* Number of files transferred by ymodem.    */
    long    size;           /* Size of upload.                           */
    ulong   flags;          /* Storage for various runtime flags.        */
    ulong   base;           /* Starting address for data transfer.       */
    ulong   dataddr;        /* Running address for data transfer.        */
    int     errcnt;         /* Keep track of errors (used in verify mode). */
    char    *firsterrat;    /* Pointer to location of error detected when */
                            /* transfer is in verify mode.               */
    char    fname[TFSNAMESIZE];
};
```

Regardless of whether the Xmodem transfer is an upload or a download, the transfer starts with a command at the MicroMonitor CLI. Once the command is issued, the Xmodem code waits for the other end (usually HyperTerminal in Windows) to connect and begin the actual transfer.

Listing 10.2 shows the Xup() function, which is called when the user requests a file transfer from the target to the host.

Listing 10.2   Xup().

```
static int
Xup(struct xinfo *xip)
{
    uchar   c, buf[PKTLEN_128];
    int     done, pktlen;
    long    actualsize;

    Mtrace("Xup starting");

    actualsize = xip->size;

    if (xip->size & 0x7f) {
        xip->size += 128;
        xip->size &= 0xffffff80L;
    }

    printf("Upload %ld bytes from 0x%lx\n",xip->size,(ulong)xip->base);

    /* Startup synchronization... */
    /* Wait to receive a NAK or 'C' from receiver. */
    done = 0;
    while(!done) {
        c = (uchar)getchar();
        switch(c) {
        case NAK:
            done = 1;
            Mtrace("CSM");
            break;
        case 'C':
            xip->flags |= USECRC;
            done = 1;
            Mtrace("CRC");
            break;
        default:
            break;
```

```
            }
    }

done = 0;
xip->sno = 1;
xip->pktcnt = 0;
while(!done) {
    c = (uchar)putPacket((uchar *)(xip->dataaddr),xip);
    switch(c) {
    case ACK:
        xip->sno++;
        xip->pktcnt++;
        xip->size -= xip->pktlen;
        xip->dataaddr += xip->pktlen;
        Mtrace("A");
        break;
    case NAK:
        Mtrace("N");
        break;
    case CAN:
        done = -1;
        Mtrace("C");
        break;
    case EOT:
        done = -1;
        Mtrace("E");
        break;
    default:
        done = -1;
        Mtrace("<%2x>",c);
        break;
    }
    if (xip->size <= 0) {
        rputchar(EOT);
        getchar();  /* Flush the ACK */
        break;
    }
```

```
        Mtrace("!");
    }
    Mtrace("Xup_done.");
    return(0);
}
```

NOTE

The Mtrace() function (see Listing 10.2) deserves a quick side note. The Xmodem code uses Mtrace() to help with debugging. The Xmodem protocol is using the same serial port as is usually used by printf(), so you can't add printf statements to debug the code because adding printf statements screws up the protocol. The Mtrace() (or memory trace) function looks like printf(), but, instead of the output going to the console, it goes to an internal RAM buffer so that after the protocol completes, you have the option to dump the contents of that buffer to see a trace log of what was happening. Mtrace() is a useful tool to have for any case where you are writing code in an area that does not allow printing through the serial port. Now back to Xup().

Right off the bat this function must deal with an Xmodem "yukism." The size of the transfer must be converted to a mod-128 size. The smallest packet size for Xmodem is 128 bytes, so if the actual transfer size is 129 bytes, Xmodem sends 256. After padding the data size, the function attempts to synchronize with the receiver by listening for the other end to connect. The program at the other end of the serial connection sends either a NAK (negative acknowledgement) to initiate a transfer using checksums or the character C to initiate a transfer using CCITT CRC16. After this synchronization is finished, the packets begin to flow. This Xmodem implementation is about as simple as it can get. Function Xup() sends each packet and then waits for a response using the putPacket() function. The putPacket() function (not shown) sends the SOH (start of header) character, increments the sequence number by one, sends the sequence number and its complement, sends the packet data and checksum or CRC, then waits for the response, and returns to the calling Xup() function. If the response is a positive acknowledgment (ACK), then Xup() continues with the next packet. Otherwise, it quits. No retransmission, nothing fancy. If a transfer fails, then it is up to the user to try again.

Xdown()

The Xdown() function (see Listing 10.3) is called from the xmodem command when the user requests a file transfer from the host to target.

Listing 10.3   Xdown().

```
/* Xdown():
 * Called when a transfer from host to target is being made (considered
 * a download).
 */

static int
Xdown(struct xinfo *xip)
{
    long    timeout;
    char    c, tmppkt[PKTLEN_1K];
    int     done;

    xip->sno = 0x01;
    xip->pktcnt = 0;
    xip->errcnt = 0;
    xip->xfertot = 0;
    xip->firsterrat = 0;

    /* Startup synchronization... */
    /* Continuously send NAK or 'C' until sender responds. */
    Mtrace("Xdown");
    while(1) {
        if (xip->flags & USECRC)
            rputchar('C');
        else
            rputchar(NAK);
        timeout = LoopsPerSecond;
        while(!gotachar() && timeout)
            timeout--;
        if (timeout)
            break;
    }

    done = 0;
    Mtrace("Got response");
```

```
   while(done == 0) {
       c = (char)getchar();
       switch(c) {
       case SOH:                   /* 128-byte incoming packet */
           Mtrace("O");
           xip->pktlen = PKTLEN_128;
           done = getPacket(tmppkt,xip);
           break;
       case STX:                   /* 1024-byte incoming packet */
           Mtrace("T");
           xip->pktlen = PKTLEN_1K;
           done = getPacket(tmppkt,xip);
           break;
       case CAN:
           Mtrace("C");
           done = -1;
           break;
       case EOT:
           Mtrace("E");
           rputchar(ACK);
           done = xip->xfertot;
           printf("\nRcvd %d pkt%c (%d bytes)\n",xip->pktcnt,
               xip->pktcnt > 1 ? 's' : ' ',xip->xfertot);
           break;
       case ESC:          /* User-invoked abort */
           Mtrace("X");
           done = -1;
           break;
       default:
           Mtrace("<%02x>",c);
           done = -1;
           break;
       }
       Mtrace("!");
   }
   if (xip->flags & VERIFY) {
       if (xip->errcnt)
```

```
            printf("%d errors, first at 0x%lx\n",
                xip->errcnt,(ulong)(xip->firsterrat));
        else
            printf("verification passed\n");
    }
    return(done);
}
```

If `Xdown()` looks similar to `Xup()`, that is because it is. `Xdown()` is just the other end of the protocol. At the top of Listing 10.3 is the synchronization step. This time this code is *sending* either the `C` or `NAK` (depending on how the transfer was configured) and then waiting for the response. Once the response is received, the packets once again begin to flow, but this time the packets flow in the other direction (into target memory). In this direction, packets are announced by either of two bytes: `SOH` and `STX`. `SOH` indicates an incoming packet of 128 bytes, and `STX` indicates a 1024-byte inbound packet. The `getPacket()` function (not shown) does the real work of pulling in the packets and sending a response character. (The `getPacket()` function is similar to `putPacket()` on the `Xup()` side.) After the sender has completed the transmission, the sender sends an end-of-transmission (EOT) character to indicate that the transfer is done. Receipt of the EOT character causes the loop to terminate, completing the transaction. A few other situations can abort the transfer, but these situations are the exception.

Notice the `VERIFY` flag check just after the loop. The `VERIFY` flag check is a useful option added to MicroMonitor's Xmodem implementation. This option allows a host to download and verify (not overwrite, just compare) the downloaded data to data already resident on the target.

Xmodem in MicroMonitor

Xmodem gives MicroMonitor the ability to transfer files to and from the target. This file transfer can be to/from files or to/from raw memory in the target. The verification option mentioned above is useful for simple memory tests or to verify that code did not overwrite some block of data. The actual implementation of Xmodem in MicroMonitor supports most of the options, such as 128/1024-byte packets, checksum and CRC, Ymodem extensions, and so forth. Refer to the CD for more detail.

One last note on MicroMonitor's Xmodem implementation. The boot monitor resides in boot flash memory and occasionally the boot flash memory might need to be updated. You could just use a programmer to burn a new device and install it; however, MicroMonitor's Xmodem hooks up with the flash driver code to allow the user to download a binary image and automatically re-burn the monitor code on board. This feature is a nice convenience, especially when you are porting the monitor to a new target. After the serial port and flash drivers are in place, you can use Xmodem to make quick boot flash updates while you are working on other aspects of the monitor port.

TFTP

Trivial File Transfer Protocol (TFTP) could be considered the Xmodem of Ethernet. TFTP is a basic lock-step protocol that supports file transfer using UDP. MicroMonitor supports both the TFTP client and the TFTP server. You can use the server to transfer files in either direction. The client can only retrieve files from a remote server. Like Xmodem, TFTP is too big a topic to cover completely in this book. However, I will touch on some of the MicroMonitor functions that support TFTP.

processTFTP()

The processTFTP() function (see Listing 10.4) is called out of processPACKET() (see Listing 9.5). For TFTP transfers, processTFTP() must handle five different standard requests (or opcodes):

- TFTP_RRQ — Read request. A remote system is requesting that a file or data be transferred from this target to the remote system.
- TFTP_WRQ — Write request. A remote system is requesting that a file or data be transferred to this target from the remote system.
- TFTP_DAT — A packet of data is incoming, as a result of acknowledging a previous WRQ or DAT.
- TFTP_ACK — A packet of data has been received at the remote system, meaning that the next packet can be sent.
- TFTP_ERR — Some type of error occurred.

The switch statement at the bottom of Listing 10.4 dispatches the processing of each of these opcodes.

Listing 10.4   processTFTP().

```
int
processTFTP(struct ether_header *ehdr,ushort size)
{
    static  uchar   *oaddr;
    struct  ip *ihdr;
    struct  Udphdr *uhdr;
```

```
uchar    *data;
int      count, tmpcount;
ushort   opcode, block, errcode;
char     *comma, *tftpp, *filename, *mode, *errstring, msg[64];

if (TftpTurnedOff) {
    SendICMPUnreachable(ehdr,ICMP_UNREACHABLE_PORT);
    return(0);
}

ihdr = (struct ip *)(ehdr + 1);
uhdr = (struct Udphdr *)((char *)ihdr + IP_HLEN(ihdr));
tftpp = (char *)(uhdr + 1);
opcode = *(ushort *)tftpp;

switch (opcode) {
```

Notice that processTFTP() (see Listing 10.4) takes arguments similar to the processPacket() arguments. The processTFTP() function does a lot of structure overlays onto the incoming packet. If the TFTP facility is disabled for some reason, the TftpTurnedOff flag is set. When this flag is set, the target responds to incoming packets with an ICMP Unreachable Port message.

Listing 10.5   Initiating a Download.

```
case htons(TFTP_WRQ):
    filename = tftpp+2;
    if ((EtherVerbose & SHOW_TFTP) || (!MFLAGS_NOTFTPPRN()))
        printf("TFTP rcvd WRQ: file %s\n", filename);

    if (!tftpStartSrvrFilter(ehdr,uhdr))
        return(0);

    mode = filename;
    while(*mode)
        mode++;
    mode++;
```

```
/* Destination of WRQ can be an address (0x...), environment
 * variable ($...) or a TFS filename...
 */
if ((filename[0] == '$') && (getenv(&filename[1]))) {
    TftpAddr = (uchar *)strtol(getenv(&filename[1]),(char **)0,0);
}
else if ((filename[0] == '0') && (filename[1] == 'x')) {
    TftpAddr = (uchar *)strtol(filename,(char **)0,0);
}
else {
    if (MFLAGS_NOTFTPOVW() && tfsstat(filename)) {
        SendTFTPErr(ehdr,6,"File already exists.",1);
        return(0);
    }
    TftpAddr = (uchar *)getAppRamStart();
    strncpy(TftpTfsFname,filename,sizeof(TftpTfsFname)-1);
    TftpTfsFname[sizeof(TftpTfsFname)-1] = 0;
}
TftpCount = -1; /* not used with WRQ, so clear it */

/* Convert mode to lower case... */
strtolower(mode);
if (!strcmp(mode,"netascii"))
    TftpWrqMode = MODE_NETASCII;
else if (!strcmp(mode,"octet"))
    TftpWrqMode = MODE_OCTET;
else {
    SendTFTPErr(ehdr,0,"Mode not supported.",1);
    TftpWrqMode = MODE_NULL;
    TftpCount = -1;
    return(0);
}
block = 0;
tftpLastblock = block;
oaddr = TftpAddr;
TftpChopCount = 0;
break;
```

The first opcode processed is TFTP_WRQ (Listing 10.5). Notice immediately that the switch tests htons(TFTP_WRQ), not just TFTP_WRQ. Wrapping the reference in this macro guarantees that the incoming opcode value and the opcode value on the target have the same endian-ness. The first step is to verify that the local TFTP server is in the proper state to deal with a WRQ request (the call to TftpStartSrvrFilter(), not shown). If the state is incorrect, the response is a TFTP_ERR message (in Tftp-StartSrvrFilter()), and the return value is zero.

The incoming packet contains the filename and the mode by which the file is to be transferred. This implementation accepts three different types of file names and two different modes, as follows:

Filename options:

- a standard name, in which case the data is first copied to RAM and then transferred via tfsadd() to TFS.
- a hexadecimal address, assumed to start with 0x, in which case the data is transferred directly to the specified location.
- an address stored in a shell variable, assumed to start with $, in which case the data is transferred to the hexadecimal address contained in the shell variable.

Mode options:

- netascii for transfer of ASCII files. Incoming \r\n is replaced with \n.
- octet for transfer of binary files. Incoming data is left untouched.

These options give the user the ability to transfer directly to RAM through a hard-coded address or through the contents of a shell variable. (Yes, this statement does mean that you cannot transfer a file whose name starts with 0x or $, but this restriction is reasonable.) Notice the macro MFLAGS_NOTFTPOVW(). This line tests whether the requested file transfer is to a file that already exists. If a flag in the system has been set that disallows the overwrite of an existing file through TFTP, the monitor returns TFTP_ERR. That's about it for TFTP_WRQ. The server state advances to "receiving" and the request is acknowledged (with ACK).

Listing 10.6   Initiating an Upload.

```
case htons(TFTP_RRQ):
    filename = tftpp+2;
    if ((EtherVerbose & SHOW_TFTP) || (!MFLAGS_NOTFTPPRN()))
        printf("TFTP rcvd RRQ: file %s\n",filename);
    if (!tftpStartSrvrFilter(ehdr,uhdr))
        return(0);
```

```
        mode = filename;
        while(*mode) mode++;
        mode++;
        comma = strchr(filename,',');
        if (!comma) {
            TFILE   *tfp;
            tfp = tfsstat(filename);
            if (!tfp) {
                SendTFTPErr(ehdr,0,"File not found, try 'address,count'",1);
                TftpCount = -1;
                return(0);
            }
            TftpAddr = (uchar *)TFS_BASE(tfp);
            TftpCount = TFS_SIZE(tfp);
        }
        else {
            comma++;
            TftpAddr = (uchar *)strtol(filename,(char **)0,0);
            TftpCount = strtol(comma,(char **)0,0);
        }
        if (strcmp(mode,"octet")) {
            SendTFTPErr(ehdr,0,"Must use binary mode",1);
            TftpCount = -1;
            return(0);
        }
        block = tftpLastblock = 1;
        tftpGotoState(TFTPACTIVE);
        SendTFTPData(ehdr,block,TftpAddr,TftpCount);
        return(0);
```

Listing 10.6 shows the code that processes TFTP_RRQ requests. The code once again begins with some state verification (the call to tftpStartSrvrFilter().) The format for an incoming packet is similar to that recognized by TFTP_WRQ. This implementation accepts two different filename syntaxes:

- a standard file name, in which case the data is read from a file in TFS.
- a hexadecimal address and size formatted as 0xADDR,SIZE. This syntax supports the ability to use a TFTP client to retrieve a raw block of memory from the target. (Once again, the syntax does preclude certain filenames).

After determining the address and size of the data to be transferred, the code checks the mode. In this direction, only `octet` is supported. Finally, state is logged, the first data block is sent, and the monitor enters a wait state, pending an incoming `TFTP_ACK` opcode.

Listing 10.7   Receiving a Data Packet.

```
case htons(TFTP_DAT):
      block = ntohs(*(ushort *)(tftpp+2));
      count = ntohs(uhdr->uh_ulen) - (sizeof(struct Udphdr)+4);

      if (EtherVerbose & SHOW_TFTP)
          printf("  Rcvd TFTP_DAT (%d,blk=%d)\n",count,block);


      /* This TFTP_DAT may be from a local "get" request... */
      if (TftpState == TFTPSENTRRQ) {
          tftpLastblock = 0;
          if (block == 1) {
              TftpRmtPort = ntohs(uhdr->uh_sport);
              tftpGotoState(TFTPACTIVE);
          }
          else {
              SendTFTPErr(ehdr,0,"invalid block",1);
              return(0);
          }
      }
      /* Since we don't ACK the final TFTP_DAT from the server until after
       * the file has been written, it is possible that we will receive
       * a re-transmitted TFTP_DAT from the server.  This is ignored by
       * Sending another ACK...
       */
      else if ((TftpState == TFTPIDLE) && (block == tftpLastblock)) {
          SendTFTPAck(ehdr,block);
          if (EtherVerbose & SHOW_TFTP)
              printf("  (packet ignored)\n");
          return(0);
      }
```

```
    else if (TftpState != TFTPACTIVE) {
        SendTFTPErr(ehdr,0,"invalid state",1);
        return(0);
    }


    if (ntohs(uhdr->uh_sport) != TftpRmtPort) {
        SendTFTPErr(ehdr,0,"invalid source port",0);
        return(0);
    }
    if (block == tftpLastblock) {     /* If block didn't increment, assume */
        SendTFTPAck(ehdr,block);      /* retry.  Ack it and return here.   */
        return(0);                    /* If block != tftpLastblock+1,      */
    }                                 /* return an error, and quit now.    */
    else if (block != tftpLastblock+1) {
        SendTFTPErr(ehdr,0,"Unexpected block number",1);
        TftpCount = -1;
        return(0);
    }
    TftpCount += count;
    oaddr = TftpAddr;
    tftpLastblock = block;
    data = (uchar *)(tftpp+4);


    /* If count is less than TFTP_DATAMAX, this must be the last
     * packet of the transfer, so clean up state here.
     */
    if (count < TFTP_DATAMAX) {
        tftpGotoState(TFTPIDLE);
    }
```

Listing 10.7 shows how TFTP_DAT opcodes are handled. To determine which end initiated the transfer, the code tests TftpState. If this state variable has been set to TFTPSENTRRQ then the current TFTP_DAT packet is the result of the target TFTP client issuing a "tftp get" to a remote server. Otherwise the data packet was sent in response to a TFTP_WRQ from a remote client. The code must also cover the case of the remote machine sending a duplicate TFTP_DAT. Often packets are retransmitted because a write to TFS is so large that the remote host times out before the target can finish transferring it to flash. Note that the receiving computer does not send the ACK until *after* the file has been successfully written to TFS; hence, large files can trigger retransmissions. The final state check just makes sure that the system is already in the active mode waiting for data. Further sanity checks verify that the host sending the data is the same host that sent the RRQ previously. The receiving code also verifies the block number.

Listing 10.8   Saving the Data.

```
/* Copy data from enet buffer to TftpAddr location... */
    tmpcount = count;
    while(tmpcount) {
        if (TftpWrqMode == MODE_NETASCII) {
            if (*data == 0x0d) {
                data++;
                tmpcount--;
                TftpChopCount++;
                continue;
            }
        }

        *TftpAddr = *data;
        if (*TftpAddr != *data) {
            sprintf(msg,"Write error at 0x%lx",(ulong)TftpAddr);
            SendTFTPErr(ehdr,0,msg,1);
            TftpCount = -1;
            return(0);
        }
        TftpAddr++;
        data++;
        tmpcount--;
    }

    /* If the transfer is complete and TftpTfsFname[0] is non-zero,
     * then write the data to the specified TFS file... Note that a
     * comma in the filename is used to find the start of (if any)
     * the TFS flags string.  A second comma, marks the info field.
     */
```

```
    if ((count < TFTP_DATAMAX) && (TftpTfsFname[0])) {
        char *fcomma, *icomma, *flags, *info;
        int err;

        info = (char *)0;
        flags = (char *)0;
        fcomma = strchr(TftpTfsFname,',');
        if (fcomma) {
            icomma = strchr(fcomma+1,',');
            if (icomma) {
                *icomma = 0;
                info = icomma+1;
            }
            if (tfsctrl(TFS_FATOB,(long)(fcomma+1),0) != -1) {
                *fcomma = 0;
                flags = fcomma+1;
            }
            else {
                SendTFTPErr(ehdr,0,"Invalid flag spec.",1);
                TftpTfsFname[0] = 0;
                break;
            }
        }
        if ((EtherVerbose & SHOW_TFTP) || (!MFLAGS_NOTFTPPRN()))
            printf("TFTP adding file: '%s' to TFS.\n",TftpTfsFname);
        err = tfsadd(TftpTfsFname,info,flags,
            (char *)getAppRamStart(),TftpCount+1-TftpChopCount);
        if (err != TFS_OKAY) {
            sprintf(msg,"TFS err: %s",
                (char *)tfsctrl(TFS_ERRMSG,err,0));
            SendTFTPErr(ehdr,0,msg,1);
        }
        TftpTfsFname[0] = 0;
    }
break;
```

After all the sanity checks for TFTP_DAT state, the code in Listing 10.8 can assume that it is time to start the transfer of data from Ethernet packet buffer space to some other target memory. If netascii mode is set, 0x0d (\r) characters are dropped as necessary. An incoming packet size less than the max size of TFTP_DATAMAX (512) signals the end of the transfer. If appropriate, the data is transferred to a file in TFS.

NOTE

To support TFS's flags and info fields, the filename can be comma-delimited as follows: filename, flags, info ; where filename is the name of the file, flags is a string with all of the flags (or attributes) associated with the file, and info is the information field associated with the TFS file (whitespace is illegal in this comma-delimited string). This format allows a standard TFTP client to specify a destination file (in TFS) with flags and info fields included in the string. The only (reasonable) limitation is that the comma must be used as a field delimiter.

Listing 10.9   Processing and ACK.

```
case htons(TFTP_ACK):
    block = ntohs(*(ushort *)(tftpp+2));
    if (TftpState != TFTPACTIVE) {
        SendTFTPErr(ehdr,0,
            "Illegal server state for incoming TFTP_ACK",1);
        return(0);
    }
    if (EtherVerbose & SHOW_TFTP)
        printf("  Rcvd TFTP_ACK (blk#%d)\n",block);

    if (block == tftpLastblock) {
        if (TftpCount > TFTP_DATAMAX) {
            TftpCount -= TFTP_DATAMAX;
            TftpAddr += TFTP_DATAMAX;
            SendTFTPData(ehdr,block+1,TftpAddr,TftpCount);
            tftpLastblock++;
        }
        else if (TftpCount == TFTP_DATAMAX) {
            TftpCount = 0;
            tftpGotoState(TFTPIDLE);
            SendTFTPData(ehdr,block+1,TftpAddr,0);
            tftpLastblock++;
```

```
        }
        else {
            TftpAddr += TftpCount;
            TftpCount = 0;
            tftpGotoState(TFTPIDLE);
        }
    }
    else if (block == tftpLastblock-1) {
        SendTFTPData(ehdr,block+1,TftpAddr,TftpCount);
    }
    else {
        SendTFTPErr(ehdr,0,"Blockno confused",1);
        TftpCount = -1;
        return(0);
    }
    return(0);
```

The TFTP_ACK acknowledgment notifies the recipient that the previous packet was
received and that the other end is ready for another packet. Thus, each ACK potentially triggers another packet transmission. Like the other handlers, this code begins
with sanity checks. If all is well, the code then decides whether enough data remains
to fill a packet. If not, this packet is the last. Note that a final packet of exactly 512
bytes is processed as a special case. The value in TftpCount keeps track of how much
data is left to be sent, and TftpAddr is the location from which the data is to be sent.
If the block number is correct, the handler sends a new packet. If the block number is
one less than expected, then the code resends the previous packet. All other block
numbers trigger an error response.

Listing 10.10   Handling Errors.

```
    case htons(TFTP_ERR):
        errcode = ntohs(*(ushort *)(tftpp+2));
        errstring = tftpp+4;
        if (EtherVerbose & SHOW_TFTP)
            printf("  Rcvd TFTP_ERR #%d (%s)\n",errcode,errstring);
        TftpCount = -1;
        tftpGotoState(TFTPERROR);
        strncpy(TftpErrString,errstring,sizeof(TftpErrString)-1);
        TftpErrString[sizeof(TftpErrString)-1] = 0;
```

```
            return(0);
        default:
            if (EtherVerbose & SHOW_TFTP)
                printf("  Rcvd <%04x> unknown TFTP opcode\n", opcode);
            SendTFTPErr(ehdr,0,"Unexpected opcode received.",1);
            TftpCount = -1;
            return(-1);
        }
    SendTFTPAck(ehdr,block);
    return(0);
}
```

The TFTP_ERR opcode requires very little programming. As shown in Listing 10.10, the header merely changes the state to error, records the incoming error, and prints an error message to the console. Listing 10.10 also shows how the default handler deals with an unexpected opcode.

Field Upgrade Capability

In this chapter, I have discussed some of the implementation details of Xmodem and TFTP. Both protocols are "old reliables" and both protocols within the MicroMonitor package provide a target with the ability to update files on the target system. The code described in this chapter can be the basis for a field upgrade mechanism for an application that resides on top of MicroMonitor. Similar to the way in which I combined TFS with the CLI to form a script runner in Chapter 8, you can combine TFS with either Xmodem or TFTP (or both) to form a field upgrade mechanism. Depending on the needs of the application, the application can be left unaware of the monitor's ability to perform the upgrade, or it can become part of the upgrade facility itself. I'll discuss these two alternatives in the following sections.

Application Unaware of the Underlying Upgrade Path

The simpler way to provide for application upgrades is to keep the application unaware of the upgrade path. The application is just plain dumb. This model is similar to the model used by just about any other program on a PC or other host system. The program is installed on the system to do a job. If that job changes or if a bug is found, the program is stopped, a new program is installed, and the new program is restarted. The program code itself is totally unaware of the fact that some installation process just took place. The underlying platform (Windows, DOS, or UNIX for example) provided the capability. MicroMonitor provides this capability, assuming of course, that the target has either a serial port or Ethernet connection.

With this approach, the application resides in TFS as an executable file. The file is autobootable, so when MicroMonitor starts, it automatically starts the application. At startup, the monitor provides a mechanism to allow the autoboot sequence to abort. When the autoboot aborts, MicroMonitor is left running in a standalone mode. The TFTP and Xmodem facilities are working on the monitor, so the host can simply download a new application file as a replacement for the current application. After this download is complete, you can restart the target, and the autoboot sequence starts the new application.

Application Is Part of the Upgrade Path

An alternative approach is to build the Xmodem or TFTP code into the application. While the application is running, these facilities can be used to download files into TFS flash space. Recall that TFS executables are stored in flash memory but are executed out of RAM, so the files in TFS can be manipulated while the application is running. The advantage of this approach is that the application might be able to stay up while the upgrade is in progress; then, at some later off-hours time, the target can be reset, and the new application, which is already in TFS, can autoboot.

Summary

While you could do all of your development using an external programmer (and many have), the development process is much more efficient if you can download new code directly to the target and update the flash memory using its in-circuit programming capability. Thus, getting some kind of file transfer working should be one of your top priorities. MicroMonitor supplies support for the two most universal file transfer protocols: Xmodem and TFTP.

Typically, when bringing up a new installation of MicroMonitor, I begin by getting the serial port and Xmodem working. Even if the board includes an Ethernet interface, I often use the serial port (if available) for the initial development efforts. The Xmodem code is much smaller and simpler, and the Mtrace feature makes it easier to debug the link. Moreover, until recently at least, host-based development tools are more apt to expect a serial link to the target than a network link. Later, when I have richer debugging support functioning, I might install the TFTP support and switch to TFTP for file download.

Both protocols give you good interconnectivity. While the Xmodem implementation deliberately excludes the error handling normal in a modem-oriented implementation, it is still a compatible implementation. So long as you use it over a direct, error-free line, it should work with most Xmodem packages. The TFTP implementation is much larger, but it complies fully with the relevant request for comments (RFC). Both options include features that make them useful in the early stages of development, even when TFS isn't present or isn't fully operational.

Chapter 11

Adding the Application

I've mentioned several times that an application resides on top of the monitor. The monitor supports an application much like DOS does, with many of the same benefits. The monitor provides a platform on which the application runs. Because the application can use the monitor's API to access platform resources, it is insulated from the gory details of the underlying hardware. This chapter shows how the application and monitor can live happily together on the target system.

Different Memory Map

Because I am building an application to run on top of the monitor and because the model of the monitor is that the application is loaded from TFS to RAM space, the application's memory map becomes much simpler. As a matter of fact, all of the application can reside in the same block of RAM or DRAM space. The monitor's loader (part of TFS) automatically transfers the contents of the executable file in TFS flash to the RAM space.

Figure 11.1 Monitor Transfers File from Flash to DRAM.

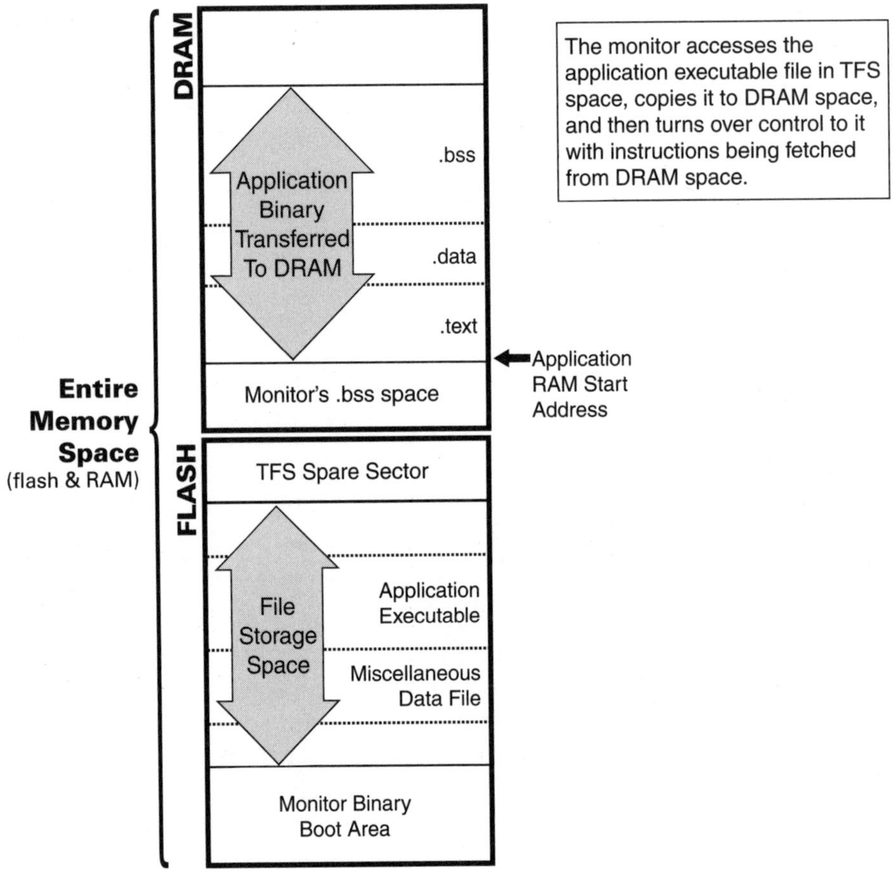

The monitor accesses the application executable file in TFS space, copies it to DRAM space, and then turns over control to it with instructions being fetched from DRAM space.

Less Intense Startup

The application can assume that it is being run out of an environment that has already booted the target. Thus, many things can be left untouched, since the monitor already takes care of them at boot time. The application doesn't need to worry about the reset vector. In fact, because the monitor has initialized all of the exception handlers, the application can ignore all but the exception handlers that are specific to its needs.

Recall that, for the monitor, all initialized data is not writable because initialized data was left in flash memory to avoid the step of copying the initialized data from boot flash to RAM. With the application loaded from TFS, this problem disappears because by default all of the text and data sections are copied from flash memory to

RAM, so immediately and without any copying by the application itself, all initialized data is writable at runtime.

Establishing an Application Stack

When the monitor transfers control to the application, the application will be using the stack space allocated to the monitor. If the application is a simple, single-threaded program, this action might be all that is needed. Thus, the application might not need to worry about creating a stack area. On the other hand, if an RTOS is to run in the application, then it is likely that the RTOS's API will deal with the per task stack allocation. Either way, it's pretty easy!

Connecting to the Monitor's API

MicroMonitor provides a hookup mechanism through which the application accesses the MicroMonitor API. This mechanism is similar in purpose to the BIOS jump table on a DOS PC. The goal is to provide a mechanism that allows the application to use some of the functionality of the monitor, without having the application know anything about where the functionality actually resides in the monitor's instruction space. A second goal is to make this hookup entirely independent of the underlying CPU. Thus, the BIOS approach, which uses a CPU-specific software interrupt, is not an option.

As you recall from Chapter 4, the reset code contains a tag called moncomptr. An excerpt from that code is repeated in Listing 11.1.

Listing 11.1   Another look at moncomptr.

```
coldstart:
    Initialize "something" to store away a state variable.
    StateOfTarget = INITIIALIZE
    JumpTo warmstart


moncomptr:
    .long moncom
```

```
warmstart:
    /* Load into StateOfTarget the parameter passed
     * to warmstart as if it was the C function:
     * warmstart(unsigned long state).
     */
```

The `moncomptr` tag is a location in the boot flash memory that does not move even if the monitor is rebuilt. The location does not change because of the tag's position relative to the reset vector code.[1] The location of this pointer is at a fixed location in the monitor's memory map, and that fixed location contains a pointer to the `moncom()` function. The location of the `moncom()` function can change each time the monitor is rebuilt, but that doesn't matter. Because the pointer is in a fixed location, the function is accessible.

The `moncom()` Function

The application must be aware of this one fixed address in the monitor (`moncomptr`) that contains a pointer to a function. This function's API is known to the application, and the hookup is made through that API. A few header files from the monitor are shared with the application, and one function, `monConnect()`, is provided to the application in source code form. The application does not need to know anything else about the memory map of the monitor.[2] The function in monitor space is called `moncom()`, for monitor communication. Listing 11.2 is a snippet of the `moncom()` function.

Listing 11.2   Function-to-Function Pointer Connection.

```
#include "monlib.h"

int
moncom(int cmd, void *arg1, void *arg2, void *arg3)
{
    int retval;

    retval = 0;
```

---

1.   The `reset` vector is at a fixed location, and `moncomptr` is at a fixed position relative to the reset vector address; hence, the address of `moncomptr` is fixed.

2.   Not quite true but accurate for the context of this discussion. The application does need to know of the monitor's memory map so that it does not use space that is already occupied by the monitor.

```
    switch(cmd) {
        case GETMONFUNC_PUTCHAR:
            *(ulong *)arg1 = (ulong)rputchar;
            break;
        case GETMONFUNC_GETCHAR:
            *(ulong *)arg1 = (ulong)getchar;
            break;
        case GETMONFUNC_GOTACHAR:
            *(ulong *)arg1 = (ulong)gotachar;
            break;
        etc......
    }
}
```

The monConnect() Function

The application knows where this monmcom() function is in monitor space because a pointer to this function is stored in the well-known address (the application must know this well-known address). Now, other functions in application space can use this function to "connect" the application to the monitor, and this juncture is where monConnect() comes in. The monConnect() function takes as one of its arguments, the well-known address.

Listing 11.3   The monConnect() Function.

```
static int  (*_rputchar)(), (*_getchar)(), (*_gotachar)();

/* monConnect():
 * This must be the first call by the application code to talk to the
 * monitor.  It is expecting three incoming function pointers:
 *
 * mon: Points to the monitor's _moncom function;
 *      This is a "well-known" address because the monitor and
 *      application code (two separately linked binaries) must
 *      know it.
 * lock:   Points to a function in the application code that will be
 *      used by the monitor as a lock-out function (some kind of
 *      semaphore in the application).
```

```
 * unlock:  Points to a function in the application code that will be
 *       used by the monitor as an un-lock-out function (undo
 *       whatever lock-out mechanism was done by lock).
 */
void
monConnect(int (*mon)(), void (*lock)(), void (*unlock)())
{
    /* Assign incoming lock and unlock functions... */
    _monlock = lock;
    _monunlock = unlock;

    /* If the mon pointer is non-zero, then make the
     * mon_ connections...
     */
    if (mon) {

        _moncom = mon;

    /* Make the connections between "mon_" functions that are
     * symbolically accessible by the application and the
     * corresponding functions that exist in the monitor...
     */
        _moncom(GETMONFUNC_PUTCHAR,&_rputchar,0,0);
        _moncom(GETMONFUNC_GETCHAR,&_getchar,0,0);
        _moncom(GETMONFUNC_GOTACHAR,&_gotachar,0,0);

    }

}
```

Both the monconn() function in the monitor and the monConnect() function in the application compile with the same monlib.h file. This header file contains all of the GETMONFUNC_XXX definitions. When the application calls monConnect, the application connects the function pointers _rputchar, _getchar, and _gotachar to the corresponding rputchar, getchar, and gotachar functions in the monitor's space. At this point, the application could just use those function pointers. However, it would be nicer for the application to have functions (not pointers) to access the monitor code. Moreover, if the monitor is used in a multitasking environment, then it (and all of its API) becomes a shared resource requiring some form of synchronized access control. If the application always accessed the monitor through a function, then that function could wrap the monitor access with a semaphore or some other synchronization mechanism prior to entering monitor code space. This code resides in application space and can be used to call the monitor `rputchar` service. The code in Listing 11.4 implements this kind of protection.

Listing 11.4   **Adding Locking to** `putchar()`.

```
int
mon_putchar(uchar c)
{
    int ret;

    if (_monlock)
        _monlock();

    ret = _rputchar(c);

    if (_monunlock)
        _monunlock();

    return(ret);
}
```

The monitor synchronization functions are optional and would be set up using the second and third arguments of the `monConnect()` function (see Listing 11.3).

To summarize the mechanism:

- At startup, the application calls `monConnect()`, passing it the well-known address and pointers to lock and unlock functions (NULL pointers will effectively disable this synchronization feature.).

- The `monConnect()` function calls `moncom()` in monitor space through the well-known address. Each call to `moncom()` loads a function pointer in application space with the address of the corresponding function in monitor space, using the `GETMONFUNC_XXX` macro referenced in the call to `moncom()`.

- When `monConnect()` completes, the application can call directly to a full set of mon_xxx functions (like `mon_putchar()`, see Listing 11.4) in application space.

monConnect() establishes a lot more than the three functional connections shown in Listing 11.3. The other connections are all constructed in the same way as the three shown in this example.

The Application start() Function

The entry point of a simple application is typically called start. When booting an application through MicroMonitor, start can immediately be a C function. The address of start is the entry point that the monitor calls after the application is loaded. A typical start() function is shown in Listing 11.5.

Listing 11.5   A Typical start() Function.

```
#include "monlib.h"


int
start(void)
{
    char    **argv;
    int     argc;

    /* Connect the application to the monitor.  This must be done
     * prior to the application making any other attempts to use the
     * "mon_" functions provided by the monitor.
     */
    monConnect((int(*)())(*(unsigned long *)0xfffc0000),(void *)0,(void *)0);

    /* Extract argc/argv from structure and call main(): */
    mon_getargv(&argc,&argv);

    /* Call main, then return to monitor. */
    return(main(argc,argv));
}
```

Notice in Listing 11.5 that the application doesn't even need to initialize its own .bss space. When MicroMonitor loads the application from flash to RAM, it has access to the memory map of the application and can automatically clear all .bss sections of the application prior to transferring control to the entry point.

The Application `main()` **Function**

The `main()` function of the application (see Listing 11.6) is called from `start()`. The `start()` function established the connection with the monitor through the `monConnect()` call and immediately executed the `mon_getargv()` API function to retrieve an argument list from the monitor's space. This argument list can be built by the monitor's `argv` command, or it is automatically loaded when a TFS-based executable is called from the monitor command line. Thus a `main()` function in an application running on the monitor basically looks like any other `main()` function.

Listing 11.6   `main()`.

```
#include "monlib.h"

main(int argc,char *argv[])
{
    int     i;
    char    *env;

    for(i=0;i<argc;i++) {
        mon_printf("argv[%d] = %s\n",i,argv[i]);
    }

    mon_printf("Hello embedded world!\n");
    env = mon_getenv("ENV");
    if (env) {
        mon_printf(" The ENV variable is : %s\n",env);
    }
    mon_appexit(0);
}
```

The three different `mon_xxx` calls in the example of Listing 11.6 demonstrate additional API functions available to the application when the monitor is present. Some key features are:

- applications that are loaded from TFS can be passed different argument lists to invoke different actions depending on the need;
- the application immediately has access to the monitor's console interface through `mon_printf()`;

- shell variables created in monitor space are accessible by the application through the `mon_getenv()` API call;
- the application can return control to the monitor by either returning to the caller of `start()` or by issuing the `mon_appexit()` API call.

Application-Originated Drivers

The monitor has its own set of drivers for serial ports and Ethernet. Chapter 9 discussed MicroMonitor's Ethernet features. As you have seen, some of the functionality of the serial port connected to the console is made available to the application (through `mon_printf()` and `mon_putchar()`, for instance). Recall that all of MicroMonitor's drivers are polled, so high performance applications probably need to override the monitor and establish new, probably interrupt-driven, drivers. Establishing new drivers is perfectly acceptable because the monitor imposes no kernel-level/user-level restriction. Hence, interfacing to the device directly is fine. The driver interface depends on RTOS and hardware details beyond the scope of this discussion. The point is that the application is not forced to use the facilities provided by MicroMonitor (refer to Figure 3.1, page 67, for a better view of this).

Application-Based CLI Uses Monitor CLI

Assume I have an application that wants to interface to the console port with its own CLI. The application has installed its own serial port drivers and uses its own interface to the user. However, I still want the application to be able to use some of the commands in the monitor. The application has application-specific commands, but the monitor still has a lot of useful facilities for software/hardware analysis and easy interface to the file system. It's very easy to extend the application's command set to include the monitor's command set because the CLI processing of MicroMonitor can be accessed by one function (`docommand()`) and because the application can access `docommand()` through the monitor API function called `mon_docommand()`. So, the application's CLI can simply pass all unknown command strings (strings that do not parse into an application-specific command) to `mon_docommand()` for further processing by the monitor's CLI.

In the CLI chapter, I pointed out that the monitor ignores (or strips off) a leading underscore from the incoming command string. Now, given the context of an application running on top of the monitor, I can better explain why this behavior is useful. It is very possible that there are duplicate command names in the application and monitor (The `help` command is a good example.). To access the monitor's version of the command, the user precedes the command with an underscore. The application's command processor does not recognize the token; it is passed to `mon_docommand()`,

and the underscore is stripped off. Thus, help is processed by the application's CLI, and _help is passed to the monitor's CLI.

This case where the application's CLI falls through to the monitor's CLI deserves closer inspection. The interface to the serial port that the monitor normally uses is now changed (because the application has most likely established a new serial driver). If a monitor command is called through the application's CLI, how can it print to the console? We can address this problem through a small modification to the putchar() function (see Listing 11.7).

Listing 11.7   putchar().

```
int
putchar(int C)
{
    extern int  (*remoteputchar)();
    int timeout;

    if (remoteputchar) {
        return(remoteputchar(C);
    }

    for(timeout=0;timeout<MAX_WAIT;timeout++) {
        if (XMIT_HOLD_EMPTY())
            break;
    }

    if (timeout == MAX_WAIT) {
        ERROR();
    }

    STORE_XMIT_HOLD_REG((char)C);
    return((int)C);
}
```

Now putchar() includes references to the remoteputchar() function pointer. If this pointer is non-NULL, then instead of using the monitor-specific code for interfacing to the serial port, some other remote function is used. The remote function pointer is assigned to the monitor through a mechanism similiar to that used to set up the mon_XXX functions. The only difference is that this function pointer is in monitor space instead of application space. The `mon_com()` function is a wrapper around the `_moncom()` function pointer used by `monConnect()`.

```
#include "monlib.h"
mon_com(CHARFUNC_PUTCHAR,appPutchar,0,0);
```

This call tells the monitor to use the function `appPutchar()` instead of its own device interface. The function pointer `remoteputchar` (in monitor space) is loaded with the address of `appPutchar()` (in application space). Similar function replacements exist for a few other monitor device interfaces, and the logic is the same.

Scripts Run Through the Application's CLI

One last hook in MicroMonitor is worth mentioning. Suppose you are now at the application's CLI (not the monitor's CLI), and you have a script in TFS that you want to execute. You give the script some name that does not conflict with any other command name, say `widget_script`. You type `widget_script` at the application's CLI, and, through the mechanism discussed above, the command passes through to the monitor. The monitor's CLI passes it to TFS for execution as a script.

This design works fine, as long as the script contains only monitor commands. You cannot, however, use this approach to get free scripting for your applications, because, by default, the script runner uses `docommand()` (in monitor space) to process each line of the script. Application-specific commands in the script are not recognized.

However, the script runner already has provisions to address this situation. The script runner always uses a function pointer to access a CLI function. By default, this function pointer is loaded with the monitor's `docommand()` function, but this pointer can be overridden to reference a function in application space.

```
#include "tfs.h"
#include "monlib.h"
mon_tfsctrl(TFS_DOCOMMAND,(long)appDocommand,0);
```

The preceding code tells the monitor's script runner to use the function `appDocommand()` instead of the default `docommand()`. (`tfsDocommand()` is the function pointer used by the script runner.) With this single modification, the application can get free scripting. At the application's CLI, you issue the command `widget_script`. This command falls through to the monitor, and the script runner executes each command through the `appDocommand()` function that was assigned to the `tfsDocommand` function pointer. The application's CLI processes commands for both the application and monitor. Hence, the script runner in the monitor can be configured to execute commands from both the application's CLI and the monitor's CLI.

Summary

It should be evident at this point that the application can now do whatever it wants to do. You might decide not to use any of the monitor facilities, or you might choose to use only a subset of them (refer to Figure 3.1). The real point is that you can build a variety of different applications onto the underlying platform, and building on the monitor brings substantial benefits. The monitor insulates the application from many hardware details. It simplifies the application by creating a convenient execution context. Finally, it makes some advanced features, like scripting, seem almost free.

Chapter 12

Monitor-Based Debugging

I discussed some fundamental debugging steps in an earlier chapter but in the context of debugging the boot code. In this chapter, I will discuss debugging an application residing on top of MicroMonitor, using only the monitor's debugging facilities.

Unlike remote, host-directed debugging, monitor-based debugging uses only target resources and only the capabilities built into the target microprocessor. In most cases (not always), monitor-based debugging requires the ability to write into the application's instruction space. Typically, when a breakpoint is set using the monitor's command line interface (CLI), the monitor modifies the application's text space or sets some special registers in the processor. The monitor then transfers control to the application. If the instruction at the breakpoint location is executed, control is returned to the monitor's CLI.

It is relatively straightforward to give the monitor the ability to display memory. Depending on the complexity of the application being debugged, it may even be reasonable to single step and resume execution following a breakpoint. Thus the monitor can supply the minimal necessary tools for debugging. Because the monitor, however, doesn't have access to the symbolic information in the source code (nearly all of that information remains on the host with the compiler), monitor-based debugging poses some serious challenges.

For example:

- How do you display memory? Because you are running at the CLI of the target, you can't just ask for a structure by name. Instead, you probably need to look up the symbol's address in the output map file generated by the linker and ask the debugger to display memory at that address. Moreover, the monitor doesn't know anything about variable types. Because it doesn't know the symbol type, it won't know how many bytes to fetch for shorts, longs, or char strings. And you can forget about structure display.

- How do you specify a breakpoint location? Again, the lack of symbolic information changes everything. You can't just say "set a breakpoint at function foo." Instead, you must first look up the address of the function. After you know the load address, then you can issue some command, such as b 0x123456 where 0x123456 is the address where you want the breakpoint. Keep in mind, you probably need to perform this lookup every time you want to set a breakpoint at foo(), because each time you rebuild the application, the address could be different. The simplest steps can turn into tedious processes.

- How do you correlate the assembly language execution with your source code? Single-stepping is now at the assembler level, not the C level. Single-stepping at the assembler level isn't very useful for a high-level programmer.

- How does the monitor talk to the serial port? When the breakpoint occurs, the monitor takes over, but the application now owns the serial port. If the monitor reinitializes the serial port for its use, the interface between the application and the serial port is likely to be lost, which means returning control to the application is difficult.

- How does the monitor temporarily shut down the application? When the breakpoint occurs, the monitor takes over the system. If the application is an RTOS-hosted task, with interrupts enabled and a variety of different peripherals configured, how does the monitor deal with shutting all this stuff down?

The preceding list explains why monitor-based debugging isn't that popular. It ain't easy! Before you give up on it though, I'd like to re-investigate the topic and see if there just might be some breath left in the old beast.

Different Type of Debug Philosophy

First, let's be realistic about our expectations. A monitor-based debugging environment can't do everything. It's not meant to compete with a top-of-the-line in-circuit emulator (ICE). After you put aside this expectation and re-think the way certain debugging tasks are performed, I think you'll agree that monitor-based debugging offers quite a bit of functionality.

So what do you think of when you think about debugging an embedded system? You might think of a JTAG/BDM-based debug port, an emulator or logic analyzer, the `printf()` statement, or one of the many sophisticated source-level debuggers available today. Each of these has its own advantages and disadvantages. Some debuggers are very powerful but come at a hefty price. Some are tied to a particular compiler tool set, while others are only useful on certain CPU families. The JTAG-based debug port is probably the most common now because it is a good balance between cost and capability. These devices can still cost a thousand dollars, and then they are only useful if they are connected to the system, usually requiring some bulky pod to hang fairly close to the target.

I'll begin by establishing a debugging model for the boot monitor. Instead of thinking within the confines of a typical breakpoint, think about a runtime analysis that includes the breakpoint as one of its features. I will not consider single stepping, and I will not allow an application to be continued after a breakpoint turns control over to the monitor CLI. I will, however, consider auto-return breakpoints used for runtime analysis. I will also provide a certain amount of access to the symbol table (variables will be displayable as something more than just a basic memory dump). I will even support the ability to do a stack trace. The major limitation is that the monitor debugger is not able to return control to the running application after a hard breakpoint occurs (see the following Breakpoints section). If you can live with that, you will see that a lot can be done within the so-called limitations of a monitor-based debug environment.

Breakpoints

A breakpoint provides the ability to tell the application that at a particular address or event, control is to be turned over to some other authority (in this case, the monitor/debugger). When the application relinquishes control, all context is made available to the debugger so that the debugger can display local variables, dump a stack trace, and so forth. For this discussion, I will describe two distinct types of breakpoints:

- *Hard breakpoints* — Established by the monitor so that when the breakpoint occurs, the monitor's CLI takes control. There is no way to return to the application code after this breakpoint occurs unless the application is restarted.

- *Soft breakpoints* — Established by the monitor for runtime analysis (referred to before as an *auto-return* breakpoint). When the instruction at the breakpoint executes, control transfers to the monitor code (through the exception handler). After storing some information, the monitor returns control to the application in real time. Soft breakpoints come in several different types. Each type alters some state maintained by the monitor. This state information can be statistics that reflect execution behavior or control values used by the monitor itself (possibly to change the action taken by the soft breakpoint handler). For reasons I'll explain later, a soft breakpoint is harder to implement than a hard breakpoint.

The breakpoint is usually inserted into the application by replacing the instruction at the specified address with some other instruction that triggers an exception.[1] From this point on, I refer to this instruction as a *trap*. The exception handler for this trap should save the entire execution context (or register set) of the CPU. It then transfers control to some debugger-specific entry-point in the monitor. If the trap was triggered by a hard breakpoint, the monitor then presents its CLI. If the trap was triggered by a soft breakpoint, the monitor logs some state and returns control to the application. The difficulty of returning control to the application is what makes soft breakpoints more difficult than hard breakpoints.

Before returning control to the application the monitor must restore the code at the breakpoint (remember, a trap was inserted to create the breakpoint), restore all the registers that were active at the time of the breakpoint, and resume execution at the address of the breakpoint.

This last step is somewhat tricky. If the monitor simply replaces the trap with the original code, then the breakpoint is erased. To resume execution and keep the breakpoint, the monitor must somehow execute only the instruction at the breakpoint, recover control long enough to re-insert the trap instruction, and then allow the application to continue execution. Also, because changing the instruction at the breakpoint amounts to an exercise in self-modifying code, the monitor might need to take special actions to preserve cache coherency.

The full algorithm for breakpoints consists of these steps:

1. Configure the exception handler that corresponds to the trap so that it points to code owned by the monitor. To support soft breakpoints, you must also configure the processor's trace (or single-step) exception handler owned by the monitor.

2. Insert trap(s) into the instruction address space (be aware of cache).

3. Transfer control to the application you are debugging.

4. At the time of the exception, copy all registers to a local area accessible by the monitor.

5. Determine the type of exception and take the appropriate action. If the breakpoint is a hard breakpoint, branch to the monitor's CLI; otherwise, take the appropriate action based on the type of soft breakpoint and continue with Step 6.

---

1. On the 68000, the appropriate instruction is trap. For the x86, use INT3. Most CPUs have some instruction that can cause an exception, even if it's nothing more than an intentional divide by zero.

6. Install the original instruction back into the address space (be aware of cache).

7. Restore the register context.

8. Put the processor into trace mode and return from the exception to the address that now contains the original instruction. Executing the original instruction now causes a trace exception.

9. When the trace exception occurs, reinstall the trap instruction and again return control to the application. (The trap must be re-installed so that the breakpoint is active for the next time the CPU fetches from that address.)

You can avoid some of the complexity by only implementing the functionality you need. For instance, the soft breakpoint could be limited to a single break per setting. After the breakpoint is reached, your monitor would restore the original instruction (disabling the breakpoint) and resume full speed execution. This approach eliminates the complexity of Steps 8 and 9 but also eliminates the ability to take the breakpoint again in real time. To simplify things further, the whole soft breakpoint mechanism can be omitted, eliminating everything after Step 4.

Because the code for this part of the monitor is complex and extremely dependent on processor-specific techniques, I have chosen not to present any code examples here. If you are interested in the details, you can explore specific implementations on the CD.

Using Breakpoints for Code Analysis

I suspect most programmers think of breakpoints purely as tools for tracing program execution. The code analysis model I'm going to describe views the breakpoint more as an event that can be used to trigger some activity. The idea behind code analysis is to provide the developer with some convenient mechanism for gathering runtime information. This information might indicate which path the code executed, but it might also reflect other information about the executing program, such as how much stack space was used or whether a particular data structure was changed. Code analysis requires the use of the soft breakpoint mechanism described above. The important result, however, isn't that some breakpoint was encountered. The important result is the information that is collected as a result of the breakpoint events.

This section assumes that you are going to bite the bullet and implement the whole soft breakpoint mechanism discussed in the previous section. Note that the implementation of this portion of the debugger is available only with certain ports of the monitor on the CD.

To enable this style of debugging, the monitor must support some means of associating some user-defined, breakpoint-specific code with each breakpoint. In MicroMonitor, the at command creates this association. For added flexibility, the code can always perform the action or else selectively perform the action based on some condition.

The monitor command syntax is as follows

```
at {breakpoint tag} [if condition] {action}
```

The three parameters after the command are

- *Breakpoint tag* — This is the name of a particular breakpoint. The existence of a tag implies that the at command must be coordinated with some other processor-specific mechanism that sets breakpoints (using some of the methods discussed before). This tag is processor-specific because the breakpoint mechanism is processor-specific.

- *If condition* — This is an optional test that can become part of the logic to decide whether or not to perform the action. The conditions can be the non-zero return of a specified function call, an at variable reaching some count, or the at flag containing some predetermined bit setting.

- *Action* — This is the operation controlled by the command. The action can adjust state maintained by the command or simply return control to the monitor.

The following examples illustrate how to use this facility.

Example 1:

The following sequence of at commands establishes a counting breakpoint based on the exception that occurs as a result of a DATA_1RD breakpoint. The breakpoint mechanism is CPU-dependent, so, for the sake of this discussion, it might be an exception that occurs using the first data breakpoint provided by the CPU. When the exception occurs, the at handler logic is part of the exception handler, and, for each at statement established by the user, there is one pass through the logic. The first pass increments the ATV1 variable (within the context of the at command), and the second pass checks to see if ATV1 is 5. If ATV1 is 5, the logic halts the application and turns over full control to the monitor's CLI.

```
at DATA_1RD ATV1++          # Increment internal AT variable one
at DATA_1RD if ATV==5 BREAK # If ATV1 equals 5, then break
```

Example 2:

The following set of at commands breaks (transfers control to monitor CLI) when
breakpoint ADDR_1 is executed after breakpoint ADDR_2 has executed.

```
at ADDR_1 FSET01        # Set bit zero of the internal AT flag
at ADDR_1 FALL03 BREAK  # If both bits are set, then break
at ADDR_2 FCLR01        # Clear bit zero of the internal AT flag
at ADDR_2 FSET02        # Set bit 1 of the internal AT flag
```

Example 3:

The following example demonstrates the idea of using functionality within the application to aid in the code analysis. The break occurs if the function at address 0x1234
returns 1.

```
at ADDR_1 0x1234()==1 BREAK
```

Example 4:

As a final example, I'll use the at command to help detect a memory leak. Assume
ADDR_1 is malloc, ADDR_2 is free and, at the time ADDR_3 is hit, I expect there to be no
allocated memory. I can verify the differential between malloc/free calls by observing the content of the ATV1 variable after the breakpoint.

```
at ADDR_1 ATV1++        # Increment ATV1 at ADDR_1 (malloc)
at ADDR_2 ATV1--        # Decrement ATV1 at ADDR_2 (free)
at ADDR_3 BREAK         # Break at ADDR_3
```

The point of these examples is to show the power and flexibility that you get with
the at command. The backend, CPU-specific code is similar to what would be used
to implement basic breakpoints, but adding this at [if-condition] {action}
extension puts a whole new spin on monitor-based breakpoints. While the code
overhead isn't great, at actions can impose a significant real-time hit, because they
insert extra code into the runtime stream every time the breakpoint event occurs.
Whether this overhead is tolerable depends on the requirements of the application,
but, because all processing is on-board, the performance hit is usually acceptable.

Some CPUs Provide Debug Hooks

Historically, the use of monitor-based debugging has been limited by the requirement
that the instruction space be modifiable. For the vast majority of embedded systems
designs, the instruction space is not modifiable. Typically instructions are stored in
flash[2] memory or EPROM, and the CPU executes the code directly from that space.

Modern processor designs are addressing this issue. Many of today's processors are equipped with special debug capabilities that overcome this limitation. (Plus, under MicroMonitor, the application is transferred to RAM anyway, so the instruction space of an executing application is writable.)

Debug registers add to the versatility of the monitor-based debugger because now the CPU can be configured to take a breakpoint based on one instruction address (or a range) without the requirement that the instruction space be written. Additionally, some processors support data breakpoints (sometimes referred to as watchpoints). A data breakpoint triggers a trap any time a particular piece (or range) of data is accessed. Data breakpoints can usually be qualified to specify whether a trap occurs only on reads, only on writes, or on both.

The monitor must be able to deal with these added debug capabilities (different capabilities from different CPUs). Instead of implementing a generic mechanism for inserting some trap into the instruction space, a monitor for one of these machines should exploit these extra capabilities.

Data breakpoints add even more complexity to the monitor code (but they're worth it). Data breakpoints are more difficult to support because the monitor cannot use the address at which the exception occurred to determine what breakpoint triggered the exception. With data breakpoints, the breakpoint exception handler must be smart enough to look into the CPU state to determine if a data breakpoint occurred and, if multiple breakpoints were set, be able to determine which one caused the trap.

Adding Symbolic Capabilities

Though I won't go into the coding details here, it is relatively straightforward to give the monitor some symbolic capabilities. The CLI already has the plumbing necessary to recognize and evaluate script variables. It doesn't take much to extend this mechanism so that it also searches a special file for otherwise undefined symbols.

For example, if I have a file called `symtbl` in flash memory and it has the following lines in it:

```
main        0x123456
func1       0x123600
func2       0x123808
varA        0x128000
varB        0x128004
varC        0x12800c
```

---

2. Yep, flash memory can be written but not in a way that would allow our implementation of a breakpoint to be practical.

Then I execute a script with the following two lines in it:

```
echo The address of main() is %main
echo The variable 'varA' is located at %varA
```

The output

The address of main() is 0x123456
The variable varA is located at 0x128000

MicroMonitor even allows me to change the previous at command from

```
at ADDR_1 0x1234()==1 BREAK
```

to

```
at ADDR_1 %{func_name}()==1 BREAK
```

because I can replace 0x1234 with the real function name. The only thing I need is the ability to generate, from an application, the symtbl file. This ability to generate the symtbl file is dependent on the tool set (compiler/linker) that you're using, but it should be a simple process regardless.

Displaying Memory

Almost any boot monitor you use with an embedded system provides some type of memory display command. The memory display command can be a very useful tool, even for the high-level software developer. If the memory display command supports the hexadecimal and decimal display of address space and provides for 1-, 2-, and 4-byte data units, the CLI's fundamental ability to deal with symbols allows the monitor to display variables in their basic symbolic form. For example, assume I have a short variable called varB and I want to display it in decimal. I could use the following command:

```
dm -2d %varB 1
```

where dm is the display memory command, -2d is an option string indicating that the data is to be displayed in two-byte decimal units, %varB is the name of the variable to be displayed, and 1 indicates that only one unit is to be displayed. The result is that you have the ability to display variables just as you would with a high-level debugger, and all you need to do is make sure that your on-board symtbl file is synchronized with the application you're debugging.

You could go one step further and build a few simple scripts that save on the typing. For example, the following scripts display different integer formats
file int2:

```
dm -2d $ARG1 1     #Decimal 16-bit integer
```

file uint4:

```
dm -4 $ARG1 1      #Hex 32-bit integer (no -d option, means display
in hexadecimal)
```

Now instead of typing dm -2d %varB 1, the int2 script could be used:

```
int2 %varB
```

A simple -s option could also be incorporated into dm so that memory could be displayed as character strings instead of raw hexadecimal. Listing 12.1 is the start of the code for the monitor command that implements this display memory command, dm.

Listing 12.1   Code for Display Memory Command.

```
char *DmHelp[] = {
    "Display Memory",
    "-[24bdefs] {addr} [cnt]",
    " -2    short access",
    " -4    long access",
    " -b    binary",
    " -d    decimal",
    " -e    endian swap",
    " -f    fifo mode",
    " -m    use 'more'",
    " -s    string",
    " -v {var} quietly load 'var' with element at addr",
    0,
};

#define BD_NULL        0
#define BD_RAWBINARY   1
#define BD_ASCIISTRING 2

int
Dm(int argc,char *argv[])
{
    int     i, count, count_rqst, width, opt, more, size, fifo;
    int     hex_display, bin_display, endian_swap;
    char    *varname, *prfmt, *vprfmt;
    uchar   *cp, cbuf[16];
    ushort  *sp;
    ulong   *lp, add;
```

```
    width = 1;
    more = fifo = 0;
    bin_display = BD_NULL;
    hex_display = 1;
    endian_swap = 0;
    varname = (char *)0;
    while((opt=getopt(argc,argv,"24bdefmsv:")) != -1) {
        switch(opt) {
        case '2':
            width = 2;
            break;
        case '4':
            width = 4;
            break;
        case 'b':
            bin_display = BD_RAWBINARY;
            break;
        case 'd':
            hex_display = 0;
            break;
        case 'e':
            endian_swap = 1;
            break;
        case 'f':
            fifo = 1;
            break;
        case 'm':
            more = 1;
            break;
        case 'v':
            varname = optarg;
            break;
        case 's':
            bin_display = BD_ASCIISTRING;
            break;
        default:
            return(CMD_PARAM_ERROR);
```

```
        }
    }

    add = strtoul(argv[optind],(char **)0,0);

    if (argc-(optind-1) == 3) {
        count_rqst = strtoul(argv[optind+1],(char **)0,0);
        count_rqst *= width;
    }
    else
        count_rqst = 128;
```

Listing 12.1 details the argument option processing. The first few lines are a default initialization. A call to getopt() allows the user to override the default options. Options include specification of the width of the accesses (default is 1 byte; short and long accesses can be set). The ability to dump from FIFO is provided, as are a few other variations on the format of the output, such as dumping raw binary, endian-swapping the data, dumping ASCII strings, or presenting the values in decimal (instead of the default ASCII-coded hexadecimal). The final half-dozen lines of Listing 12.1 retrieve arguments from the command line to establish the address of the memory dump and the size.

Listing 12.2 lists the code that formats the result. The content of the hex_display and width variables are used to build a format string that printf uses later in the function. Two format strings are built in Listing 12.2. One format string is for the output of the data to the console (prfmt), and the other is for formatting the content of a shell variable that might have been specified by the -v option (vprfmt).

Listing 12.2   Formatting the Results.

```
    if (hex_display) {
        switch(width) {
        case 1:
            prfmt = "%02X ";
            break;
        case 2:
            prfmt = "%04X ";
            break;
        case 4:
            prfmt = "%08X ";
```

```
            break;
        }
        vprfmt = "0x%x";
    }
    else {
        switch(width) {
        case 1:
            prfmt = "%3d ";
            break;
        case 2:
            prfmt = "%5d ";
            break;
        case 4:
            prfmt = "%12d ";
            break;
        }
        vprfmt = "%d";
    }
```

Listing 12.3   Binary and ASCII Formatting.

```
    if (bin_display != BD_NULL) {
        cp = (uchar *)add;
        if (bin_display == BD_ASCIISTRING) {
            puts(cp);
            if (varname) {
                shell_sprintf(varname,vprfmt,cp+strlen(cp)+1);
            }
        }
        else {
            for(i=0;i<count_rqst;i++) {
                putchar(*cp++);
            }
        }
        putchar('\n');
        return(CMD_SUCCESS);
    }
```

If the option to display as binary or ASCII string is set, the code of Listing 12.3 is executed, and the command is completed. Note that for either of these display modes, the access width is 1 byte only.

The final loop (see Listing 12.4) is the code that dumps memory in 1-, 2-, or 4-byte units. The listing shows only the code for width = 2. The other width options are processed similarly. Every 16 bytes, a new line is started. If the -v option is used, then there is no display. The content of the specified address is simply placed into a shell variable, and the command completes. The loop itself is used to support the -m option, which, if used, prompts the user for more data to be dumped.

Listing 12.4   Controlling Data Width.

```
    do {
        count = count_rqst;

        if (width == 1) {
            ...
        }
        else if (width == 2) {
            sp = (ushort *)add;

            if (varname) {
                shell_sprintf(varname,vprfmt,
                    endian_swap ? swap2(*sp) : *sp);
            }
            else {
                while(count>0) {
                    printf("%08lx: ",(ulong)sp);
                    if (count > 16)
                        size = 16;
                    else
                        size = count;

                    for(i=0;i<size;i+=2) {
                        printf(prfmt,
                            endian_swap ? swap2(*sp) : *sp);
                        if (!fifo)
                            sp++;
```

```
                }
                putchar('\n');
                count -= size;
                if (!fifo) {
                    add += size;
                    sp = (ushort *)add;
                }
            }
        }
    }
    else if (width == 4) {
        ...
    }
} while (more && More());
return(CMD_SUCCESS);
}
```

Overlaying a C Structure onto Memory

Wouldn't it be nice to be able to display memory as structures and linked lists? The problem with doing this action at the monitor level is that the monitor doesn't usually have access to the information that the compiler/linker provides regarding the format of a structure. Because I am now assuming I have a file system, one might think that I could put the tool set-generated data in a file and allow the monitor to parse through it. I could, but parsing this data (the symbol table generated by the compiler) can be complicated, especially when you consider the fact that the format of this file could be very different from one compiler to the next. Even if I limit myself to a particular file format (say, ELF), the symbol table format might not be the same from one compiler to the next. A simpler approach is to create a command in the monitor that can look to a structure-definition file in the file system to determine how to overlay a structured display on top of a block of memory on the target. This approach eliminates all dependency on some external file format; hence, it works regardless of CPU type or toolset.

The structure definition file is an ASCII file that contains structure definitions almost as they would be seen within a C header file. The command in the monitor, called cast, can then use this file as a reference when asked to display a particular block of memory. This structure information, combined with the monitor's use of the symtbl file, allows me to issue commands like, such as

```
cast abc %InBuf
```

This command looks for the file structfile in the flash file system, and, if the file is found, the command overlays the structure defined as abc on top of the address associated with the symbol %InBuf (from the monitor's symtbl file). By enhancing this command so that you can specify which member of the structure is the next pointer, you can turn the cast command into a linked list display tool with almost no additional coding effort.

MicroMonitor expects the structure definition to be in the file structfile. In general, the format of this file is similar to that of standard C structure definitions but with some limitations. The types char, short, and long are supported, and they are displayed as a 1-, 2-, or 4-byte decimal integers, respectively. Hexadecimal and character display formats are specified with a member-like notation: the types char.x, short.x, and long.x display hexadecimal representations; the char.c type displays the value as a character.

The example structure definition in Listing 12.5 displays the member i in decimal format, j in hexadecimal, c as a character, d in hexadecimal, and e as a one-byte decimal integer.

Listing 12.5   Structure Definition.

```
struct abc {
    long    i;
    long.x j;
    char.c c;
    char.x d;
    char    e;
}
```

If a structure contains an array, the user must define the array as one of the fundamental types described above and give it an appropriate size. The cast command does not display arrays within structures because of the complexity of the output generated. Thus, the size associated with an array member is treated like padding, and only the name and array size are displayed. Listing 12.6 is an example of a structure definition file that demonstrates all of the functionality of the cast command. Note that the # sign signifies a comment.

Listing 12.6   A Structure Definition File Used by the cast
Command.

```
struct abc {
    long      I;
    char.c    c1;
    pad[3];          # Not displayed, just adds padding
    struct def d;
}

struct def {
    short   s1;
    short.x s2;
    long    ltbl[5]; # Data is not displayed
    short   s3;
}
```

In Listing 12.6, notice the embedded structures, the use of the .x suffix, and the
pad[] descriptor. The pad[] descriptor is used for CPU/compiler-specific padding.
The cast command is totally unaware of compiler-specific padding and CPU-specific
alignment requirements. If the structure definition puts a long on an odd boundary
and the CPU does not support that, cast still attempts the access, generating an
exception. The user must add the appropriate padding to reflect actual alignment
requirements. If the member is of type char.c * or char.c [], cast displays the
ASCII string. (If you don't want the pointer to be dereferenced, use char.x *.)

Listing 12.7   cast Command.

```
static   ulong memAddr;
static   int castDepth;

#define OPEN_BRACE  '{'
#define CLOSE_BRACE '}'

#define STRUCT_SEARCH    1
#define STRUCT_DISPLAY   2
#define STRUCT_ALLDONE   3
#define STRUCT_ERROR     4
```

```c
#define STRUCT_SHOWPAD  (1<<0)
#define STRUCT_SHOWADD  (1<<1)
#define STRUCT_VERBOSE  (1<<2)


#define STRUCTFILE "structfile"

struct mbrinfo {
    char *type;
    char *format;
    int size;
    int mode;
};

struct mbrinfo mbrinfotbl[] = {
    { "char",     "%d",       1 },       /* decimal */
    { "char.x",   "0x%02x",   1 },       /* hex */
    { "char.c",   "%c",       1 },       /* character */
    { "short",    "%d",       2 },       /* decimal */
    { "short.x",  "0x%04x",   2 },       /* hex */
    { "long",     "%ld",      4 },       /* decimal */
    { "long.x",   "0x%08lx",  4 },       /* hex */
    { 0,0,0 }
};

char *CastHelp[] = {
    "Cast a structure definition across data in memory.",
    "-[apv] {struct type} {address}",
    "Options:",
    " -a   show addresses",
    " -l{linkname}",
    " -n{structname}",
    " -p   show padding",
    " -t{tablename}",
    0,
};
```

```c
int
Cast(int argc,char *argv[])
{
    long    flags;
    int     opt, tfd, index;
    char    *structtype, *structfile, *tablename, *linkname, *name;

    flags = 0;
    name = (char *)0;
    linkname = (char *)0;
    tablename = (char *)0;
    while((opt=getopt(argc,argv,"apl:n:t:")) != -1) {
        switch(opt) {
        case 'a':
            flags |= STRUCT_SHOWADD;
            break;
        case 'l':
            linkname = optarg;
            break;
        case 'n':
            name = optarg;
            break;
        case 'p':
            flags |= STRUCT_SHOWPAD;
            break;
        case 't':
            tablename = optarg;
            break;
        default:
            return(0);
        }
    }
    if (argc != optind + 2)
        return(-1);

    structtype = argv[optind];
    memAddr = strtoul(argv[optind+1],0,0);
```

The cast command begins in Listing 12.7. The command supports a few options that offer display of linked lists, inclusion of the address of the data in the display, and display of the padding. As with most of MicroMonitor commands, the cast function begins by performing some default initialization, a call to getopt() to override the defaults, and retrieval of the necessary command line arguments.

Listing 12.8   Checking for a Structure File.

```
/* Start by detecting the presence of a structure definition file... */
    structfile = getenv("STRUCTFILE");
    if (!structfile) {
        structfile = STRUCTFILE;
    }


    tfd = tfsopen(structfile,TFS_RDONLY,0);
    if (tfd < 0) {
        printf("Structure definition file '%s' not found\n",structfile);
        return(0);
    }
```

Because this command requires a structure definition file, the command must verify that a structure definition file is present (Listing 12.8). The default name of the file is defined by STRUCTFILE, but can be overridden by the environment variable STRUCTFILE if present. This technique is used in several places in MicroMonitor, where a hardcoded value is available but can be overridden by the content of a shell variable.

Listing 12.9   Displaying Multiple Structures.

```
    index = 0;
    do {
        castDepth = 0;
        showStruct(tfd,flags,structtype,name,linkname);
        index++;
        if (linkname) {
            printf("Link #%d = 0x%1x\n",index,memAddr);
        }
        if (tablename || linkname) {
```

```
            if (askuser("next?")) {
                if (tablename) {
                    printf("%s[%d]:\n",tablename,index);
                }
            }
            else {
                tablename = linkname = (char *)0;
            }
        }
    } while(tablename || linkname);

    tfsclose(tfd,0);
    return(0);
}
```

The loop at the end of the cast command (see Listing 12.9) allows multiple structures or table entries to be displayed by calling showStruct(). After each structure display, the user can abort or continue with the next entry.

Listing 12.10   showStruct().

```
/* castIndent():
 *  Used to insert initial whitespace based on the depth of the
 *  structure nesting.
 */
void
castIndent(void)
{
    int i;

    for(i=0;i<castDepth;i++) {
        printf("  ");
    }
}


/* strAddr():
 *  Called by showStruct().  It will populate the incoming buffer pointer
 *  with either NULL or the ascii-hex representation of the current address
```

```
 *  pointer.
 */
char *
strAddr(long flags, char *buf)
{
    if (flags & STRUCT_SHOWADD) {
        sprintf(buf,"0x%08lx: ",memAddr);
    }
    else {
        buf[0] = 0;
    }
    return(buf);
}


int
showStruct(int tfd,long flags,char *structtype,char *structname,char *linkname)
{
    struct mbrinfo *mptr;
    ulong  curpos, nextlink;
    int    i, state, snl, retval, tblsize;
    char   line[96], addrstr[16], format[64];
    char   *cp, *eol, *type, *eotype, *name, *bracket, *eoname, tmp;

    type = (char *)0;
    retval = nextlink = 0;
    curpos = tfsctrl(TFS_TELL,tfd,0);
    tfsseek(tfd,0,TFS_BEGIN);
    castIndent();

    if (structname) {
        printf("struct %s %s:\n",structtype,structname);
    }
    else {
        printf("struct %s @0x%lx:\n",structtype,memAddr);
    }
    castDepth++;
```

The function showStruct() (Listings 12.10–12.15) is the workhorse of the cast command. The showStruct() function uses recursion to display structures within structures. The showStruct() function parses the structure definition file (tfd is the descriptor), while looking for the structure type specified by structtype. The function then attempts to display the memory block that begins at memAddr as if it were the structure. Note that showStruct() does not verify the syntax of the structure definition in structfile. It is up to the user to avoid confusing this function.

The showStruct() function records the current position in structfile so the position can be retrieved in the event of recursion. The function then seeks to the beginning of the file and calls castIndent(). The castIndent() function keeps track of the depth (or recursion level) of showStruct() and, based on that depth, prints out a related number of spaces. As the recursion depth increases, the space count increases. This process allows the embedded members to be indented, as one would expect. Next, showStruct() prints out either the name of the structure or its address and starts searching for the incoming structure type in the structure definition file.

Listing 12.11   Searching Through the Structure Definition File.

```
state = STRUCT_SEARCH;
snl = strlen(structtype);

while(1) {
    if (tfsgetline(tfd,line,sizeof(line)-1) == 0) {
        printf("Structure definition '%s' not found\n",structtype);
        break;
    }
    if ((line[0] == '\r') || (line[0] == '\n')) { /* empty line? */
        continue;
    }

    eol = strpbrk(line,";#\r\n");
    if (eol) {
        *eol = 0;
    }

    if (state == STRUCT_SEARCH) {
        if (!strncmp(line,"struct",6)) {
            cp = line+6;
```

```
            while(isspace(*cp)) {
                cp++;
            }
            if (!strncmp(cp,structtype,snl)) {
                cp += snl;
                while(isspace(*cp)) {
                    cp++;
                }
                if (*cp == OPEN_BRACE) {
                    state = STRUCT_DISPLAY;
                }
                else {
                    retval = -1;
                    break;
                }
            }
        }
    }
```

Initially, showStruct() is in state (STRUCT_SEARCH), looking for the specified structure. In this state, the function steps through each line of the file (using the TFS API function tfsgetline()), until the structure definition is found (Listing 12.11). After the definition is found, showStruct() changes state to STRUCT_DISPLAY to indicate that it is now displaying the specified memory using the specified structure.

Listing 12.12   Displaying the Structure.

```
        else if (state == STRUCT_DISPLAY) {
            type = line;
            while(isspace(*type)) {
                type++;
            }

            if (*type == CLOSE_BRACE) {
                state = STRUCT_ALLDONE;
                break;
            }
```

```
        eotype = type;
        while(!isspace(*eotype)) {
            eotype++;
        }
        *eotype = 0;
        name = eotype+1;
        while(isspace(*name)) {
            name++;
        }
        bracket = strchr(name,'[');
        if (bracket) {
            tblsize = atoi(bracket+1);
        }
        else {
            tblsize = 1;
        }

        if (*name == '*') {
            castIndent();
            printf("%s%-8s %s: ",strAddr(flags,addrstr),type,name);
            if (!strcmp(type,"char.c")) {
                printf("\"%s\"\n",*(char **)memAddr);
            }
            else {
                printf("0x%1x\n",*(ulong *)memAddr);
            }
            memAddr += 4;
            continue;
        }
```

After showStruct() is in the state STRUCT_DISPLAY (Listing 12.12), each line is parsed to filter white space and properly align character pointers on tokens within the line. Note that this mechanism is not very robust. To maintain a reasonable level of simplicity, the code assumes a sane structure definition file.

The parsing code first looks for a leading asterisk, which indicates that a pointer needs to be dereferenced. If there is no leading asterisk, the raw memory is formatted, based on each member of the structure. The table mbrinfotbl[] (see Listing 12.13) is used to scan the line of the structure definition file for one of the possible data display formats supported. Listing 12.12 also detects the presence of square brackets ('[' & ']') to support array specifications.

Listing 12.13 Using `mbrinfotbl[]`.

```
mptr = mbrinfotbl;
while(mptr->type) {
    if (!strcmp(type,mptr->type)) {
        castIndent();
        eoname = name;
        while(!isspace(*eoname)) {
            eoname++;
        }
        tmp = *eoname;
        *eoname = 0;

        if (bracket) {
            if (!strcmp(type,"char.c")) {
                printf("%s%-8s %s: ",
                    strAddr(flags,addrstr),mptr->type,name);
                cp = (char *)memAddr;
                for(i=0;i<tblsize && isprint(*cp);i++) {
                    printf("%c",*cp++);
                }
                printf("\n");
            }
            else {
                printf("%s%-8s %s\n",
                    strAddr(flags,addrstr),mptr->type,name);
            }
            memAddr += mptr->size * tblsize;
        }
        else {
            sprintf(format,"%s%-8s %%s: %s\n",
                strAddr(flags,addrstr),mptr->type,mptr->format);
            switch(mptr->size) {
                case 1:
```

```
                    printf(format,name,*(uchar *)memAddr);
                    break;
            case 2:
                    printf(format,name,*(ushort *)memAddr);
                    break;
            case 4:
                    printf(format,name,*(ulong *)memAddr);
                    break;
        }
        memAddr += mptr->size;
    }
    *eoname = tmp;
    break;
    }
    mptr++;
}
```

Listing 12.14   Dealing with an Embedded Structure.

```
if (!(mptr->type)) {
    int padsize;
    char *subtype, *subname, *eossn;

    if (!strcmp(type,"struct")) {
        subtype = eotype+1;
        while(isspace(*subtype)) {
            subtype++;
        }
        subname = subtype;
        while(!isspace(*subname)) {
            subname++;
        }
        *subname = 0;

        subname++;
        while(isspace(*subname)) {
            subname++;
        }
```

```
        eossn = subname;
        while(!isspace(*eossn)) {
            eossn++;
        }
        *eossn = 0;
        if (*subname == '*') {
            castIndent();
            printf("%s%s %s %s: 0x%08lx\n",
                strAddr(flags,addrstr),
                type,subtype,subname,*(ulong *)memAddr);
            if (linkname) {
                if (!strcmp(linkname,subname+1))
                    nextlink = *(ulong *)memAddr;
            }
            memAddr += 4;
        }
        else {
            for (i=0;i<tblsize;i++) {
                if (bracket) {
                    sprintf(bracket+1,"%d]",i);
                }
                if (showStruct(tfd,flags,subtype,subname,0) < 0) {
                    state = STRUCT_ALLDONE;
                    goto done;
                }
            }
        }
    }
    else if (!strncmp(type,"pad[",4)) {
        padsize = atoi(type+4);
        if (flags & STRUCT_SHOWPAD) {
            castIndent();
            printf("%spad[%d]\n",strAddr(flags,addrstr),
                padsize);
        }
        memAddr += padsize;
    }
```

```
            else  {
                retval = -1;
                break;
            }
        }
    }
    else {
        state = STRUCT_ERROR;
        break;
    }
}
```

If showStruct() cannot find a match between the content of the line and the mbrinfotbl[] array, the only other acceptable possibilities are another structure (in which case recursion occurs and the process just deepens) or an invisible padding request (Listing 12.14). The pad entry in the structure definition file tells show-Struct() to skip over some specified number of bytes without displaying anything. This option is useful for two reasons:

1. Sometimes you must insert padding to align members of a structure properly, as the C compiler would.
2. Sometimes you are only interested in a small section of a large structure. This pad[] feature reduces the unwanted visual noise.

When the loop ends (see Listing 12.15), if all went well, the value of state is STRUCT_ALLDONE. Otherwise, the switch statement prints an error message.

Listing 12.15   showStruct().

```
done:
    switch(state) {
        case STRUCT_SEARCH:
            printf("struct %s not found\n",structtype);
            retval = -1;
            break;
        case STRUCT_DISPLAY:
            printf("invalid member type: %s\n",type);
            retval = -1;
            break;
```

```
        case STRUCT_ERROR:
            printf("unknown error\n");
            retval = -1;
            break;
    }
    tfsseek(tfd,curpos,TFS_BEGIN);
    if (linkname)
        memAddr = nextlink;
    castDepth--;
    return(retval);
}
```

Some Example Output

To illustrate the flexibility of the cast and dm commands, I will use them to generate some example displays. I'll first show a memory dump using dm and then display the same memory using cast.

Assume I want to look at the structure type abc (as defined in Listing 12.6), located at location 0x5d000 in system memory. If I dump the data as raw memory, using dm it displays as

```
uMON> dm 0x5d000 48
0005d000: 00 01 00 00 64 00 00 00   04 01 12 34 00 00 00 00   ....d......4....
0005d010: 00 00 00 00 00 00 00 00   00 00 00 00 00 00 00 00   ................
0005d020: be ef 00 00 00 00 00 00   00 00 00 00 00 00 00 00   ................
```

The output format is clean and easy to read, as long as you want to read raw memory. Each line starts with a hexadecimal address, followed by 16 bytes of ASCII-coded hexadecimal data, followed by the same 16-byte block displayed in ASCII. If the ASCII is a non-printable character, then a dot (.) is printed as a placeholder. If you look closely, you can see the data in the block of memory. Wouldn't it be nicer to look at output such as the following

```
uMON>cast abc 0x5d000

struct abc @0x5d000:
    long     I: 65536
    char.c   c1: d
    struct def d:
```

```
short    s1: 1025
short.x  s2: 0x1234
long     ltbl[5]
short    s2: 48879
```

Notice member I printed as a long decimal value (0x10000 = 65536)

0005d000: <u>00 01 00 00</u> 64 00 00 00   04 01 12 34 00 00 00 00   ....d......4....

Notice member c1 printed as an ASCII character (0x64 = d)

0005d000: 00 01 00 00 <u>64</u> 00 00 00   04 01 12 34 00 00 00 00   ....d......4....

Notice that the three bytes of padding were silently ignored

0005d000: 00 01 00 00 64 <u>00 00 00</u>   04 01 12 34 00 00 00 00   ....d......4....

Notice short member s1 displayed as a decimal number (0x401 = 1025)

0005d000: 00 01 00 00 64 00 00 00   <u>04 01</u> 12 34 00 00 00 00   ....d......4....

and so on through the structure. As you can see, it is easier to look at a structure with cast than through a raw memory dump.

Stack Trace

The stack trace exception handler is probably the most useful tool in the firmware developer's bag of tricks. The stack trace allows the developer to view the function nesting whenever the program is stopped at a breakpoint. Because the stack trace gives an instant view of the calling history, a stack trace can save gobs of debug and analysis time.

Stack trace capability is usually considered something that is only offered by a high-level debug environment. This doesn't have to be the case. Having implemented stack trace for a few different CPUs, I can tell you that implementing stack trace is a pain in the neck; once it works, however, you just can't live without it.

The monitor-based stack trace I discuss in this chapter extracts symbol information from the symbol table file, as have other commands. The stack trace, though, requires that the symbols be sorted in ascending address order. I also limit the monitor-based stack trace to provide function nesting only.

I limit the stack trace to function nesting because deciphering variables in the stack is a bit more complicated. Think about it for a minute: return addresses must be easy to find because the hardware must use a return address every time it returns from a function call. On the other hand, finding a variable within the stack isn't a hardware function — it's part of the virtual machine fabricated by the compiler. In fact, different compilers for the same CPU can use different conventions for placing variables on the stack. Thus, the ability to display variables within a particular function's stack frame is not a natural thing for the CPU nor for the monitor. Any stack trace that displays variables requires information from the compiler regarding how and where the variables are stored in the frame.

The majority of the code for a stack trace implementation is compiler and CPU specific. Some of the parsing of the symbol file is generic and can be reused on multiple implementations. As I mentioned above, I found the stack trace feature to be a challenge, but it has been well worth it. Listing 12.16 is the code for the MicroMonitor `strace` command (for a PowerPC).

Listing 12.16   `strace` **Command.**

```
int
Strace(int argc,char *argv[])
{
    char    *symfile, fname[64];
    TFILE   *tfp;
    ulong   *framepointer, pc, fp, offset;
    int     tfd, opt, maxdepth;

    tfd = fp = 0;
    maxdepth = 20;
    pc = ExceptionAddr;
    while ((opt=getopt(argc,argv,"d:F:P:rs:")) != -1) {
        switch(opt) {
        case 'd':
            maxdepth = atoi(optarg);
            break;
        case 'F':
            fp = strtoul(optarg,0,0);
            break;
        case 'P':
            pc = strtoul(optarg,0,0);
            break;
        case 'r':
            showregs();
            break;
        default:
```

```
            return(0);
        }
    }

    if (!fp) {
        getreg("R1", &framepointer);
    }
    else {
        framepointer = (ulong *)fp;
    }

    /* Start by detecting the presence of a symbol table file... */
    symfile = getenv("SYMFILE");
    if (!symfile) {
        symfile = SYMFILE;
    }

    tfp = tfsstat(symfile);
    if (tfp)  {
        tfd = tfsopen(symfile,TFS_RDONLY,0);
        if (tfd < 0) {
            tfp = (TFILE *)0;
        }
    }

    /* Show current position: */
    printf("   0x%08lx",pc);
    if (tfp) {
        AddrToSym(tfd,pc,fname,&offset);
        printf(": %s()",fname);
        if (offset) {
            printf(" + 0x%lx",offset);
        }
    }
    putchar('\n');

    /* Now step through the stack frame... */
    while(maxdepth) {
```

```
        framepointer = (ulong *)*framepointer;

        if ((!framepointer) || (!*framepointer) || (!*(framepointer+1))) {
            break;
        }

        printf("   0x%08lx",*(framepointer+1));
        if (tfp) {
            int match;

            match = AddrToSym(tfd,*(framepointer+1),fname,&offset);
            printf(": %s()",fname);
            if (offset) {
                printf(" + 0x%lx",offset);
            }
            if (!match) {
                putchar('\n');
                break;
            }
        }
        putchar('\n');
        maxdepth--;
    }

    if (!maxdepth) {
        printf("Max depth termination\n");
    }

    if (tfp) {
        tfsclose(tfd,0);
    }
    return(0);
}
```

As is the case with most MicroMonitor commands, strace (see Listing 12.16) starts with default initialization and processing of command line options and arguments. Because strace always runs after some exception has occurred, the current address is taken from the global variable ExceptionAddr (which was loaded by the exception handler.) The command accepts several options but usually the defaults are appropriate.

After the options are processed, the code retrieves the stack pointer. The stack is basically organized as a linked list of stack frames. Later, the code uses this pointer to find the first frame.

Before processing the stack though, the code looks for the symtbl file and initializes the tfd descriptor. This descriptor is later passed to AddrToSym() each time the monitor wants to find the symbolic equivalent of an address. If the symtbl file is not present, only the addresses are displayed. The processing loop walks through the currently nested stack frames until some termination criteria is met, either a null frame pointer or a maximum frame depth.

Listing 12.17   AddrToSym().

```
/* AddrToSym():
 *  Assumes each line of symfile is formatted as...
 *      synmame SP hex_address
 *  and that the symbols are sorted from lowest to highest address.
 *  Using the file specified by the incoming TFS file descriptor,
 *  determine what symbol's address range covers the incoming address.
 *  If found, store the name of the symbol as well as the offset between
 *  the address of the symbol and the incoming address.
 *
 *  Return 1 if a match is found, else 0.
 */
int
AddrToSym(int tfd,ulong addr,char *name,ulong *offset)
{
    int     lno;
    char    *space;
    ulong   thisaddr, lastaddr;
    char    thisline[84];
    char    lastline[sizeof(thisline)];

    lno = 1;
    *offset = 0;
    lastaddr = 0;
    tfsseek(tfd,0,TFS_BEGIN);
```

```
    while(tfsgetline(tfd,thisline,sizeof(thisline)-1)) {
        space = strpbrk(thisline,"\t ");
        if (!space) {
            continue;
        }
        *space++ = 0;
        while(isspace(*space)) {
            space++;
        }
        thisaddr = strtoul(space,0,0);  /* Compute address from        */
                                        /* entry in symfile.           */

        if (thisaddr == addr) {     /* Exact match, use this entry     */
            strcpy(name,thisline);  /* in symfile.                     */
            return(1);
        }
        else if (thisaddr > addr) { /* Address in symfile is greater   */
            if (lno == 1) {         /* than incoming address...        */
                break;              /* If first line of symfile        */
            }                       /* then return error.              */
            strcpy(name,lastline);
            *offset = addr-lastaddr;/* Otherwise return the symfile    */
            return(1);              /* entry previous to this one.     */
        }
        else {                      /* Address in symfile is less than */
            lastaddr = thisaddr;    /* incoming address, so just keep  */
            strcpy(lastline,thisline);  /* a copy of this line and     */
            lno++;                      /* go to the next.             */
        }
    }
    strcpy(name,"???");
    return(0);
}
```

The stack trace function uses AddrToSym() (see Listing 12.17) to convert an address to a function name. This conversion is done by stepping through each line of the symtbl file (using the TFS API function tfsgetline() and assuming that the symbols are sorted in ascending address order). When the address in the symbol table is greater than or equal to the incoming address, the address is considered a match, and the string and offset are returned. The offset is returned only if the address is not an exact match. When there is no exact match, the name of the nearest match is displayed with an offset, as in this example:

```
uMON> strace
0x8018844a: errCheck() + 0x18
0x800c7f40: serialTest() + 0x40
0x8004006c: TaskAudit() + 0x88
```

This example shows that function TaskAudit() called function serialTest() and that serialTest() called function errCheck(). The exception (or breakpoint) occurred within errCheck().

NOTE

What do you do if your customers report that your product is occasionally "just resetting." If the problem occurs only "occasionally," it can be very hard to reproduce, and sometimes is related to some event unique to the customer site. So how do you catch such a bug in the act? You probably can't leave an emulator (or an engineer) at the customer's site.

With this stack trace capability and some of the other capabilities in MicroMonitor, you can configure the environment so that any exception automatically causes the monitor to dump a stack trace to a file in the file system and then will restart the application. You can later retrieve the file and analyze it in your lab.

Testing for Stack Overflow

Programs use two different kinds of variables: static (or global) and stack variables. Static variables are assigned a fixed address. Regardless of what functions execute, a static variable always resides at the same address. Stack variables (local or auto variables in C) always belong to a specific function and are only accessible during the life of the function that declared them. The stack variables for a function are created from scratch (on the stack) each time the function runs. Depending on the stack depth when the function starts, its stack variables can very well be placed in a different location in memory.

Static variables are easy to work with but take up memory space all the time. Stack variables are temporarily allocated by the currently running function and are very convenient for temporary storage. The space allocated to a stack variable is given up and used by other functions as soon as the function that declared the variable completes. Both types of variables are necessary, and both have good and bad points.

The allocation and deallocation of stack variables is handled by code at the beginning and end of every function, called, respectively, the *prolog* and the *epilog*. This invisible code is generated by the compiler and is part of the function overhead, not part of the function's logic. In most cases, the prolog and epilog allocate and deallocate a stack frame large enough to accommodate the variables declared inside the function. The allocation adjusts the current stack pointer and frame pointer (usually downward) and provides a frame of memory space to be used by the currently running function. When an embedded system is first built, a limited amount of memory is assigned to the stack. If, in the process of executing functions, some function nesting combination causes the stack pointer to go beyond the end of the space that was allocated to the stack, the result is a stack overflow — one of the hardest-to-find bugs you can encounter.

What happens following a stack overflow depends on what the target's memory map looks like. In many single-threaded systems, the stack pointer is set to the top of memory (allowing it to grow downward), and the heap (space given to the application by malloc)[3] starts just above the end of the process text/data/BSS space and grows upward (see Figure 12.1). The point in memory at which the stack overflow occurs varies greatly depending on how much memory is allocated on the heap. Remember that the heap grows upward, the stack grows downward, and somewhere in the middle they meet. The point where heap and stack meet is the point of corruption, and this point is very hard to identify because it depends on the dynamics of your stack and heap.

A multi-tasking environment complicates things even further. In a multi-tasking environment, you have a separate logical stack for each task. Usually, each task is configured with some stack size that you are able to specify based on what the task is going to do. This design can make things more confusing because now you have potential for T different stacks to overflow (where T is the number of tasks in the system). What the stack overflows into depends on where the stack is. If the system is set up with task stacks allocated from a common block of memory, the overflow of one task stack is likely to corrupt the stack of some other task that is not currently running. If stack frames are scattered throughout memory (Figure 12.2), an overflow can corrupt other variables in the system. Either way, a stack overflow can be extremely hard to track down, primarily because the code that appears to be failing is probably not doing anything illegal on its own; it is instead crashing because some other task's stack overflowed and corrupted its variables.

---

3. A good rule for embedded systems is to avoid using malloc entirely. However, since some applications will require malloc, in this discussion I'll assume it's needed.

Figure 12.1 Single-Threaded Application Memory Map.

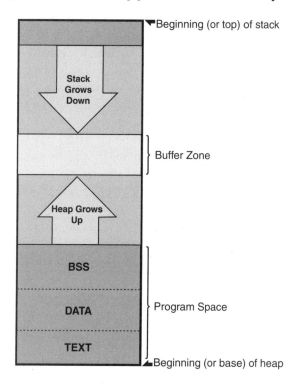

In a single-threaded application, the stack and heap often grow toward each other in the unused portion of data space.

This elusive quality of stack overflows gets worse. Almost all embedded systems have interrupts. Interrupt handlers are generally asynchronous to what is going on in application space, and usually the interrupt handler is written in C. The C code in the interrupt handler is no different from any other C code. The interrupt handler code creates a stack frame by adjusting the current stack pointer. The current stack pointer in this case is the stack pointer of the task that was interrupted. If this task's current function nesting brings its stack pointer close to the end of its allocated memory space, the occurrence of the interrupt causes a stack overflow because that interrupt handler code grows on that stack.

How do we deal with this problem? Ideally, it would be nice just to allocate a lot of memory to each stack. In some cases that's all that is needed. In other cases, you have to spend time figuring out what function nesting, task, and interrupt conditions caused the problem.

Prefill the Stack Memory or Buffer Zone

The most common way to detect a stack overflow is to prefill the RAM space used by the stack with some known pattern and then to detect if this pattern becomes entirely overwritten. For example, you could load the stack's memory space with 0x55 as the pattern. Then you could create an additional task, a buffer checker, that knows the location of each stack, and uses a timer or other event to execute this task periodically. If the buffer checker detects that the end of any of the stacks has been modified, you have detected a stack overflow.

Note that this test only detects the evidence of an overflow — you still haven't caught the offending application in the act. (It is possible a wild pointer or other fault is responsible for the detected change.) Now you know, however, what task is causing the problem based on which stack overflowed. You can investigate the code that is specific to that task. If there is good reason for the stack usage, however, just increase that task's stack size. In the case of a single-threaded application memory arrangement shown in Figure 12.1, you might want to prefill a buffer zone. If that buffer zone is ever modified, you then know you had a stack overflow.

Figure 12.2   Multi-Threaded Application Memory Map.

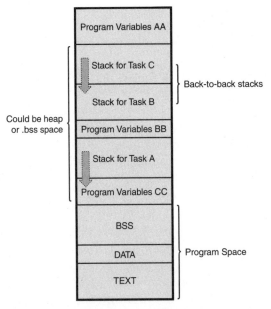

In a multi-threaded application, each task has its own stack, greatly complicating the difficulty of detecting an overflow.

On the proactive side, you can also use this method for general-purpose stack size adjustment. Prefill all stacks or buffer zones with a pattern and then adjust allocated stack sizes based on the point at which the pattern is overwritten in each stack. Keep in mind that this scheme is not perfect. Unfortunately, it is very possible that a function can overflow the stack without corrupting the pattern. This is the case if there is a function with an unused array in its frame. For instance, see Listing 12.18.

Listing 12.18   Undetected Stack Overrun.

```
func(int arg)
{
    char buffer[32];
    int  val;

    if (arg > 45) {
        sprintf(buffer,"hey, arg is greater than 45!\n");
        func1(buffer);
    }
    val = func2(arg);
    return(val);
}
```

The 32 bytes set aside for buffer might not be modified. If you are near the end of your stack frame and call the function in Listing 12.18 with arg < 45, and the end of stack space overlaps with the space allocated to buffer, the 0x55 pattern would be left intact, but the overflow would still corrupt the memory space below the end of the stack.

NOTE

Try to avoid large arrays on the stack. Sometimes you "just gotta have 'em" but be careful.

Use a Per Function Stack Frame Checker

An alternative technique for finding stack overflow is to insert a stack check function at the top of every function. This stack-check function is likely to be an assembler function that is capable of looking at the current stack pointer and determining if it is beyond the end of the stack. For multi-tasking systems, this function would also need to be aware of what task is running because different tasks use different stacks.

A stack-check function is ideal for catching an overflow where it actually happens. You can design the function to raise an exception automatically and to perform a stack trace to capture the function nesting that caused the overflow.

Unfortunately, the stack-check function can impose extreme runtime overhead. The execution time of the stack-check function is added to every function call in your system. One option is to use it selectively; some functions might not be suspect. However, the more selective you are, the less likely you are to catch the bug. Also, if you decide to be selective, be aware that even if the function doesn't have any large arrays, it still might be the offending function. Also, it might be the function that called the current function that is really to blame. Referring to Listing 12.18, if func2() does nothing but increment arg and return the value (using very little stack), it still can be the offending function because of the stack depth caused by func().

A stack-check function may be impractical for other reasons. You might not have source for all the code, so you don't have the option of installing this function everywhere. You might have all the source but might have coded large parts of the project without using the stack check macro. Adding the calls late in a large project is both tedious and error prone.

One Way To Be Prepared

Rather than find out too late that you should have made provisions for a stack check, you might want to make a suitable macro part of your project's coding standard. Because the call is a macro, including it in the code doesn't mean it gets used by the code. Most of the time, you use an empty definition for STKCHK(). With an empty definition, the call does not generate any code. When you encounter a stack problem, you can activate the macro by changing its definition (see Listing 12.19).

Listing 12.19   Creating a Stack-Check "Hook."

```
#include "stackchecker.h"

func()
{
    STKCHK();

    yada, yada, yada
}
```

System Profiling

Assume that you are on a firmware development project and that you are working on a hardware platform that has been completed and successfully deployed to the field, but there are new features yet to be delivered. Your assignment is to add some new feature, but when your feature is added, current features start to fail because you don't have enough horsepower to support the additional capability, or you don't have enough memory space left to add your feature.

One solution is to throw up your hands at the hardware people and tell them they need to give you more. This tactic often doesn't go over too well, so you need an alternative. You need to determine if you can rearrange things a bit so that you can get some more bandwidth out of the current implementation. You also need to determine if any functions in the system can be removed because they aren't used. These questions are best answered through a technique known as *system profiling* (sometimes called *runtime analysis*).

Function counting, *task-ID activity*, and *basic block coverage* are some basic system profiling capabilities. Some of the information you uncover through system profiling is useful for verifying that all code has been executed, and some information is useful for determining where to focus optimization time if you need to speed things up. Note that some of the more sophisticated RTOS packages provide various types of system profiling as a standard component or an optional extension. These tools can shed a lot of light on an RTOS-based firmware project, and, depending on what is used, system profiling might or might not insert additional load on the system. The following sections discuss some system profiling techniques for the developer who does not want to worry about implementing an externally purchased package.

NOTE

By using external hardware to analyze and display the runtime statistics of a system (based on tracing instruction fetches), you can profile a system without any runtime overhead. This hardware technique is only practical, though, if the address bus is externally accessible and there is some way to deal with the instruction cache.

Use the System Tick

If you are programming an embedded system, it is very likely that your target has some heartbeat or system tick interrupt. This interrupt is usually established in hardware as the highest-level interrupt in the system. You can use this interrupt to log what code segment or task was interrupted each time the interrupt occurs.

The simplest application of this technique is to gather task statistics. When any given task is in the running state, there is some global pointer in the system (usually referred to as a task ID, or TID) that can be made accessible to the system tick handler to let the system tick handler know what task was active at the time of the tick. The interrupt handler can then increment by one some counter (one per task) to keep track of task activity.

This information might or might not be valuable, depending on what's going on. Also, the value of this information depends on the degree of correlation between a given task and certain pieces of code. For example, if many tasks are active but most of the tasks call the same functions, knowing what task is most active doesn't do much good because it doesn't point you to the function that needs to be optimized. If, on the other hand, each task is primarily executing some unique block of code, then task ID logging might be enough to point you in the right direction.

An alternative to logging the task ID statistics is to build in the ability to log what function is active at each system tick. Following are two different ways to log the active function. One method puts the burden on the system tick, and the other method is dependent on the availability of a fairly large amount of RAM.

For the first case, start by building the application and gathering function statistics (location and size). After you know the function statistics, insert into the system tick a function call that passes the address of the code that was interrupted by the system tick to some function that knows the location and size of all of the functions in the build. By comparing this address to what is known about the build, this function can identify which function was executing and can increment the associated counter. Because this technique adds a fairly complex search or lookup to every clock tick, it can seriously burden the processor.

The second technique offers better performance but requires more RAM. To use this technique, you must have a block of extra RAM equal in size to your .text space (the area that has the functions in it). The system tick would then pass the address of the code that was interrupted to a function that would treat this block of RAM as a table of counters. The function would use the incoming address as an offset into this table and would modify the counter at that offset. This solution is quick and gives a really clear picture of what code is most active.

A command in MicroMonitor called prof supports some of the preceding concepts. Listing 12.20 shows some of the associated code.

Listing 12.20   The prof **Command.**

```
struct pdata {
    ulong   data;       /* Start of symbol or tid. */
    int     pcount;     /* Pass count.             */
};
```

```
/* prof_FuncConfig():
 * This function builds a table of pdata structures based on the
 * content of the symbol table.
 * It assumes the file is a list of symbols and addresses listed
 * in ascending address order.
 */
void
prof_FuncConfig(void)
{
    int     tfd, i;
    struct  pdata *pfp;
    char    line[80], *space;

    tfd = prof_GetSymFile();
    if (tfd < 0) {
        return;
    }

    prof_FuncTot = 0;
    pfp = prof_FuncTbl;

    while(tfsgetline(tfd,line,sizeof(line)-1)) {
        space = strpbrk(line,"\t ");
        if (!space) {
            continue;
        }
        *space++ = 0;
        while(isspace(*space)) {
            space++;
        }
        pfp->data = strtoul(space,0,0);
        pfp->pcount = 0;
        pfp++;
        prof_FuncTot++;
    }
    tfsclose(tfd,0);
```

```
        /* Add one last item to the list so that there is an upper limit for
         * the final symbol in the table:
         */
        pfp->pdata = 0xffffffff;
        pfp->pcount = 0;

        /* Test to verify that all symbols are in ascending address order...
         */
        for (i=0;i<prof_FuncTot;i++) {
            if (prof_FuncTbl[i].data > prof_FuncTbl[i+1].data) {
                printf("Warning: function addresses not in order\n");
                break;
            }
        }
        prof_FuncTot++;
}
```

The prof command calls the function prof_FuncConfig() when the user wants to build a table of pdata structures based on the content of the symtbl file. Similar to the stack trace facility, prof_FuncConfig() assumes that the symbols are in the file in ascending address order. The prof_FuncConfig() function then steps through the file and creates one pdata entry for each line in the symbol table file. The table is built at a location specified by prof_FuncTbl, which is also established by the user by using the prof command.

Listing 12.21   profiler().

```
#define HALF(m) (m >> 1)

static int prof_Enabled;       /* If set, profiler runs; else return.        */
static int prof_BadSymCnt;     /* Number of hit, but not in a symbol.        */
static int prof_CallCnt;       /* Number of times profiler was called.       */
static int prof_FuncTot;       /* Number of functions being profiled.        */
static int prof_TidTot;        /* Number of TIDs being profiled.             */
static int prof_TidTally;      /* Number of unique TIDs logged so far.       */
static int prof_TidOverflow;   /* More TIDs than the table was built for.    */
```

```
static struct pdata *prof_FuncTbl;
static struct pdata *prof_TidTbl;
static char prof_SymFile[TFSNAMESIZE+1];

void
profiler(struct monprof *mpp)
{
    struct pdata *current, *base;
    int nmem;

    if (prof_Enabled == 0)
        return;

    if (mpp->type & MONPROF_FUNCLOG) {
        nmem = prof_FuncTot;
        base = prof_FuncTbl;
        while(nmem) {
            current = &base[HALF(nmem)];
            if (mpp->pc < current->data) {
                nmem = HALF(nmem);
            }
            else if (mpp->pc > current->data) {
                if (mpp->pc < (current+1)->data) {
                    current->pcount++;
                    goto tidlog;
                }
                else {
                    base = current + 1;
                    nmem = (HALF(nmem)) - (nmem ? 0 : 1);
                }
            }
            else {
                current->pcount++;
                goto tidlog;
            }
        }
        prof_BadSymCnt++;
```

```
        }
tidlog:
    if (mpp->type & MONPROF_TIDLOG) {
        /* First see if the tid is already in the table.  If it is,
         * increment the pcount.  If it isn't add it to the table.
         */
        nmem = prof_TidTally;
        base = prof_TidTbl;
        while(nmem) {
            current = &base[HALF(nmem)];
            if (mpp->tid < current->data) {
                nmem = HALF(nmem);
            }
            else if (mpp->tid > current->data) {
                base = current + 1;
                nmem = (HALF(nmem)) - (nmem ? 0 : 1);
            }
            else {
                current->pcount++;
                goto profdone;
            }
        }
        /* Since we got here, the tid must not be in the table, so
         * do an insertion into the table.  Items are in the table in
         * ascending order.
         */
        if (prof_TidTally == 0) {
            prof_TidTbl->pcount = 1;
            prof_TidTbl->data = mpp->tid;
            prof_TidTally++;
        }
        else if (prof_TidTally >= prof_TidTot) {
            prof_TidOverflow++;
        }
        else {
            current = prof_TidTbl + prof_TidTally - 1;
            while(current >= prof_TidTbl) {
```

```
                if (mpp->tid > current->data) {
                    current++;
                    current->pcount = 1;
                    current->data = mpp->tid;
                    break;
                }
                else {
                    *(current+1) = *current;
                    if (current == prof_TidTbl) {
                        current->pcount = 1;
                        current->data = mpp->tid;
                        break;
                    }
                }
                current--;
            }
            prof_TidTally++;
        }
    }
profdone:
    prof_CallCnt++;
    return;
}
```

The function `profiler()` (see Listing 12.21) would be called by the application's system tick (through the MicroMonitor API `mon_` hookup discussed in Chapter 11). The application code would populate a `monprof` structure to tell the profiler to do TID and/or function profiling and to specify the TID and/or PC.

The function profiling (`MONPROF_FUNCLOG`) uses the table built by `prof_FuncConfig()`. For this service, `profiler()` searches the table (using a binary search) for a match between the incoming address and the address range of one of the symbols. After a match is found, the matching symbol's pass count is incremented.

The TID profiling assumes that the user has established some maximum number of expected unique TID values. A table of `pdata` structures of that size is assumed to exist (and to be initialized to `NULL`) starting at the location specified by `prof_TidTbl`. At each call to `profiler()`, the table is built with each unique TID value inserted in the table so that the entries are in ascending order. This approach allows the `profiler` to then do a quick binary search for a match between the incoming TID and the entries in the table already. If a match is found, that pass count is incremented; if no match is found, the TID is added to the list, and the pass count is set to one.

Listing 12.22   Printing the Profile Statistics.

```
void
prof_ShowStats(int minhit, int more)
{
    int     i, tfd, linecount;
    ulong   notused;
    char    symname[64];
    struct  pdata   *pptr;

    printf("FuncCount Cfg: tbl: 0x%08x, size: %d\n",
        prof_FuncTbl, prof_FuncTot);
    printf("TidCount  Cfg: tbl: 0x%08x, size: %d\n",
        prof_TidTbl, prof_TidTot);

    if (prof_CallCnt == 0) {
        printf("No data collected\n");
        return;
    }
    linecount = 0;
    tfd = prof_GetSymFile();
    if ((prof_FuncTbl) && (prof_FuncTot > 0)) {
        printf("\nFUNC_PROF stats:\n");
        pptr = prof_FuncTbl;
        for(i=0;i<prof_FuncTot;pptr++,i++) {
            if (pptr->pcount < minhit) {
                continue;
            }
            if ((tfd < 0) ||
                (AddrToSym(tfd,pptr->data,symname,&notused) == 0)) {
                printf(" %08x    : %d\n",pptr->data,pptr->pcount);
            }
            else {
                printf(" %-12s: %d\n",symname,pptr->pcount);
```

```
                }
            if ((more) && (++linecount >= more)) {
                linecount = 0;
                if (More() == 0) {
                    goto showdone;
                }
            }
        }
    }

    if ((prof_TidTbl) && (prof_TidTot > 0)) {
        printf("\nTID_PROF stats:\n");
        pptr = prof_TidTbl;
        for(i=0;i<prof_TidTot;pptr++,i++) {
            if (pptr->pcount < minhit) {
                continue;
            }
            printf(" %08x    : %d\n",pptr->data,pptr->pcount);
            if ((more) && (++linecount >= more)) {
                linecount = 0;
                if (More() == 0) {
                    goto showdone;
                }
            }
        }
    }
showdone:
    putchar('\n');
    if (prof_BadSymCnt) {
        printf("%d out-of-range symbols\n",prof_BadSymCnt);
    }
    if (prof_TidOverflow) {
        printf("%d tid overflow attempts\n",prof_TidOverflow);
    }
    printf("%d total profiler calls\n",prof_CallCnt);

    if (tfd >= 0) {
```

```
        tfsclose(tfd,0);
    }
    return;
}
```

When profiling is completed, the statistics gathered by these two functions can be dumped to the user through the prof command. The prof command ultimately calls prof_ShowStats(). Function prof_ShowStats() (Listing 12.22) prints the contents of the two tables of pdata structures to the console. The user can specify the minimum number of hits so that only the big hitters are printed. Also, the user can specify some more throttling because the output could be fairly large, depending on the number of functions in the application.

Basic Block Coverage

The basic block coverage (BBC) capability depends on the compiler and certainly adds runtime overhead to the application. For each basic block in the code, the compiler inserts a counter. This counter can be used by the system test team to verify that all code under test has been covered. After you put the target through a test suite, you can use the results of the BBC to see what lines of code were missed. This solution is not perfect, but it is a step towards completion. The BBC approach does not cover all functional routes, just code.

NOTE

A basic block is a sequence of code that is always executed as a (potentially interruptable) unit. In other words, if any one line of code within the block has been executed, then every line of code in the block was executed. In C, a basic block is generally enclosed in braces.

Listing 12.23   BBC Example.

```
void
funcX(void)
{
    if (aa == 15)
    {
        Block 1 of funcX().
    }
    if ((aa == 15) || (bb == 35))
```

```
    {
        Block 2 of funcX().
    }
}
```

In Listing 12.23, the BBC technique indicates that both blocks have been executed even if only the aa == 15 case was invoked; hence, the case of bb == 35 and aa != 15 (which would pass through funcX but only invoke Block 2) is not tested.

Summary

Monitor-based debugging certainly does not provide all of the capability that comes with some of the desktop development environments available today. However, monitor-based debugging does provide an environment that can reside in the system with the application. Monitor-based debugging, therefore, lets you debug in the field without the need for a pod connection or even an additional serial port. This convenience can prove priceless. Monitor-based debugging does not prevent any of the more sophisticated development environments from just lying on top of the monitor platform.

Chapter 13

Porting MicroMonitor to the ColdFire™ MCF5272

In this chapter, I'll walk through the process of porting the MicroMonitor boot monitor to a Motorola ColdFire MCF5272C3 evaluation board. I'll assume you have some familiarity with the MicroMonitor command set and that you have access to the source code (all of which is on the CD). I'll limit my discussion of the ColdFire to those details that are necessary to the porting process. Consider this chapter a lesson on the monitor porting process rather than on the MCF5272C3 or the ColdFire architecture.

I chose the MCF5272C3 evaluation board because:

- The MCF5272C3 CPU has a good set of built-in peripherals. Its size and complexity are a good match for MicroMonitor;

- The MCF5272C3 core is very similar to the popular Motorola 68000 series of microprocessors;

- Motorola's support web sites provide a lot of information on the CPU and the evaluation board, including the source code for their boot monitor;

- Although it is not used in this port, the ColdFire's BDM interface is top of the line;
- The facilities built into the monitor shipped with the board make it very easy to install MicroMonitor. In fact, I can install MicroMonitor without even needing to overwrite the default boot monitor.

Since I am working with an evaluation board, I can immediately make a few convenient assumptions that could not be made if this were brand new hardware. I can assume the hardware design has been tested, I can assume I have correct schematics, and I can assume the example code in Motorola's boot monitor truly does illustrate how to manipulate the hardware correctly.

TIP

If your project includes building new hardware and you are writing the firmware, try really hard to get an evaluation board for the CPU and to get the hardware designers to follow the evaluation board design as a reference. If the new hardware follows the evaluation board as a reference, you can work on firmware on the evaluation board, and, when the real hardware becomes available, the transition to the real hardware will be easy.

Source Code Directory Tree

Before I can start writing code for the evaluation board, I must step back and look at the tree of source code that comes with MicroMonitor on the CD. There are basically two high-level directories: common and targets. The common directory contains the code that is reusable across several different platforms. The targets directory contains subdirectories, each of which are specific to a particular target. Separating the code into these two main directories allows you to port the monitor source to several very different architectures with minimal changes to the code.

Figure 13.1 MicroMonitor Source Tree.

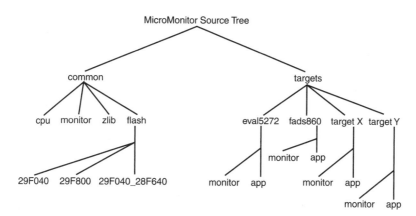

The subdirectories under the common and targets directories are as follows:

- common/cpu — contains code that is CPU-specific but not target-specific. Things like the disassembler, exception handling, and CPU-specific commands for the CLI are here.

- common/monitor — contains the bulk of the code. All facilities that are 100% target/CPU-independent reside in this directory. This includes TFS, the Ethernet facilities, file editor, the majority of the monitor commands, memory allocator, CLI handler, and so forth. All of the core monitor facilities are in this directory.

- common/zlib — contains almost entirely untouched material from the zlib public domain code. I have made only the bare minimum changes needed to get zlib code to fit into the monitor. The changes are isolated to one file.

- common/flash — contains subdirectories that support specific flash architectures. The architecture might be a single 29F040 or 29F800, or it might be a target that has a 29F040 boot device with a 28F640 device used for TFS storage. Each subdirectory represents one flash configuration; each flash configuration might be applicable to several target systems.

- targets/fads860 — contains (along with the other targets/xxx directories) code that is specific to one particular target system. All of the non-generic, non-reusable stuff for a given target (In this case, the FADS860 evaluation board) is here.

- targets/eval5272 — like the other target-specific directories, this contains the reset code, communications drivers (serial port and Ethernet), and main(). Also, the linker map file, makefile, and most other build-related files are located here. This directory is where I do the majority of the work related to this port.

Beneath each `targets/XXX` directory is a *monitor* and *app* directory. The `monitor` directory contains all of the target-specific code used by the monitor for the specific target, and the `app` directory is intended to contain a very basic example of an application that could reside in and execute out of TFS after the monitor is ported and running on the target.

The Makefile

The makefile includes a few other .make files found in some of the common directories. Every target-specific makefile includes `common/monitor/common.make`, `common/zlib/zlib.make`, and `common/monitor/tools.make`. These three .make files keep the target-specific makefile minimal by putting the common stuff in one place. There are fancier ways to do this; however, keeping things simple works just fine for me.

NOTE

I was "born and raised" on UNIX, using one of a few different UNIX-based shells and the many wonderful tools that UNIX weenies have grown to love (with good reason!) Despite this, I still wanted to have my embedded development setup on a PC so that I could work more portably. Being very comfortable with the UNIX shell, I was very happy to come across the MicroCross GNU X-Tools, which provide a UNIX-like cross development environment for the PC. The X-Tools package includes pre-built GNU cross compilers for several CPU architectures, the bash shell, and other UNIX tools (`find`, `grep`, `rm`, `cp`, `ls`, `awk`, `sed`, etc.) available for a Win32 platform. With this `bash` shell as my console on a Win32 platform, I get the best of both worlds. Thus, even though I am working on a PC, I use `make` to drive my builds, and I assume that the UNIX-like tools are available. The basic Micro-Cross toolset and installation instructions are included on the book's CD.

The `common.make` file includes all of the make targets for the common modules, plus some conveniences that use the GNU cross development tools to build a variety of different output listings. These ancilliary build targets include helpful things like symbol tables, S-records, and C/disassembler mixed files. The `common.make` file also provides for the common `clobber` and `clean` facilities (to remove unwanted object and executable files) and a target that builds a .tar file for the target-specific source.

To implement all of these conveniences, the target-specific makefile must follow some guidelines. The majority of these guidelines involve initializing certain `make` variables within the makefile so that the `common.make` file can use them. The only other guideline is that all object modules are placed under an *obj* directory beneath the target-specific monitor directory.

Listings 13.1 through 13.4 present the basic makefile to be used for this port.

Listing 13.1   Basic Makefile.

```
#############################################################################
#
# Makefile for building a monitor for the MCF5272 evaluation platform.
#
# Currently, the only target supported for 5272 platform is EVAL.  When
# the platform count increases to more than 1, the target name should be
# specified on the command line.
#
# NOTE: This port has only been tested running in RAM space of the
# MCF5272 eval board.  It is downloaded using the DBUG command "DL" or "DN".
#
PLATFORM    = CFEVAL

FLASH       = 29pl160c
TGTDIR      = eval5272


MONBASE     = ../../..
TGTBASE     = $(MONBASE)/targets/$(TGTDIR)
COMBASE     = $(MONBASE)/common
COMCPU      = $(COMBASE)/cpu
ZLIB        = $(COMBASE)/zlib
COMMON      = $(COMBASE)/monitor
FLASHDIR    = $(COMBASE)/flash/$(FLASH)
INFO        = info


TARGET      = m68k-coff
include     $(COMMON)/tools.make


CFLAGS      = -Wall -D PLATFORM_$(PLATFORM)=1 -Wno-format \
              -fno-builtin -msoft-float -g -c -m5200 -I. -I$(COMMON) \
              -I$(COMCPU) -I$(FLASHDIR) -o $@
ASFLAGS     = -m5200 -o $@
ASMCPP      = cpp -D PLATFORM_$(PLATFORM)=1 -D ASSEMBLY_ONLY \
```

```
                -I$(COMCPU) -I$(COMMON)
LDFLAGS      = -Map=$(AOUT).map
AOUT         = mon$(PLATFORM)
LIBS         = libz.a $(LIBGCC)
```

In Listing 13.1, the top set of variables are used to identify the environment within which the monitor source code resides. This environment supports convenient -I arguments for directories that have include files and allows the common.make file to perform some common tasks based on these variables. The rest of these variables are typical for a makefile. The value of the PLATFORM variable is used to allow this directory and makefile to support more than one platform potentially. I'll talk more about this feature when I get to the config.h file.

The pre-built tools in the MicroCross X-Tools package are distinguished by names of the form <target><output file type><base tool name>. Thus, to generate code for an ARM board using ELF format object files, you would invoke the compiler named arm-elf-gcc. In Listing 13.1, the included file tools.make uses the value of the TARGET variable to build X-Tools compatible tool names (for CC, LD, ASM, etc.) For the ColdFire port, the CPU is a member of the Motorola 68K family (m68k) and I want to generate COFF output files, so TARGET is set to m68k-coff.

Listing 13.2   Object List for the ColdFire 5272 Make File.

```
OBJS=obj/reset.o obj/start.o obj/cpuio.o obj/chario.o obj/mprintf.o \
obj/main.o obj/mstat.o obj/sbrk.o obj/malloc.o obj/docmd.o obj/cmdtbl.o \
obj/go.o obj/env.o obj/memcmds.o obj/xmodem.o obj/flash.o obj/except.o \
obj/flashpic.o obj/flashdev.o obj/ethernet.o obj/reg_cache.o obj/vectors.o \
obj/tfs.o obj/if.o obj/misccmds.o obj/genlib.o obj/edit.o obj/lineedit.o \
obj/tfsapi.o obj/tfsclean1.o obj/tfscli.o obj/tfslog.o obj/symtbl.o \
obj/tfsloader.o obj/redirect.o obj/monprof.o obj/bbc.o obj/etherdev.o \
obj/icmp.o obj/arp.o obj/nbuf.o obj/dhcpboot.o obj/dhcp_00.o obj/tftp.o \
obj/tcpstuff.o obj/crypt.o obj/password.o obj/moncom.o obj/cache.o \
obj/misc.o obj/dis_cf.o

include $(ZLIB)/zlib.objlist
```

The object list of Listing 13.2 is based on the features that are to be part of the monitor build. The majority of these files are object files that are built from the common space. The objects are specified here so that each target can be built to include only the features that are needed for that application. Hence, this list is very target specific. The one important thing to note is that the build assumes that reset.o is the first module in the list. This assumption allows the linker to place the code that is in reset.s at the beginning of the memory map. Notice the inclusion of zlib.objlist. The zlib.objlist file (in the common/zlib directory) contains the objects that make up the zlib compression facility. This list is kept in common space because it is always used the same way. It can simply be included here if you use it.

Listing 13.3   Release vs. Development Build Versions.

```
#HHHHHHHHHHHHHHHHHHHHHHHHHHHHHHHHHHHHHHHHHHHHHHHHHHHHHHHHHHHHHHHHH
#
# rom:
# Standard monitor build, destined for installation using newmon tool.
#
rom: $(INFO) $(OBJS) libz.a makefile
    $(LD) $(LDFLAGS) -TROM.lnk -nostartfiles -e coldstart \
    -o $(AOUT) $(OBJS) $(LIBS)
    coff -m $(AOUT)
    coff -B $(AOUT).bin $(AOUT)


#HHHHHHHHHHHHHHHHHHHHHHHHHHHHHHHHHHHHHHHHHHHHHHHHHHHHHHHHHHHHHHHHH
#
# ram:
# Version of monitor for download into RAM.
#
ram: $(INFO) $(OBJS) libz.a makefile
    $(LD) $(LDFLAGS) -TRAM.lnk -nostartfiles -e coldstart \
    -o $(AOUT) $(OBJS)
    coff -m $(AOUT)
    coff -B $(AOUT).bin $(AOUT)
```

For each monitor build, I usually have the option of building a release version of the monitor that boots out of flash memory (the rom tag in Listing 13.3) or a development version that loads in RAM (the ram tag in Listing 13.3). (I often use the RAM resident version when I'm testing some new monitor feature. For this example port, I use the ram tag to create a monitor that can be downloaded into RAM space not used by the evaluation board's DBUG monitor.) The rom make tag is the top tag in the makefile, so it is the default.

The coff tool (referenced in Listing 13.3) could be replaced by various GNU tools with similar capabilities. I wrote the coff tool as an exercise to improve my own understanding of the COFF file format. The -m option dumps a memory map of the executable, and the -B option builds a binary image based on the executable, as I discussed in one of the earlier chapters of the book. This same capability is available for COFF, ELF, and A.OUT file formats. The source and executables are on the CD.

Notice the use of the $(AOUT) variable. This variable is used throughout the target makefile and common.make file as the base name for various files created by the make process. In this case, AOUT is set to mon$(PLATFORM), and PLATFORM is set to CFEVAL; AOUT then, is monCFEVAL. This base name is used for several other outputs, such as monCFEVAL.bin for the raw binary image, monCFEVAL.srec for an S-record, monCFEVAL.sym for a symbol file, and so on. I find that this simple naming scheme keeps things a bit more organized from one target to the next, plus using a common base name makes it very convenient for the clobber tag to remove all of the files related to a particular target.

Listing 13.4   Miscellaneous Rules Section.

```
#############################################################
#
# Miscellaneous rules:
#
include $(COMMON)/common.make
include $(ZLIB)/zlib.make

libz.a: $(ZOBJS)
    m68k-coff-ar rc libz.a $(ZOBJS)

info:
    defdate -f %H:%M:%S BUILDTIME >info.h
    defdate -f %m/%d/%Y BUILDDATE >>info.h
```

The miscellaneous rules section (see Listing 13.4) includes the two other common .make files. Including these files pulls in the core set of targets and their dependencies. The libz.a tag builds the list of libz objects into a library. The info tag builds a simple header file (info.h) that contains the time and date of the build. This info.h file is then included by one of the source files of the monitor to provide part of the information reported by MicroMonitor's version command.

A Cross-Platform Date Tool
The info.h file is built with another home-grown tool called defdate (source and executable on CD). I wrote defdate because I build on both UNIX and Win32 and could not find a good cross-platform means of creating a date string that could be included in an #include file. If you look at the source on the CD, you'll see it took a total of about five minutes to write defdate.

Listing 13.5 info.h.

```
info.h:


#define BUILDTIME "12:26:16"
#define BUILDDATE "12/23/2000"


function called by 'Version' command:


void
ShowVersion(void)
{
    printf("Monitor built: %s @ %s\n",BUILDDATE, BUILDTIME);
}
```

Listing 13.5 shows the typical content of info.h (as it would be built by the def-date tool) and how it is used by the monitor's version command. Note that most compilers provide the __DATE__ and __TIME__ intrinsic definitions. One of my earlier projects used a compiler that did not support these definitions, and defdate become very handy; so I've been sticking with it.

The (incomplete) list of individual module tags shown in Listing 13.6 demonstrates the use of the various shell variables established at the top of the file. Notice in the last rule that I make assembly a two-step process. The source file is first passed through the C preprocessor (ASMCPP) and then through the assembler. Depending on the assembler, this process could be reduced to a single step. I chose to use the two-step process, however, rather than have toolset dependencies in the makefile. Notice that all modules are in the obj directory. This partitioning keeps the object module clutter out of the directory that holds the source code.

Listing 13.6   Individual Module Targets.

```
#############################################################
#
# Individual modules:
#
obj/dis_cf.o:   $(COMCPU)/dis_cf.c $(COMMON)/genlib.h config.h
    $(CC) $(CFLAGS) $(COMCPU)/dis_cf.c


obj/flashdev.o: $(FLASHDIR)/flashdev.c
    $(CC) $(CFLAGS) $(FLASHDIR)/flashdev.c


obj/main.o: main.c config.h cpu.h $(COMMON)/tfs.h \
    $(COMMON)/genlib.h $(COMMON)/ether.h \
    $(COMMON)/monflags.h $(COMMON)/stddefs.h
    $(CC) $(CFLAGS) main.c


obj/reset.o:    reset.s  config.h
    $(ASMCPP) reset.s >tmp.s
    $(ASM) tmp.s
    rm tmp.s
```

The final section of the makefile (see Listing 13.7) sets up a make tag that is used by the common.make clobber tag. As you will see shortly, common.make has the clobber target, but, to allow clobber to be customized, it depends on clobber1, which must be provided by the target makefile.

Use cpp with Assembly Language

I find the trivial differences among assemblers annoying. Different assemblers use different comment delimiters and different directives. Rather than deal with these nuisance differences, I write my assembly code in a partially "normalized" syntax and then use the C preprocessor to translate my code to the form that the particular assembler wants. This translation tactic lets me use the familiar c-style comment delimiters (/* and */). More importantly, I can use #include at the top of the assembler file, letting me share the same header files across both assembly and C code. Sharing headers is a great convenience when writing firmware.

This technique is common enough that many compilers support the ability to pre-process assembly files through some command line option. Even if your compiler doesn't support this feature, you can still accomplish the same goal by using a two step translation process. Run CPP on the "normalized" assembly file, then assemble the output of the preprocessor.

Listing 13.7 `clobber1` **Target.**

```
##############################################################################
#
# Miscellaneous utilities:
# (generic utilities are in $(COMMON)/common.make)
#
clobber1:
    rm -f $(AOUT).map
```

Listing 13.8 shows what I consider to be the most interesting parts of the common.make file. The first portion of common.make (not shown in the listing) consists of tags for each of the common modules and tags for a bunch of common tools. The tools (as can be seen from the text in the help tag in common.make) provide the facilities that are most commonly used in the cross compilation-process: conversion to S-records or binary, generation of a symbol table, generation of a file that contains both C-source and assembly language mixed, and so forth. Note that this portion of common.make depends on some of the variables that were established at the top of the makefile.

Listing 13.8   Common Miscellaneous Targets.

```
##############################################################################
#
# COMMON miscellaneous targets:
#
clean:
    rm -rf obj
    rm -rf libz.a symtbl
    mkdir obj


clobber:    clean clobber1
```

```
    rm -f $(AOUT)
    rm -f $(AOUT).bin $(AOUT).srec $(AOUT).fcd $(AOUT).dis $(AOUT).sym

tar:    clean
    rm -f $(AOUT).srec $(AOUT).sym  $(AOUT).fcd $(AOUT).dis $(AOUT).tar
    /bin/sh -c "cd $(MONBASE) ; \
    tar -cf $(AOUT).tar common/monitor common/zlib common/cpu \
    common/flash/$(FLASH) targets/$(TGTDIR)/app targets/$(TGTDIR)/monitor"
    mv $(MONBASE)/$(AOUT).tar .

gnusrec:
    $(OBJCOPY) -F srec $(AOUT) $(AOUT).srec

bin2srec:
    bin2srec $(AOUT).bin > $(AOUT).srec

bindump:
    $(OBJDUMP) --full-contents $(AOUT) >$(AOUT).fcd

showmap:
    $(OBJDUMP) --section-headers $(AOUT)

dis:
    $(OBJDUMP) --source --disassemble $(AOUT) >$(AOUT).dis

disx:
    $(OBJDUMP) --source --disassemble --show-raw-insn $(AOUT) >$(AOUT).dis

sym:
    $(NM) --numeric-sort $(AOUT) >$(AOUT).sym

symtbl: sym
    monsym -p0x $(AOUT).sym >symtbl

help:
    @echo "gnusrec  : use objcopy to produce $(AOUT).srec"
    @echo "bin2srec : use bin2srec to produce $(AOUT).srec"
```

```
        @echo "showmap  : display section headers"
        @echo "dis      : source/assembly dump to $(AOUT).dis"
        @echo "disx     : like dis, but show instruction in hex & symbolic"
        @echo "sym      : numerically sorted symbol table dump to $(AOUT).sym"
        @echo "symtbl   : rearrange output of sym to create monitor's symtbl file"
        @echo "bindump  : ascii-coded hex full-content dump to $(AOUT).fcd"
        @echo "clean    : delete entire obj directory"
        @echo "tar      : create a tar file of the current source and binary."
```

That's it for the makefile and its components. Absolutely no rocket science, just simple and easy-to-duplicate rules for other targets and compilers and for both Win32 and UNIX.

The Configuration Header File

To maintain some type of global configuration control over all files in the monitor build, one file, mysteriously named config.h, should be at the top of the #include list for every file in the build. The following sections walk through each of the sets of definitions in config.h and explains how to adjust various operational parameters.

FORCE_BSS_INIT

When the CPU resets, it transfers control to the non-volatile code located at the address of the CPU's reset vector. The code in the file reset.s is supposed to be mapped to that location. After the lowest level of initialization, reset.s calls start() (the first C function). The start() function depends on a parameter passed to it by the reset code to know what type of startup (warm or cold) just occurred. If the reset is a cold start (meaning that the power was just applied or the system reset button was pushed), then all of the monitor's .bss space must be initialized to zero. If the reset is not a cold start, then the .bss is left as is so that state already established before the reset remains available. The decision whether or not to initialize .bss is based on an incoming parameter set up by assembly language code in reset.s.

When bringing up a new piece of hardware, this .bss initialization should be independent of the type of startup to avoid the case where .bss is erroneously not initialized when it should be. Defining FORCE_BSS_INIT makes this brute force .bss initialization occur in start(). Once the target boot source code has stabilized, this definition should be removed so that .bss is appropriately touched or left alone.

PLATFORM_XXX

In general, each directory below the targets directory is for one specific target system. This directory structure keeps target-specific interfaces cleanly in their own directory space. However, sometimes multiple targets are so close in architecture that it just doesn't make sense to isolate them by directory. The PLATFORM_XXX definition (see Listing 13.9) in config.h, the makefile, and any of the target-specific files support the need for minor differences between nearly identical targets.

At reset, the monitor dumps a verbose header to the console port. One of the lines in the header is the name of the platform, derived from the PLATFORM_NAME definition (see Listing 13.9.) The ColdFire port only supports one platform, so this definition isn't absolutely necessary. However, following the established model just makes things consistent from one port to the next. Also, if a future design comes up that is very close to the evaluation platform, we are ready for it.

Listing 13.9   PLATFORM_XXX **Definition.**

```
#if PLATFORM_CFEVAL
#define PLATFORM_NAME      "Coldfire 5272 Evaluation Board"
#else
#error                     "Platform name is not specified"
#endif
```

Flash Configuration

Because the flash drivers are written to be independent of the address space they use, they must be supplied with some basic information about where the devices reside in the target memory space. This information is provided by the definitions in Listing 13.10.

Listing 13.10   Flash Bank Configuration Definitions.

```
/* Flash bank configuration:
 */
#define FLASHBANKS              1
#define FLASH_BANK0_WIDTH       2
#define FLASH_BANK0_BASE_ADDR   0xFFE00000
#define FLASH_PROTECT_RANGE     "0-6"
```

Recall from the chapter on flash drivers that there can be multiple banks of flash memory. This platform contains only one flash device. If there were more than one,

FLASHBANKS would reflect that, and there would be multiple sets of FLASH_BANKX_WIDTH (in bytes) and FLASH_BANKX_BASE_ADDR (starting point of the device in CPU memory space) definitions. The final definition of FLASH_PROTECT_RANGE is used to tell the flash driver which sectors to apply software protection (refer to the chapter on flash drivers for details on software protection). This sector range can span multiple banks and/or devices and can specify multiple ranges (use a hyphen for a multi-sector range and a comma to separate multiple ranges).

TFS Configuration

When TFS is compiled, it must be told where in memory it is to exist and where in memory the spare sector is to reside. The config.h definitions specific to TFS allow TFS to configure itself for optionally multiple, non-contiguous blocks (TFS devices) of memory. The configuration data here works in coordination with information in the tfsdev.h header file, which defines the structure — or table of structures if more than one TFS device is supported — that describes each block.

Listing 13.11   TFS Definitions in config.h.

```
Portion of config.h:

/* TFS definitions:
 */
#define TFSSPARESIZE         0x40000
#define TFSSECTORCOUNT       2
#define TFSSTART             0xfff40000
#define TFSEND               0xfffbffff
#define TFSSPARE             0xfffc0000
#define TFS_EBIN_COFF        1
#define TFSNAMESIZE          23

Portion of tfsdev.h:

/* TFS Device table:
 */
struct tfsdev tfsdevtbl[] = {
    {   "//AM29160/",
```

```
        TFSSTART,
        TFSEND,
        TFSSPARE,
        TFSSPARESIZE,
        TFSSECTORCOUNT,
        TFS_DEVTYPE_FLASH, },

    /* If there was another TFS device, an
     * additional tfsdev entry would be here.
     */

    { 0, TFSEOT,0,0,0,0,0 }
};

#define TFSDEVTOT ((sizeof(tfsdevtbl))/(sizeof(struct tfsdev)))
```

Listing 13.11 shows the related portions of config.h and tfsdev.h. The entries in config.h are used by tfsdev.h and in other parts of the TFS code. In the majority of cases, the file system is built with only one TFS device, so there is a one-to-one mapping of start, end, spare size, and sector count between config.h and tfsdev.h. If I were building a system for multiple TFS devices, then there would be an additional tfsdev structure in the tfsdevtbl[] array for each additional device. Also, there would be additional definitions in config.h that tfsdev.h would reference.

The TFS definitions establish the target-specific information needed to compile the file system. The parameters include the base and end address of the flash space used by TFS (TFSSTART and TFSEND), the address and size of the spare sector (TFSSPARE and TFSSPARESIZE), and the number of sectors allocated to TFS for storage space (TFSSECTORCOUNT), which does not include the spare sector. The definition of TFSNAMESIZE is only needed if the size is to be something other than the default of 23. (For all systems so far, 23 has been fine. However, if there ever is a need to make it bigger or smaller, TFSNAMESIZE is where you do it. The only requirement is that the size be one less than some value divisible by four.)

One additional TFS definition, TFS_EBIN_COFF, tells TFS what loader to include with TFS when built. Currently COFF, ELF, and A.OUT are supported; others are easily added to the platform.

The INCLUDE List

The monitor can be built with a fairly wide variety of options. In general, the options' specific capabilities are supported by corresponding CLI commands. The first obvious advantage to being able to configure different capabilities selectively is that eliminating unneeded capabilities saves memory space. The less obvious advantage is that during a port to a new target, fewer capabilities means less complexity in the initial build and less debugging. At the start, all but the most basic features can be configured out, and then, one by one, features that correspond to specific hardware peripherals can be added. For example, when I start the port, I don't want to have to worry about TFS and Ethernet or even flash memory when I don't even know how to configure the RAM and serial port, so I start with these other components disabled. Then, one by one, I enable the features. This approach allows me to tackle one problem at a time as I continue the port.

The definitions in Listing 13.12 show an example configuration for a monitor platform. The included `inc_check.h` header file, found in the common/monitor directory, is used to do a sanity check on the list. The majority of these definitions would be set to zero at the start of a port, and then one by one they can be enabled to add functionality. An early configuration for starting a port would be to set `INCLUDE_MEMCMDS` and `INCLUDE_XMODEM`, which allows me to start the port working on `reset.s` and the serial port. After the target boots with the serial port working, I can use some of the memory `modify` and `display` commands to look around at the address space. If memory seems to be correctly configured, then I can use `xmodem` to download small test programs into RAM.

NOTE

The inclusion of `inc_check.h` below the list of `INCLUDE_XXX` definitions enforces the requirement that these defines in Listing 13.12 be set to zero or one not just omitted. I chose this alternative because it forces the user to be aware of the configuration and reduces the likelihood that a section is omitted just because the user was unaware of the option.

Listing 13.12

```
/* INCLUDE_XXX Macros:
 * The sanity of this list is tested through the inclusion of
 * "inc_check.h" at the bottom of this list...
 */
#define INCLUDE_MEMCMDS          1
#define INCLUDE_PIO              0
```

```
#define INCLUDE_EDIT            1
#define INCLUDE_DEBUG           0
#define INCLUDE_DISASSEMBLER    0
#define INCLUDE_UNPACK          0
#define INCLUDE_UNZIP           1
#define INCLUDE_ETHERNET        0
#define INCLUDE_TFTP            0
#define INCLUDE_TFS             1
#define INCLUDE_FLASH           1
#define INCLUDE_XMODEM          1
#define INCLUDE_LINEEDIT        1
#define INCLUDE_CRYPT           0
#define INCLUDE_DHCPBOOT        0
#define INCLUDE_TFSAPI          1
#define INCLUDE_TFSAUTODEFRAG   1
#define INCLUDE_TFSSYMTBL       0
#define INCLUDE_TFSSCRIPT       0
#define INCLUDE_TFSCLI          1
#define INCLUDE_EE              0
#define INCLUDE_GDB             0
#define INCLUDE_STRACE          0
#define INCLUDE_CAST            0
#define INCLUDE_EXCTEST         0
#define INCLUDE_IDEV            0
#define INCLUDE_REDIRECT        0
#define INCLUDE_QUICKMEMCPY     1
#define INCLUDE_PROFILER        0

#include "inc_check.h"
```

Miscellaneous Configuration

This section discusses two important definitions required by the platform:

ALLOCSIZE — The monitor comes with its own memory allocator because, although I don't advocate use of malloc all over the place in an embedded system, intelligent use of memory allocation can be very handy in some situations. The definition of ALLOCSIZE tells the monitor how much memory to allocate statically to the heap in the monitor. The block of memory used for the `malloc` heap is part of the static memory configured into the monitor. I chose to keep the memory allocated to the heap within the monitor's `.bss` space so that an application can reside in memory space after the monitor without worrying about clashing with a heap growing from the monitor. In addition, the monitor's allocator supports the ability to allocate from two different non-contiguous blocks of memory (two heaps essentially). This design is useful for cases where the monitor is built with a small heap to keep RAM usage low but occasionally runs an application that needs a larger heap. The application can use the monitor's allocator and add more to the heap by simply expanding the heap into some new address space assigned by the application.

SYMFILE — If the shell variable `SYMFILE` is not set as an override, then this definition will set the default name for the symbol table file, usually symtbl.

Stepping Through the Port

Now I'm ready to start with the port. I will depend on the vendor for information about the evaluation system. The most critical resources are

- the CPU data sheet
- the flash (AM29PL160C) data sheet
- serial port (part of processor) data sheet
- Ethernet device (part of processor) data sheet
- the schematics of the evaluation board
- the source code for the board's monitor

(The `.pdf` files for each of these documents can be retrieved from Motorola and AMD's web sites.)

The text that follows is specific to the MCF5272C3 evaluation board. I keep the descriptions as general as possible, so that it is clear how the steps apply to other systems. If you plan to use this example as a guide while porting to some other evaluation board, then it is important that you be familiar with the board and its documentation before you start.

Downloading the First Image

First, I need to establish some plan regarding how I am to get the code (in binary form) onto the target. In earlier chapters, I mentioned three alternatives: BDM, JTAG, and manual flash burning with an external programmer and a socketed boot ROM. In this case, I have a fourth alternative. The evaluation board ships with a boot monitor (not MicroMonitor) in flash memory, so I can use this boot monitor to download the programs to test them out.

If I develop in this mode, I need to be careful about one important hazard. As I write and test my boot firmware and device drivers, I need to be careful that I don't inadvertently make them dependent on the original firmware or on some value it leaves behind. A nice feature of the MCF5272C3 is that the flash memory can be configured as two separate blocks, either of which can be mapped into the space containing the reset vector (depending on the setting of a jumper.) This approach allows you to boot into the provided monitor while loading your code but to boot into your code for testing. The process is

- boot with the provided monitor handling the reset,
- download your code into RAM,
- transfer your code to the alternate block of flash,
- change the jumper, and
- reset the board.

At the reset, the system is executing (booting from) the newly downloaded code, which is a really nice way to test your own boot code. If your code works when tested using this approach, you know that it works on its own — that it's not inadvertently benefiting from some setup performed by the original monitor. If your code doesn't work, then all you need to do is change the jumper back to the original position and you have the original monitor on which to fall back. This feature is really handy!

Before transferring to flash memory, I need the ability to download code and execute the code at the location to which I just downloaded it. The MCF5272CE monitor has a command called dl that allows you to transfer S-record files from a host and a command called go that allows you to transfer control to a specified address in the memory space.

With these facilities in the monitor, most terminal emulation programs should be able to transfer a file in its raw mode to the target. I chose to use my own tool (called com) simply because using something I wrote allows me to be certain of what is happening on the serial port connection. Plus, since com comes on the CD, it's a tool you will have at your disposal. To prepare for the transfer, I connect an RS-232 cable from the PC's COM port to the terminal DB9 connector on the evaluation board and apply power to the evaluation board. For this particular hardware, there is no need for a NULL modem. The target's monitor is expecting the host to transmit at 19,200 baud, no parity, 8-bit chars, 1 stop bit. All normal stuff. To connect to COM port 2 at 19,200, I enter this command line (on the host) at a console prompt: com -b19200 -p2 .

NOTE

The monitor shipped with the MCF5272CE also has facilities that support a network download (the dn command) in conjunction with a small TFTP server. We will stick with the serial port downloader just to keep things simple and to eliminate the unknowns of the Ethernet connection at this point.

At this point, the com program is waiting for characters from the COM port or the console port. If com gets a character from the COM port, com displays the character at the console. If com gets a character from the console port, com transfers the character to the COM port interface. If you hit return now, you should see the dBUG> prompt displayed. This prompt confirms connectivity between the host and the target evaluation board. I can now start building the monitor and testing it, piece by piece.

Referring to code in the targets/eval5272/monitor directory, the config.h file should be configured with all INCLUDE_XXX macros set to 0 and FORCE_BSS_INIT defined. This process builds an absolutely minimum monitor. The file reset.s is based on a few files from the MCF5272CE monitor.[1] The reset.s file calls peripheral initialization functions (also part of the MCF5272CE monitor) and eventually calls start(). After I get to start() and get the serial port running, I am over a major hurdle. For the this evaluation board, writing the code for the serial port was simple because the code for the MCF5272CE monitor is organized quite well. I extracted functions to perform serial port putchar/getchar/gotachar functionality and inserted them into the MicroMonitor framework (cpuio.c). If this code works, I have an initialized target with a working serial port. So I need to build it, download it, and see if it runs.

The makefile can build a RAM- or ROM- (flash memory) based image. At this point I want a RAM-based image, so I execute make ram. This make process compiles each of the monitor modules, links all of the modules to a particular memory map (RAM.lnk), and then converts the COFF file, first to binary and then to S-records (because that's what the dl command is expecting).

Now I am ready to download the first test image. At the dBUG> prompt, I type dl, and then ctrl-x to tell the com program what file to transfer to the target. Next I type monCFEVAL.srec because that's the file that the bin2srec tool in the makefile created.

This procedure causes a lot of dots (one per S-record line) to be printed on the console window of the PC. The dots let me know that the data is being transferred.

---

1. If you compare the target-specific code used for MicroMonitor in this port to the code used to initialize the shipped DBUG monitor, you will see that I shamelessly reused as much of the Motorola code as possible.

After the process completes, I see a message that indicates that the S-record file transfer completed successfully, and the dBUG> prompt returns.

At this point, the image is at location 0x80000 in the DRAM space of the evaluation board (refer to evaluation board documentation for more details if interested). I can now use the go command to execute some function or set of functions in the downloaded space. I need to determine the address of the start function, so I search (using grep) the symbol file created by the makefile (monCFEVAL.sym) for the address. I then type go 0xADDR where ADDR is the address of the start function. This action results in startup of the MicroMonitor in the RAM space of the evaluation board. The output looks something like Listing 13.13.

Listing 13.13   Output for MicroMonitor Startup.

```
dBUG> go 80450


                        MICRO MONITOR
                     CPU: ColdFire 5272
            Platform: Coldfire 5272 Evaluation Board
                Built: 09/14/2001 @ 21:16:42
              Monitor RAM: 0x091310-0x0a4234
              Application RAM Base: 0x0a5000

uMON>
```

The text of Listing 13.13 illustrates a few neat steps. I started off with the monitor that is installed on the boot flash of the evaluation board (dBUG). This monitor produced the dBUG> prompt at the top of the listing. The go command is issued with the address of the start() function (in the monitor binary that I just downloaded), which transfers control to the MicroMonitor. The first visual thing that MicroMonitor does is print a header, reporting the platform and CPU name and followed by a description of where it thinks its memory is. The final thing to notice in this listing is the new prompt, uMON>. This prompt lets me know that MicroMonitor is now running.

I've verified a lot already. I can build and download a monitor image, plus the code I built actually works. If the code didn't work, then I would not have seen the MicroMonitor header and uMON> prompt. Just as a sanity check, I can type help at the uMON> prompt, and I should see something like Listing 13.14.

Listing 13.14   Type help as a Sanity Check.

```
uMON>help
call        echo        heap        help        ?           mstat
reg         reset       set         sleep       ulvl        version


uMON>
```

Notice that not many commands are available at this point, which is because all the INCLUDE_XXX macros were set to zero. I can now start enabling some additional features. The next major feature should be flash memory, but, before working on that, turn on INCLUDE_MEMCMDS and INCLUDE_XMODEM. After enabling these two #defines, I rebuild and download as before. The help list (Listing 13.15) now includes cm, dm, fm, mt, pm, and sm. These commands make up the memory display, test, and modify commands pulled in by INCLUDE_MEMCMDS. The additional xmodem command is pulled in as a result of setting INCLUDE_XMODEM.

I now have a system that can run as a functional boot monitor. I have the ability to issue commands (obviously), display/modify/test memory (cm, dm, fm, mt, pm, and sm), download data into RAM (xmodem), and jump into the downloaded data (call). Note that all of these new commands are from source code in the common directory. They involve absolutely no target-specific code, so as soon as I have the basic serial port driver working, I can immediately throw in INCLUDE_MEMCMDS and INCLUDE_XMODEM.

At this point, if we weren't running on top of another monitor, I would begin using xmodem to download small programs using MicroMonitor's xmodem and call commands (similar to the way I am downloading the whole monitor using Motorola's dl and go).

Listing 13.15   Expanded Help List.

```
uMON>help
call        cm          dm          echo        fm          heap
help        ?           mstat       mt          pm          reg
reset       set         sleep       sm          ulvl        xmodem
version
uMON>
```

Enabling the Flash Driver

Next in the list of drivers is the flash device. Getting these drivers running is a multi-step process. The first step is to get to know the device and how it is connected to the CPU. In this case, the flash device has a 16-bit connection to the CPU, starting at address 0xffe00000. The device has 11 sectors with the sizes (in bytes) specified in the SectorSizes160C[] array of common/flash/29pl160c/flashdev.c (also shown in Listing 13.16). Because the driver functions are copied to RAM, I must make sure that during FlashInit() (front end of the flash driver initialization) the instruction and data caches are disabled.

I construct my first iteration of the driver by defining INCLUDE_FLASH to 1 in config.h and executing the rebuild/download steps, which pulls in the flash code from common/monitor/flash.c and common/flash/29pl160c/*.*.

Listing 13.16   Sector Size Array.

```
/* SectorSizes160C:
 *  There are a total of 11 sectors for this part.  This table reflects the
 *  size of each sector in bytes.
 */
int SectorSizes160C[] = {
        0x4000,  0x2000,  0x2000,  0x38000, 0x40000,
        0x40000, 0x40000, 0x40000, 0x40000, 0x40000,
        0x40000
};

struct sectorinfo sinfo160[sizeof(SectorSizes160C)/sizeof(int)];
```

Eventually this port's flash driver provides the following: device identification, sector erase, write, and atomic erase-write. I begin with device identification, because that is the easiest feature to implement and test. For the AM29PL160C, the device ID is read as a manufacturer ID and a device ID. The read involves writing the AutoSelect command to the device and is handled by the function Flashtype16() in common/flash/29pl160c/flashpic.c. I know that this ID[2] was properly received because MicroMonitor did not generate an error message when I restarted it with the new build. If the ID did not match with what the data sheet stated, the driver would indicate a device ID failure, which could mean the code is wrong or that the hardware does not properly support a write to the flash device.

---

2.   Defined in flashdev.h as: #define AM29PL160C 0x00012245 (refer to data sheet).

I can also verify that the driver has properly established the sector sizes for the device by issuing a `flash info` command. The resulting report (in Listing 13.17) shows what the monitor thinks is the sector map for the device. Before proceeding, if I were writing this code from scratch, I would step back and verify that each sector size matches the sector size specified in the data sheet.

The next task, in order of complexity, is the `flash erase` command. However, I can't test `flash erase` if I haven't written anything to the flash memory, so I look at the `flash write` command. Having gotten through the flash type (`AutoSelect`) process, the other interfaces are similar, just a bit more involved. The `flash write` process (`Flashwrite16()` in `common/flash/29pl160c/flashpic.c`) is similar to `Flashtype16()` but uses a different command sequence and writes data after the command sequence (instead of reading, as was the case for `Flashtype16()`).

Listing 13.17   Device Sector Map.

```
uMON>flash info
Device = AMD-29PL160C
  Base addr   : 0xffe00000
  Sectors     : 11
  Bank width  : 2
  Sector     Begin       End        Size     SWProt?  Erased?
      0     0xffe00000  0xffe03fff  0x004000   yes      no
      1     0xffe04000  0xffe05fff  0x002000   yes      no
      2     0xffe06000  0xffe07fff  0x002000   yes      yes
      3     0xffe08000  0xffe3ffff  0x038000   yes      no
      4     0xffe40000  0xffe7ffff  0x040000   yes      no
      5     0xffe80000  0xffebffff  0x040000   no       no
      6     0xffec0000  0xffefffff  0x040000   no       no
      7     0xfff00000  0xfff3ffff  0x040000   no       no
      8     0xfff40000  0xfff7ffff  0x040000   no       no
      9     0xfff80000  0xfffbffff  0x040000   no       no
     10     0xfffc0000  0xffffffff  0x040000   no       no
uMON>
```

There is one added catch here. Because I am working with a 16-bit device and each write to the device is an aligned 16-bit quantity, I must deal with the possibility that the starting address might be odd or the ending address might be even. Either or both of these situations are very likely, so the driver must deal with them. The `Flashwrite16()` function has a front end that deals with the possibility of an odd starting address and a back end that deals with the possibility of not ending on an odd address. Listings 13.18 through 13.20 show the front end, middle block, and back end of the Flashwrite16() function.

Listing 13.18   Front End of Flashwrite16() Function.

```
int
Flashwrite16(struct flashinfo *fdev,uchar *dest,uchar *src,long bytecnt)
{
    ftype   val;
    long    cnt;
    int     i, ret;
    uchar   *src1;

    ret = 0;
    cnt = bytecnt & ~1;
    src1 = (uchar *)&val;

    /* Since we are working on a 2-byte wide device, every write to the
     * device must be aligned on a 2-byte boundary.  If our incoming
     * destination address is odd, then decrement the destination by one
     * and build a fake source using *dest-1 and src[0]...
     */
    if (NotAligned(dest)) {
        dest--;

        src1[0] = *dest;
        src1[1] = *src;

        /* Flash write command */
        Write_aa_to_555();
        Write_55_to_2aa();
        Write_a0_to_555();
        Fwrite(dest,src1);

        /* Wait for write to complete or timeout. */
        while(1) {
```

```
            if (Is_Equal(dest,src1)) {
                if (Is_Equal(dest,src1))
                    break;
            }
            /* Check D5 for timeout... */
            if (D5_Timeout(dest)) {
                if (Is_Not_Equal(dest,src1)) {
                    ret = -1;
                    goto done;
                }
                break;
            }
        }

        dest += 2;
        src++;
        bytecnt--;
    }
```

The front end (see Listing 13.18) checks for misalignment. If the write starts on an odd address, then the code builds and writes a fake two-byte source buffer (with one byte taken from the real source and the other byte taken from the already-written flash location). It then adjusts the beginning address of the source buffer so that the middle block always receives a block that starts on an aligned boundary. Later the back end uses the same strategy to deal with misalignments at the end of the block.

Listing 13.19   Middle Block of `Flashwrite16()` Function.

```
/* Each pass through this loop writes 'fdev->width' bytes...
 */

for (i=0;i<cnt;i+=fdev->width) {

    /* Flash write command */
    Write_aa_to_555();
    Write_55_to_2aa();
    Write_a0_to_555();
```

```
        /* Just in case src is not aligned... */
        src1[0] = src[0];
        src1[1] = src[1];

        /* Write the value */
        Fwrite(dest,src1);

        /* Wait for write to complete or timeout. */
        while(1) {
            if (Is_Equal(dest,src1)) {
                if (Is_Equal(dest,src1))
                    break;
            }
            /* Check D5 for timeout... */
            if (D5_Timeout(dest)) {
                if (Is_Not_Equal(dest,src1)) {
                    ret = -1;
                    goto done;
                }
                break;
            }
        }
        dest += fdev->width;
        src += fdev->width;
}
```

The middle block of code (see Listing 13.19) does the majority of the work associated with the flash write (depending on the size of the block being written).

Listing 13.20   Back End of `Flashwrite16()` Function.

```
/* Similar to the front end of this function, if the byte count is not
 * even, then we have one byte left to write, so we need to write a
 * 16-bit value by writing the last byte, plus whatever is already in
 * the next flash location.
 */
if (cnt != bytecnt) {
```

```
        src1[0] = *src;
        src1[1] = dest[1];

        /* Flash write command */
        Write_aa_to_555();
        Write_55_to_2aa();
        Write_a0_to_555();
        Fwrite(dest,src1);

        /* Wait for write to complete or timeout. */
        while(1) {
            if (Is_Equal(dest,src1)) {
                if (Is_Equal(dest,src1))
                    break;
            }
            /* Check D5 for timeout... */
            if (D5_Timeout(dest)) {
                if (Is_Not_Equal(dest,src1)) {
                    ret = -1;
                    goto done;
                }
                break;
            }
        }
    }

done:
    /* Read/reset command: */
    Write_f0_to_555();
    return(ret);
}
```

The back end of the function (Listing 13.19) deals with the possibility that there might be only one byte left at the end of the loop (using the same "fake buffer" technique as the front end).

I can test the flash write with the command

```
flash write 0xfff00000 0x80000 16
```

This command tells MicroMonitor to copy 16 bytes from location 0x80000 and write them to flash location 0xfff00000. If you are actually following this process with a real evaluation board, then it is possible that 0xfff00000 has data in it, so issue the command flash erase 7 to erase that sector. When doing your own port, you should devise separate tests to verify that the front and back ends of the write function work properly (using an odd destination address with an even byte count).

Tracing through the erase and erase-and-write code is a similar exercise, so refer to the CD for complete details.

Enabling TFS

Now that I've walked through some of the flash driver steps, I can turn on the flash file system. Assuming I've written the Flashwrite16() and Flasherase16() functions correctly, TFS, once configured, just works when it starts.

To enable TFS, I enable the INCLUDE_TFSXXX macros in the config.h file by setting those macros to 1. I also need to configure TFS for the target environment (more macros in config.h). The flash device spans 0xffe00000 through 0xffffffff (2MB). The installed monitor resides at 0xffe00000 and does not use the upper half of the flash memory. I allocate sectors 8 and 9 (0xfff40000 through 0xfffbffff), giving MicroMonitor .5MB for TFS file storage. The final sector (10) is used for TFS SPARE, and sector 7 (0xfff00000-0xfff3ffff) is reserved for installing a ROM-version of the MicroMonitor binary.[3] The TFS configuration entries in config.h (Listing 13.11) are adjusted to reflect these parameters.

NOTE

Keep in mind now that I am launching MicroMonitor through the monitor that comes with the evaluation board. This process is a bit unusual, but, for the sake of this discussion, it is convenient. This arrangement allows us to test our code without blowing away the boot sector that has the installed boot monitor. In a final system, this dual-monitor environment would be converted to a MicroMonitor-only environment.

Before building a new image, also turn on INCLUDE_EDIT in config.h, so that there is an easy way to create a simple text file. (The INCLUDE_EDIT parameter enables a simple but useful ASCII file editor in the monitor.) Now build, download, and start up the new MicroMonitor, which includes TFS and the file editor.

As before, first check the commands that are included as a result of TFS being included (see Listing 13.21). Notice that not only are the tfs and edit commands available, but also several commands related to scripts in TFS are now included.

---

3. This process demonstrates the versatility of TFS in on-board flash memory. In this case, it fits inside an environment using only three sectors of flash space.

Listing 13.21   MicroMonitor Command Set with TFS Included.

```
uMON>help

argv      call      cm        dm        echo      edit
exit      flash     fm        gosub     goto      heap
help      ?         if        item      mstat     mt
pm        read      reg       reset     return    set
sleep     sm        ulvl      tfs       xmodem    version

uMON>
```

Depending on the state of the flash memory assigned to TFS, at this reset MicroMonitor might report that TFS detected corrupt file space. This result is likely because the flash space allocated to TFS wasn't cleared. You can clear the flash space in one of two ways. Use `flash erase 8-10` or `tfs init` to erase the sectors (8–10) used by TFS.

After TFS space is cleaned up, files can be added. Now would be a good time to try out `tfs add` and `edit` to create files. Then delete some files. Then try to clean up with `tfs clean`. If these experiments work without errors, you can be fairly certain that TFS is installed and working properly. The output of `tfs stat` is helpful for debugging a misconfigured TFS, if there are problems.

Enabling Ethernet

Now that all of the basic stuff is in place, it's time to work on the Ethernet driver. Aside from the initial boot, this step is the trickiest in building a new port. The Ethernet device is a bit more complicated than a serial port. Plus, if something goes wrong, it's hard to know what without a good Ethernet protocol analyzer (or sniffer). Because MicroMonitor doesn't need any interrupts, the driver is about as simple as an Ethernet driver can be.

To add Ethernet support, I modify the `INCLUDE_ETHERNET` definition in `config.h`. This change enables all of the basic code for ARP, ICMP Echo (`ping`), and for a simple CLI server running on UDP port 777. The immediate goal is to get the evaluation board to respond to a `ping` (ICMP echo). If `ping` works, I know that the Ethernet transmit and receive paths are functioning, so all of the other stuff should fall into place.

NOTE

You can connect the target to the host PC directly or through a hub. However you wire it up, do what you can to confirm your cabling works. For example, `ping` some other device using the same connection mechanism you plan to use during this port. One really nice thing about connecting to the target via a hub (assuming you don't have a protocol analyzer hooked up) is that usually the hub gives you some visual feedback to let you know that traffic is on the connection. In every hub I've seen, there are a few LEDs that let the user know (at a very high level) if something is happening on the connection.

I also need to assign a MAC and IP address to the target. If you are working peer-to-peer or on an isolated hub, you can just make up a MAC address for testing; just make sure that when you go live you have an officially assigned one. For this example, the ColdFire board comes configured with a MAC address, so I use that address. I can use the DBUG command show to get the address. In the listings here, I use the value 00:60:1d:02:0b:08.

Similarly, I must set up an IP address. The same rules for creating an address apply to both MAC and IP addresses. I again assume an isolated network, but I must make sure that the target IP address is on the same subnet as the host. I have my PC configured with IP address 135.3.94.39. My PC's subnet mask is 255.255.255.0, so I establish my target's IP address as 135.3.94.40, which puts both devices on the same subnet. To get MicroMonitor to configure itself using these values, I create a monrc file with the following content

```
set IPADD 135.3.94.40
set ETHERADD 00:60:1d:02:0b:08
set NETMASK 255.255.255.0
```

Remember that the monrc file must be created executable, so the e flag must be set at time of creation.

Now I have a monitor binary with INCLUDE_ETHERNET enabled and a monrc file that has IP and MAC address information established. I have a PC connected to the target either through a hub or direct connect. The ping command can be executed, and, if everything is hooked up properly, the target responds and the ping succeeds.

Summary

That's it. I've described the directory structure, the target-specific makefile, the config.h file used to include only the portions of the monitor I need, and the major blocks of the porting process. Having walked through the steps, you can see that the config.h file also serves as a mechanism to control the complexity of the port. Instead of trying to deal with everything all in one shot, you can use config.h to add one subsystem at a time.

This example was somewhat unique because it put a monitor into a system that already had a monitor. If the DBUG monitor were removed, I would have been forced to use some facility like a BDM or JTAG downloader or a memory emulator to get the initial versions running. In the worst case, I could have just manually burned the boot flash.

Now a confession: I mentioned earlier that I shamelessly re-used code from Motorola's DBUG monitor. I went through this entire port with very little experience on the MCF5272C3. Despite this problem, I was able to cut and paste pieces of the DBUG monitor into specific points in MicroMonitor to quickly get it up and running. There are two good points to gain from this:

- The Motorola folks did a very nice job organizing the DBUG source code.
- If boot code already exists for a target (and it almost always does but maybe not always as well organized as DBUG), then porting MicroMonitor is very straight-forward.

Conclusion

So what have you learned? You have stepped through a basic CPU schematic and gained a general understanding of how the microprocessor, the RAM, and ROM all work together. You have successfully taken source code from a familiar, well-understood environment (a PC or Unix workstation) and molded it (through cross-compilation) into the raw binary data that is needed by the CPU on the circuit board. The bytes in the final file that we transferred to the device programmer a few chapters ago are the exact bytes that the CPU wants to see. They represent the instructions and data needed by the CPU to carry out the task that the C program suggests.

You've stepped through a fairly generic approach that deals with the tough problem of booting an embedded system for the first time. The approach presented in this text is useful on a wide range of CPUs. MicroMonitor provides a good set of development tools and is useful with a variety of RTOSs and hardware platforms. You've learned about some different types of debugging strategies, and you've seen, step by step, what's involved in porting the monitor to a new platform. What's left?

I recall in my second semester of college calculus asking my professor "Is there any other math stuff after this?" If she had any coffee in her mouth at the time, I would have been soaked!

An overview like this is only the beginning. Embedded systems programming involves a lot of decision-making. Some solutions might be outstanding for some situations. In other situations, the same approach might not even fit. Although no single text is able to make these decisions for you, hopefully, this book has provided some insight that helps in the decision-making process. This industry is very exciting, and it is certainly not for those who are afraid of change. On one hand, you don't

335

want to let yourself get left behind as new technologies and techniques emerge; on the other hand, you don't want to jump onto every ship that pulls in just because it's something new. Keep digging, and look to the industry to see what looks good to you. Don't just follow hype. Investigate new tools and techniques, think about new strategies, and always consider your options.

Building a Host-Based Toolbox

There is more to an embedded system than just the embedded system. Don't let yourself develop the attitude that "*I only do firmware.*" Even if the final product will be hidden inside a toaster with no interface to a user, it is still very handy during the development cycle to have a few tools on the PC for various things. In general, it's very handy to have the ability to write programs for the PC (or whatever host you are on) because, every once in a while, you will need to write something that is just begging to be a host program. Some tools are useful for modifying the binary image file created from the executable; others are useful for communicating with the target via RS-232 or Ethernet. This appendix describes some tools I have written that I have found the most useful when interfacing to a target running MicroMonitor; however, most of these tools are generic enough to be applicable regardless of the platform.

I will introduce three useful code snippets in this chapter. The snippets provide the following capabilities:

- Interfacing to a binary file on the host;
- Interfacing to a COM port on the PC;
- Interfacing to a UDP socket on the PC.

No, the code is not C++, and you don't have any GUI — I didn't even use a GUI to write these tools. I did use Microsoft Visual C++ command line tools and nmake (nothing fancy). The snippets that follow are shown for quick illustration only. For the complete working source, refer to the CD.

Interfacing to Files on the Host

In embedded systems programming, you frequently need to perform various file format conversions. For example, you might need a binary to S-record converter (bin2srec on the CD); you may need a tool that converts a binary file into a C-array so that the array can be included in a C file (bin2array on the CD).

Not too long ago I was booting a board with a 64-bit CPU. There were two boot devices, and the target was configured such that the CPU would fetch four bytes from the first device, then four bytes from the second device. This requirement meant that I had to take the binary image that I created from the ELF-formatted output of the linker and chop it into two separate files, where each file contained alternating 4-byte chunks of the original binary. To automate this partitioning, I wrote a host-based tool I call chunker. I might never use this tool again, but it sure did the trick when I needed it. The chunker tool was very simple to write, but, if I hadn't had the ability to develop for the host as well as the target (or had an equivalent tool), I would have been in trouble! Listing A.1 and Listing A.2 show the bulk of the chunker code, demonstrating the interface to a binary file.

Listing A.1   Chunker.

```
main(int argc,char *argv[])
{
    char    *ofile, *buf1, *buf2, *bp1, *bp2, *fname, ofilename[128];
    struct  stat    stat;
    int     ifd, ofd, i, j, opt, size1, size2;

    debug = 0;
    ofile = "chunk";
```

```
while((opt=getopt(argc,argv,"do:V")) != EOF) {
    switch(opt) {
    case 'd':
        debug = 1;
        break;
    case 'o':
        ofile = optarg;
        break;
    case 'V':
        showVersion();
        break;
    default:
        exit(1);
    }
}
if (argc != optind +1)
    usage(0);

fname = argv[optind];

/* Open a binary file, determine its size and
 * allocate two buffers of that size to contain the "chunks".
 * This is an over allocation, but who cares!
 */
ifd = open(fname,O_RDONLY | O_BINARY);
if (ifd == -1) {
    perror(fname);
    exit(1);
}


fstat(ifd,&stat);
if (stat.st_size % 4) {
    fprintf(stderr,"Input file must be mod 4\n");
    exit(1);
}
```

```
buf1 = bp1 = malloc(stat.st_size);
buf2 = bp2 = malloc(stat.st_size);
if ((!buf1) || (!buf2)) {
    perror("malloc");
    exit(1);
}
```

The chunker program begins with some command line processing using getopt() and the incoming argument list. The filename of the file to be processed is the first argument after the list of options processed by getopt(). The code stores the file-name locally and then opens the file after determining the size of the file (by calling fstat). The code allocates two buffers where it will collect the chunks of data from the input file (see Listing A.2).

Listing A.2   Filling the Buffers.

```
/* Now read in 4 bytes at a time from the binary file and
 * feed 4 bytes to one buffer then 4 bytes to the other buffer.
 * Keep this up till the input file is exhausted...
 */
size1 = size2 = 0;
while(1) {
    if (read(ifd,bp1,4) != 4)
        break;
    bp1 += 4;
    size1 += 4;
    if (read(ifd,bp2,4) != 4)
        break;
    bp2 += 4;
    size2 += 4;
}

/* Create 2 new files that represent the two "chunks" of the
 * original file:
 */
sprintf(ofilename,"%s1.bin",ofile);
ofd = open(ofilename,O_WRONLY|O_BINARY|O_CREAT|O_TRUNC,0777);
if (ofd < 0) {
```

```
        fprintf(stderr,"Can't open %s\n",ofilename);
        exit(1);
    }
    if (write(ofd,buf1,size1) != size1) {
        fprintf(stderr,"Can't write file %s\n",ofilename);
        exit(1);
    }
    close (ofd);

    sprintf(ofilename,"%s2.bin",ofile);
    ofd = open(ofilename,O_WRONLY|O_BINARY|O_CREAT|O_TRUNC,0777);
    if (ofd < 0) {
        fprintf(stderr,"Can't open %s\n",ofilename);
        exit(1);
    }
    if (write(ofd,buf2,size2) != size2) {
        fprintf(stderr,"Can't write file %s\n",ofilename);
        exit(1);
    }

    /* Close, free and exit.
     */
    close (ofd);
    close (ifd);
    free(buf1);
    free(buf2);
    printf("Files %s1.bin (%d) & %s2.bin (%d) created\n",ofile,size1,size2);
    exit(0);
}
```

The main loop in Listing A.2 uses read() to retrieve four bytes at a time, placing each 4-byte chunk alternately into the two different buffers. After the buffers have been loaded, two new files are created, and the data from the buffers is stored into those files. Finally, the files and buffers are released, and a status message is printed, indicating that the two chunk files have been created from the single input file.

Interfacing to the PC Serial Port

In almost all cases, when interfacing to the serial port of a PC, the tools that come with the PC are adequate. There are cases, however, when HyperTerminal isn't sufficient. For example, if you need to observe binary data on a serial line or if you need to implement a custom serial protocol on the target, you will find it quite handy to be able to manipulate the UART on the PC directly. Listing A.3 is a base for a home-grown serial port interface that you can use in place of the default Windows tools when necessary.

Listing A.3   Base for a Home-Grown Serial Port Interface.

```
HANDLE
comOpen(int portnum, int baud)
{
    DCB dcb;
    HANDLE hCom;
    char portname[16];

    sprintf(portname,"COM%d",portnum);
    hCom = CreateFile(portname,
        GENERIC_READ | GENERIC_WRITE,   // Open for read/write.
        0,                              // Sharing flags.
        NULL,                           // Security attributes.
        OPEN_EXISTING,                  // Required for serial port.
        0,                              // File attributes (NA).
        NULL);                          // Required for serial port.

    if (hCom == INVALID_HANDLE_VALUE) {
        ShowLastError("comOpen() CreatFile()");
        return(INVALID_HANDLE_VALUE);
    }

    // Fill in the DCB...
    if (!GetCommState(hCom,&dcb)) {
        ShowLastError("comOpen() GetCommState()");
        return(INVALID_HANDLE_VALUE);
    }
```

```
    dcb.BaudRate = baud;
    dcb.ByteSize = 8;
    dcb.Parity = NOPARITY;
    dcb.StopBits = ONESTOPBIT;
    dcb.fDtrControl = DTR_CONTROL_ENABLE;
    dcb.fDsrSensitivity = FALSE;
    dcb.fOutX = FALSE;
    dcb.fInX = FALSE;
    dcb.fNull = FALSE;
    if (!SetCommState(hCom,&dcb)) {
        ShowLastError("comOpen() SetCommState()");
        return(INVALID_HANDLE_VALUE);
    }

    return(hCom);
}

void
comClose(HANDLE hCom)
{
    CloseHandle(hCom);
}

int
comRead(HANDLE hCom,char *buf,int count)
{
    DWORD   bytesread;
    DWORD   tot;

    tot = (DWORD)count;
    while(tot) {
        if (ReadFile(hCom,buf,(DWORD)tot,
            &bytesread,NULL) != TRUE) {
            ShowClearCommError(hCom);
            ShowLastError("comread ReadFile()");
            return(-1);
        }
```

```
            tot -= bytesread;
            buf += bytesread;
        }
    return(count);
}


int
comWrite(HANDLE hCom, char *buffer,int count)
{
    DWORD   byteswritten;

    if (WriteFile(hCom,buffer,(DWORD)count,
        &byteswritten,NULL) != TRUE)
            return(-1);
    return((int)byteswritten);
}
```

The code in Listing A.3 depends on the Windows services: `CreateFile()`, `GetCommState()`, `SetCommState()`, `ReadFile()`, and `WriteFile()`. For details on these system calls, refer to the Visual C++ CD documentation. The `comOpen()` function is a wrapper for `CreateFile()`, `GetCommState()`, and `SetCommState()` to open a com port that creates a convenient hook to configure baud, parity, and other serial-port parameters. The `comRead()` and `comWrite()` functions create convenient wrappers for the `ReadFile()` and `WriteFile()` system calls, which are used to transmit to and receive from the serial port.

PC-Based UDP Transactions: moncmd

MicroMonitor, when built on a target with Ethernet capability, includes a small server that processes incoming packets received on UDP port 777. The server simply takes the incoming UDP packet and assumes the content of the packet is a command destined for the monitor's CLI. The server passes the whole string to the function `docommand()` and sets a flag within the monitor. This flag tells `putchar` to build UDP packets (one line per packet) to be sent back to the client that issued the command. When the flag is set, the command results are sent to the target console (if any) and to the remote UDP port that issued the command. When the final line of output is complete, the monitor clears the flag and issues one last packet containing only one `NULL` byte to signal the remote client that the response to the command is complete.

The moncmd tool (monitor command) is a specialized UDP client that runs on a PC. It is a simple program that allows a user to talk remotely to a target system running MicroMonitor. Listing A.4 demonstrates the basic functionality needed to send and receive on a UDP socket using a Win32-based host. Note that Listing A.4 is a very basic implementation meant only to illustrate the use of socket(), sendto(), and recvfrom(). (A complete implementation is on the CD.)

Listing A.4   do_moncmd().

```
/* do_moncmd():
 *  Open a socket and send the command to the specified port of the
 *  specified host.  Wait for a response if necessary.
 *
 *  hostname:
 *      Character string IP address
 *  command_to_monitor:
 *      Character string command destined for target monitor.
 *  portnum:
 *      Port number that the UDP packet is to be sent to.
 */
int
do_moncmd(char *hostname, char *command_to_monitor, short portnum)
{
    int i, lasterr;
    int msglen;
    ulong   inaddr;
    struct  hostent *hp, host_info;
    char    rcvmsg[1024];
    WSADATA WsaData;
    DWORD   tid;
    HANDLE  tHandle;

    if (WSAStartup (0x0101, &WsaData) == SOCKET_ERROR)
        err("WSAStartup Failed");

    targetHost = hostname;
```

```
/* Build the UDP destination address:
 * Accept target name as string or internet dotted-decimal address.
 */
memset((char *)&targetAddr,0,sizeof(struct sockaddr));
if ((inaddr = inet_addr(targetHost)) != INADDR_NONE) {
    memcpy((char *)&targetAddr.sin_addr,(char *)&inaddr,sizeof(inaddr));
    host_info.h_name = NULL;
}
else {
    hp = gethostbyname(targetHost);
    if (hp == NULL)
        err("gethostbyname failed");
    host_info = *hp;
    memcpy((char *)&targetAddr.sin_addr,hp->h_addr,hp->h_length);
}
targetAddr.sin_family = AF_INET;
targetAddr.sin_port = htons(portnum);

/* Open the socket:
 */
socketFd = socket(AF_INET,SOCK_DGRAM,0);

if (socketFd == INVALID_SOCKET)
    err("socket failed");

/* Send the command string to the target:
 */
msgString = command_to_monitor;
if (sendto(socketFd,msgString,(int)strlen(msgString)+1,0,
    (struct sockaddr *)&targetAddr,sizeof(targetAddr)) < 0) {
    close(socketFd);
    err("sendto failed");
}

/* Now wait for the response:
 */
while(1) {
```

```
        int j;

        /* Wait for incoming message: */
        msglen = sizeof(struct sockaddr);
        i = recvfrom(socketFd,rcvmsg,sizeof(rcvmsg),0,
            (struct sockaddr *)&targetAddr,&msglen);

        if (i == 0) {
            fprintf(stderr,"Connection closed\n");
            close(socketFd);
            exit(EXIT_ERROR);
        }

        /* If size is 1 and 1st byte is 0 assume that's the target */
        /* saying "I'm done". */
        if ((i==1) && (rcvmsg[0] == 0))
            break;

        /* Print the received message: */
        for(j=0;j<i;j++)
            putchar(rcvmsg[j]);
        fflush(stdout);
    }

    close(socketFd);
    return(EXIT_SUCCESS);
}
```

Okay, I'm gonna be honest here, I don't know what WSAStartup() actually does! And yes, I'm OK with that! Like the sneaker commercial says, "just do it!"

The do_moncmd() function processes the IP address or the hostname provided on the command line. The function then opens a socket with SOCK_DGRAM, indicating that the socket is for UDP. After the socket is opened, the code can use the functions sendto() and recvfrom() to send and receive UDP packets. The call to sendto() transfers the string on the command line to the server task on the remote target running MicroMonitor. Finally, the while() loop processes the response. Each line received is printed to the console. To support the ability to receive a multiple-line response but still know when the final line has been received, the server in the monitor terminates the message with a single 1-byte packet containing a NULL. The remote moncmd tests for this packet and exits when appropriate.

Summary

Several other tools can prove to be quite handy in a firmware development arsenal. A TFTP client server and DHCP/BOOTP server are useful when developing code on a target that runs any kind of network boot. The TFTP client alone is great for transferring files to and from the target. Servers on the PC allow you to test networked devices without getting a system administrator to set up servers on a Unix host.

The disadvantage of using your own home-grown tools is that if you do not understand something, you are propagating the error in the tool to the target firmware. The advantage of the home-grown approach, at least for some of these tools, is that they are not that complicated to write. Also, having the source code for the tools allows you to add code in the tool that simulates protocol errors or lost packets.

Tools that can parse the executable image (for instance, coff or elf) allow you to dump symbols and memory map information in formats that may be more convenient than those supported by the tools that come with the compiler. Also, in the case of MicroMonitor and TFS, some host-based tools are essential because TFS decompression requires a preprocessing step that is non-standard.

Complete source for these tools, and others, is on the CD.

Appendix B

RTOS Overview

In general terms, a realtime operating system (RTOS) is an environment that runs on an embedded system and provides facilities that allow properly written programs to react to certain stimuli within an expected time interval. In practice, when I refer to an RTOS, I mean an environment that runs on an embedded target and provides an API that includes, at a minimum, the ability to establish multiple threads of execution (commonly referred to as *tasks*). An operating system that can execute multiple tasks concurrently is referred to as a multi-tasking operating system.

The RTOS creates an execution environment for each task that makes it convenient to pass messages between tasks, pass events between an interrupt handler and a task, prioritize task execution, and coordinate multi-task usage of an I/O device. These capabilities, though, are common to most multi-tasking operating systems. To qualify as an RTOS, these facilities must be designed so that the RTOS can react to an incoming stimulus within some maximum, predictable amount of time. The name RTOS clearly suggests real time, but it is safe to say that a large percentage of the applications using an RTOS do not have very many real-time constraints.

Some realtime applications, however, are much easier to implement using an RTOS. As embedded systems get more and more complicated, so does the firmware that makes them work. Often, very large and complex embedded systems can be implemented as a number of smaller, simpler, parallel tasks, each of which is somewhat unaware of the others. Such multi-threaded solutions can often make the code less complicated and more modular by eliminating artificial dependencies among the parallel tasks. Projects with simpler, more coherent modules are easier to manage, allowing firmware programmers to get home before midnight once in a while.

As with many other topics mentioned in this book, another book could be written on the subject of the RTOS.[1] Here, however, I will limit the discussion to some basic definitions.

NOTE

> The basic building block of any multi-tasking operating system (OS) is a task. A task is a function that is allocated a certain amount of resources and/or time to do what it has to do. With most RTOSs, each task is assigned a priority. The beauty of the RTOS is that you can have several of these prioritized tasks running and they can be somewhat unaware of the fact that they are running in parallel with other tasks.

The Scheduler

The heart of the RTOS is the scheduler. The scheduler is the piece of code that figures out which task should run next. Usually at the end of every system call, the system invokes the scheduler to determine if the currently running task should be suspended in favor of some other task.

The OS views each task as being in one of several run states. Each RTOS defines its own set of run states, but three are almost universal: *running*, *ready-to-run*, and *blocked*. At any instant in time, only one task can be in the running state: namely, the currently executing active task. Tasks that would be running if the processor wasn't already being used by some higher priority task are assigned to the ready-to-run state. Tasks that are waiting for some system call to occur before they can run are assigned to the blocked state. When a blocked task becomes unblocked, it is moved to the ready-to-run state.

When the currently running task finishes or loses its claim to the processor (perhaps because some higher priority task became ready), the OS does a *context switch*. To perform a context switch, the RTOS saves the current state of the CPU (or context) in some structure dedicated to the active task (usually called a task control block — TCB). The RTOS then retrieves the context belonging to the incoming task's state (from the new task's TCB) and loads that into the CPU as the new context. If the scheduler is *priority based*, the new task must have a higher priority than the previously running task because the scheduler always selects the highest priority ready-to-run task. It is important to note that the scheduler always selects the highest

---

1. For example, see: Jean Labrosse, MicroC/OS-II, (Lawrence, KS: CMP Books, 1999.)

priority task *that is ready to run*. Frequently, there are several tasks in the system with higher priority than the current task, but these tasks are not selected by the scheduler to run because they are not in the ready-to-run state.

Depending on the particular RTOS, the scheduler might be invoked at times other than when the running task makes a system call. If the RTOS supports preemption, a context switch may also occur as the side effect of an interrupt. For example, an interrupt might occur because a peripheral device has input available. The interrupt handler captures this input, saves it for the listening task (via a system call), and then invokes the scheduler as part of its return protocol. If the listening task was blocked waiting for the input, it now becomes ready-to-run. If the listening task (or some other now-ready task) has a higher priority than the interrupted task, the scheduler performs a task switch, suspending the interrupted task and launching the higher priority task.

In cases where a system call causes the current task to be put on hold, the context switch is called *synchronous* because it occurs through in-line code. In cases where an interrupt occurs and the interrupted task is put on hold, the context switch is called *asynchronous* because it happens at some arbitrary point during the execution of the interrupted task.

Tasks, Threads, and Processes

A thread is one of potentially several tasks that run within the context of a single process. A process is one of potentially several programs that run on a platform whose operating system can take advantage of memory management unit (MMU). It is important to note the need for an MMU. An MMU is a hardware extension in the more powerful CPUs that allows a program to run in protected memory space.

Actually, a task and a thread are essentially the same thing. We usually think of tasks in embedded systems and threads in larger machines.

The protection afforded by the MMU is what distinguishes a process from a thread. Unlike a thread, no matter how confused a process gets, it cannot corrupt the memory space of another process. Processes are safe from each other because of the protection provided by the MMU. If the currently running process has a stray pointer that starts trashing memory, it can trash its own space, but it causes some type of MMU-related OS exception before it is able to access the memory space of another process.

You might be wondering why multi-threading (or multi-tasking) is even necessary in an MMU-based multi-processing environment. With the protection provided by the MMU comes a lot of overhead at context-switch time. Recall that I said before that the context of the currently running task is the state of the CPU. The context includes the register set and a few other task-specific variables. With a process, the context is all of that plus the overhead of reconfiguring the MMU and possibly pulling the incoming process back into RAM from secondary storage.

This overhead can impose a surprisingly high cost, because seemingly innocuous transactions can cause a full process switch. For example, because one process cannot touch the memory space of another process, the only way for one process to talk to another process is through some type of message-passing system call — a call that also causes a context switch.

Because of the extra overhead associated with full processes, threads are the preferred multi-tasking choice for the real-time environment. The context switch overhead is minimal, and data sharing between threads is much less complex. Running within a thread, however, has its dangers also. With multiple threads running within the same block of memory space, a bad pointer or stack overflow in one thread has the ability to trash memory in any of the other threads. As we have discussed in an earlier chapter, finding such a bug can sometimes be very challenging.

Preemption, Time Slicing, and Interrupts

While an RTOS allows concurrent tasks to remain relatively ignorant of each other, it doesn't allow the programmer to remain ignorant of the very tricky technical issues associated with concurrency. The facilities within the RTOS can be quite forgiving, but it is up to the developer to know how to use the facilities properly. It is very possible for a firmware developer to write code that brings a highly regarded RTOS to its knees.

For example, if I have three tasks in my system and each task does whatever it wants to do, then chances are good that only the task at the highest priority level will ever run. To avoid this and other potential problems, the code for each task should be written so that if the task is not performing any useful work, it returns to the scheduler and lets another task do some work. A task can surrender the processor synchronously or asynchronously. To surrender control synchronously, the task should make some system call, in essence telling the OS that the task is waiting for something. If the OS knows the current task is just waiting, it can schedule some other task to do some real work. Calling the OS to wait on something is commonly called *blocking,* and it should be the goal of every task to do whatever has to be done as quickly as possible, then block.

Alternatively, if a task is not written for blocking, some other mechanism is needed to cause the context switch to occur. Enter interrupts. Interrupts cause an asynchronous break in the currently running code. This asynchronous break can result in the current task being preempted by some other higher priority task.

An interrupt handler written for an RTOS is usually wrapped with RTOS-specific code at the beginning and end. The closing portion of these wrappers calls the scheduler. Those system calls that are legal within an interrupt handler can detect when they are being called from within an interrupt. The code within the system call knows that if it is in an interrupt handler, it should not call the scheduler, as it normally would, but rather depend on that call happening when the interrupt handler exits. When the interrupt handler has finished, it invokes the scheduler, and, if a higher priority task is now ready to run, the switch is performed. The interrupt handler returns, but to a different task.

What if there is no system call in the interrupt handler that causes this context switch? If multiple tasks are configured with the same priority and all of the tasks refuse to block, a simple tick-driven time-slicing system can still keep the system moving. Time-slicing by the RTOS is the ability to have multiple tasks with the same priority be given a slice of the CPU's time. If your system has three tasks (all of equal priority) that all want to own the processor, the RTOSs ability to time-slice allows each task to receive some fixed number of system ticks of runtime. When the tick count is reached (a time slice), then the scheduler automatically changes context to the next task of the same priority. This approach is commonly called *round-robin time-slicing*.

Semaphores, Events, Messages, and Timers

At this point, you have a basic understanding of the core parts of the RTOS. I have mentioned system calls several times but never really elaborated on what a system call is. Like threads and tasks, the definition of a system call depends on the company you keep. In general, a system call refers to an operating system facility that, when invoked, causes a context switch into the kernel because the resource with which the system call interfaces is only accessible in kernel mode. With embedded systems, the term *system call* usually just refers to one of the RTOS's API functions, and that definition is the one I've used in this book. If the RTOS has all of the nice stuff I've talked about so far, it still can't do much. Compare it to a farm tractor that has a heavy-duty motor and a lot of power but doesn't have any attachments. The attachments included with the RTOS are the system calls that allow us to communicate between tasks, to communicate between interrupt handlers and tasks, to guarantee that only one task executes a certain function at a time, to set up timers, and so forth. Every RTOS comes with some set of system calls, but, in general, all RTOSs share a few basic functions.

Semaphores can be used to synchronize access to a shared resource. A common form of synchronization is mutual exclusion, meaning that tasks coordinate their access to a resource so that only one task at a time is manipulating the resource. For example, if a semaphore-protected function has begun executing and a context switch transfers control to another section of code that also tries to call the protected function, the second call is blocked. Mutually exclusive access is needed whenever more than one task (i.e., code in separate threads or processes) is allowed to access the same resource.

For example, assume a system has some memory-mapped register that contains eight bits, each of which control an LED (1 = on), and assume that I use the function in Listing B.1 to modify those bits.

Listing B.1   LedOn().

```
unsigned char
LedOn(unsigned char onbits)
{
    unsigned char current_bits;

    current_bits = *(unsigned char *)LED_PORT;
    current_bits |= onbits;
    *(unsigned char *)LED_PORT = current_bits;
    return(current_bits);
}
```

What would happen if (referring to Listing B.1), just after the variable current_bits is loaded from the LED_PORT address, an asynchronous context switch occurred and some other task called this function, passing it a different value? Quick answer: the setting established by the second task would be lost. Let's assume that on the first call to LedOn(), the value of onbits is 0x01, and the current value in LED_PORT is 0x80. If no context switch occurred, the result would be that LED_PORT would be 0x81, meaning that two LEDs would be lit.

If, however, a context switch happens in just the right place, the result is different. On the first call to LedOn() after the line

```
    current_bits = *(unsigned char *)LED_PORT;
```

the value stored in current_bits is 0x80. Now assume that a context switch occurs after this line and that another task calls this function with 0x02 as the onbits value. The second invocation runs to completion leaving, for the momemt, the LED_PORT value at 0x82. At some point in the future, context is restored to the original task. This instance of the function resumes at the line

```
current_bits |= onbits
```

with current_bits (in the original context) set to 0x80. When this value of current_bits is logically ORed with onbits (0x01), the result 0x81 is written to the LED port. The result is that the value established by the preempting task (0x82) is lost.

The solution to this problem is mutual exclusion. If these LED operations were properly wrapped with semaphore operations (Get at the top and Release at the bottom), then when the context switch occurred, the preempting task would not have been allowed to manipulate the LEDs until the task that owned the semaphore was done.

Events are OS-provided flags that, when set by one task or interrupt handler, cause some other task to wake up (i.e., to enter the ready-to-run state). Typically, signaling with events involves two system calls: one to post an event and one to block waiting for an event. Events are typically not queued. If the same event is posted several times prior to the acknowledgment of the event by the task that is blocked while waiting for it, those additional postings are lost. Because events are a simple flag, after the flag is set, setting it again has no significance. Usually events have lower overhead than other types of interprocess communication and thus are commonly used for communication between an interrupt handler and a task.

Messages provide a mechanism that allows a task (or interrupt handler) to send some data to another task. Unlike events, messages are queued. When multiple messages are sent to some task that is blocked while waiting for the message, each message is queued by the OS for later consumption by the receiver of the message.

Most RTOSs support the ability to send a message to be posted to the end of the queue and also to be posted to the head of the queue. In some situations, it can be very handy to be able to expedite a message by posting it to the head of the queue, but this feature must not be abused.[2] Messages can be passed from task-to-task or from interrupt-to-task, but a message usually imposes more overhead than an event.

Timers are probably the most heavily used facility within an RTOS. Not only is there typically some set of system calls specifically for timers, but many of the other system calls usually provide some time-out mechanism as well. The most common timer function is the ability to put a task to sleep for some period of time or to wake a task at some time of day in the future. The simplest example would be a task that blinks an LED (see Listing B.2).

---

2. When a message is placed in a queue, it is usually on a first-in first-out (FIFO) basis. If the message is put at the top of the queue, then it becomes a last-in first-out (LIFO) basis, which is ok, but you'd better be aware of the difference.

Listing B.2 task_BLINKER().

```
void
task_BLINKER(void)
{
    while(1)
    {
        Turn_On_Led();
        GoToSleep(1000);
        Turn_Off_Led();
        GoToSleep(1000);
    }
}
```

The GoToSleep() system call is the timer function that allows the task to wake up periodically. Aside from GoToSleep(), other system calls intrinsically use timers to support the ability to time-out. For example, a task might want to wait for an incoming event, but, if the event does not occur for 30 seconds, some other action must occur. In this case, the system call is an event mechanism, but, under the hood, the event mechanism is using timers.

Reentrancy

Actually, I've discussed reentrancy already but without naming it. I've talked about interrupts and preemption, and I've talked about what semaphores do to help you make a piece of code atomic. Interrupts and multi-threaded programming environments are wonderful things, but they add complexity to your code because they create the possibility that a function can be executing simultaneously in more than one context. The error in the LED example (Listing B.1 where one function's results are lost, causing the wrong LEDs to be lit) happens because the function was not designed to handle the possibility of reentrancy. A function is considered re-entrant only if it can safely be called simultaneously from multiple threads or processes. In this case (Listing B.1), the solution was to eliminate the possibility of reentrancy by using the semaphore. In other cases, the code may be prepared to allow reentrancy.

Use of globals or statics in functions can also cause a function to be non-re-entrant. Similar to the LED state, if a function is in the process of modifying a global variable but is interrupted in the middle of the modification by some other task that tries to manipulate the same data, the data is likely to be corrupted. Generally re-entrant functions use all local (stack) variables whenever possible. (Variables on the stack are always private to the thread that created them.) When a function needs to manipulate a global resource and still needs to be re-entrant, it should use some form of mutual exclusion to serialize access to the global resource.

Good Concurrency vs. Bad Concurrency

Here's a quick good-design/bad-design example to illustrate how bad code can undermine a good RTOS. Assume that the function `task_BLINKER()` in Listing B.2 is a task in some RTOS-based application. This task's job is very simple: wake up every second and toggle the state of the LED. The LED is adjusted and immediately the `GoToSleep()` system call is invoked. This task does just what it has to do, then blocks. Now look at the alternative function shown in Listing B.3.

Listing B.3   BLINKER_BAD()

```
void
task_BLINKER_BAD(void)
{
    while(1)
    {
        int timeout;

        Turn_On_Led();
        for(timeout=0;timeout<500000;timeout++);
        Turn_Off_Led();
        for(timeout=0;timeout<500000;timeout++);
    }
}
```

If the time-out loop takes one second, the approach shown in Listing B.3 might seem like an adequate alternative. Unfortunately, however, Listing B.3 is far from adequate. Aside from the inaccuracy of the loop's timing, Listing B.3 doesn't consider the fact that there are other tasks in the system. Because it does not issue any blocking system call, it uses as much of the CPU as the OS lets it have. Under certain circumstances this poor design might still end up working, but it is still a poor design because it is not taking advantage of the resources provided by the RTOS.

In many cases, Listing B.3 won't work at all. Assume that for some reason it is extremely important that this LED blink consistently. To assure timely execution, the task is likely to be set up to run at a high priority. If that is the case, preemption won't even help other tasks gain the CPU, because preemption only causes a task switch if the currently running task is running at a lower priority than some other task that is in the ready-to-run state. The point is that the RTOS cannot overcome a poor design! The developer still must write clean, well-informed code.

Summary

While not every real-time application needs the overhead of an RTOS, a good percentage of today's embedded applications are much easier to design and code if they are implemented as several independent threads or tasks. In this chapter, I've tried to give you some idea of what an RTOS is and what it does. I've explained, in the most general terms, what the scheduler does and what kinds of services one finds in the average RTOS. You should now understand the differnce between a task and a process, and the difference between being preempted and interrupted. Hopefully this overview will help you decide whether you want to seek more detailed information about RTOSs.

In the right hands, an RTOS can be a useful tool, but it is not a silver bullet for the nasties of real-time programming, nor is it a magic potion that turns application programmers into real-time programmers. A good RTOS will allow a talented real-time programmer to more clearly express the natural concurrency in a problem and will supply structures that encapsulate important real-time primitives (like semaphores, events, messages, etc.) It is important to note, though, that no RTOS can eliminate the intrinsic complexity of concurrent programming. Even when the application is to run on top of an RTOS, the programmer must fully understand the issues of mutual exclusion, reentrancy, deadlock, etc. If you are not already comfortable with these issues, you should begin your study of RTOSs by studying basic concurrency. Once you fully understand the issues, understanding how a particular RTOS addresses those issues will be relatively straight forward.

Index

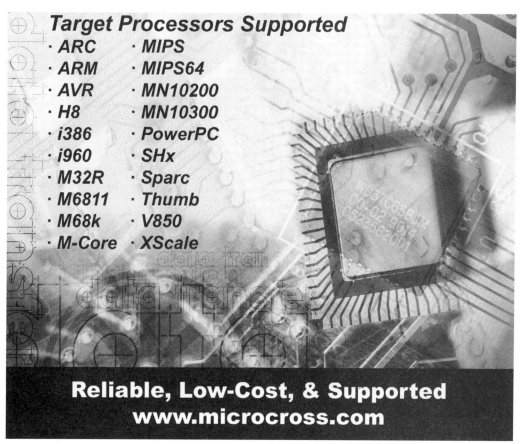

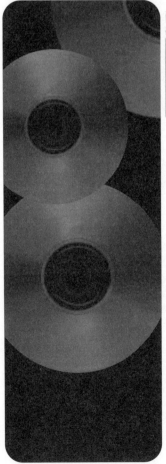

Practical Statecharts
in C/C++
Quantum Programming for Embedded Systems

by Miro Samek

Efficiently code statecharts directly in C/C++. You get a lightweight alternative to CASE tools that permits you to model reactive systems with UML statecharts. Includes complete code for your own applications, several design patterns, and numerous executable examples that illustrate the inner workings of the statechart-based framework. CD-ROM included, 388pp, ISBN 1-57820-110-1, $44.95

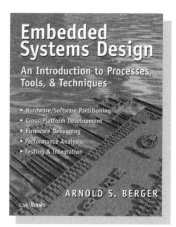

Embedded Systems Design
An Introduction to Processes, Tools, & Techniques

by Arnold S. Berger

Develop embedded systems from the ground up! This primer teaches the specialized aspects of writing software in this environment that are not covered in standard coursework for software developers and electrical engineers. It traces the software and hardware methodologies and the integration of the two disciplines. 236pp, ISBN 1-57820-073-3, $34.95

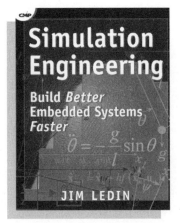

What's on the CD-ROM?

- Source code for the entire monitor package described in the book, including ports to 68K, PowerPC, ColdFire, and SH2 (roughly 50,000 lines of code).

- An HTML-based user manual for the monitor and related components.

- A full, unrestricted copy of Microcross GNU X-Tools. This GPL distribution includes cross compilers, cross-assemblers, simulators, and other embedded development tools for 21 target processors. The tools on the CD are ready-to-run binaries for Windows. The distribution includes the V Integrated Development Environment (VIDE), Cygwin B20, all source code, build instructions, and much more.

CD Includes:
Prebuilt
GNU X-Tools™
for 20+ Platforms